LIFELINE

THE GUIDE TO LIFE PROTECTION

RICHARD WATSON

Published by:

LiFETIME GUIDES

DISCLAIMER

This book is intended to provide the reader with information only. As noted throughout the book, individuals should consult appropriate professionals in each field prior to taking any particular action or treatment.

Medical information in this book should be used for reference only, and should not be considered complete nor used for treatment of any medical condition in place of a call or visit with a physician or other health-care provider. Care has been taken to confirm the accuracy of the information provided. However, the authors, editors, and publisher are not responsible for errors or omissions or for any consequences from application of the information in this publication, and make no warranty, express or implied, with respect to the contents of this publication

By using this book and the content of www.GettingSafer.com you accept the terms within this disclaimer agreement. © 2014 Lifetime Guides, LLC

Printed in the United States of America

Library of Congress Control Number: 2014909174
Published by Lifetime Guides LLC

ISBN 0976434229
ISBN 13: 9780976434221

To
First Responders

TABLE OF CONTENTS

Chapter FOUR
VEHICLE OWNERSHIP

Chapter FIVE
TRAVEL SAFELY: VACATIONS OR BUSINESS

Chapter SIX
IT'S YOUR HOME: MAKE IT SAFE!

INTRODUCTION

Ever since September 11th, 2001, the way of life, especially in America, was changed forever by several acts of war carried out by terrorists on thousands of peaceful and unsuspecting civilians in New York City, Washington, D.C., and on the four airline flights used in the assaults. Those attacks led to the greatest number of lives lost by the United States in one day, surpassing even the losses sustained at Pearl Harbor.

The result of these horrific terrorist acts instantly changed everything that Americans as well as citizens of other law-abiding countries believed about their personal safety and security. It was immediately apparent that new security measures would need to be put into effect to prevent future attacks.

The President of the United States at the time, George W. Bush, classified the attacks as 'acts of war' and said so in his address to Congress. He made it clear in that speech that "we are fighting this war on two fronts, one overseas, in countries that harbor or assist terrorist organizations, and the other on our home front".

Immediately following the attack on the World Trade Center I was inspired by the heroic work of New York Mayor Rudy Giuliani, who worked around the clock to put programs together to keep his city alive. He did so with the able help of fire, law enforcement and other agencies. I watched the mayor on TV (as did almost everyone in the nation), and saw what one person could do to help raise the spirits of New Yorkers and keep their city going. He had a tremendous positive impact, at a terrible time in America's history, on everyone throughout the country.

The example of how much one person can do in the face of tragedy to help others started me thinking about the things that I could do to help my wife and our family if we were faced with a tragic emergency.

It was shortly after 9/11 that I conceived the idea of writing this book that would be used as a personal safety and security step-by-step guide to help myself and others plan for a safer, more secure life, with fewer avoidable accidents, and peace of mind. A life made easier knowing how to make plans that will help not just ourselves but also our families and friends in emergencies. There is no doubt that if a major tragedy occurs, we can each play a part, and be helpful to others, once we have taken the time to learn what we can do to help.

In these difficult times, as part of the overall effort to be safer, we should be prepared to play our part. Whether we devote time to participate in the Citizens Corps, join volunteer organizations or develop neighborhood watch groups. It is relatively easy to become more informed about ways to prevent crimes of all types, and become better able to help ourselves, our families and our neighborhoods in a great many ways.

No doubt, each and every one of us needs to become more knowledgeable about what to do in the event of an emergency. We really should learn how to plan to do things that we probably think about but never bothered to make the time for; the things that would probably be important or vital for our own safety in an emergency.

Most of us have had great ideas from time to time about writing and organizing all the different types of information that would be needed in an emergency. Perhaps there are even notes or letters that we would want our loved ones to have in the event of a drastic accident that causes our sudden incapacity or even death. We think about listing these things and putting them in a safe place, but never get around to it.

We know that we should have details of our important documents and plans written down and put in safekeeping. However, most of us have not undertaken this daunting task because we think it is either too difficult, or we cannot decide what should be done first, or done at all. So we do little...or nothing.

This lack of personal planning became apparent when the World Trade Center was struck on 9/11. So many families had little or no idea of what to do. Too many, for example, had to start searching for DNA samples at a traumatic time to help identify loved ones. So many people did not know anything about insurance policies in effect or where to find information about assets or liabilities. It is possible now, with very little effort, to take care of these and many other potential problems by working through this book and putting everything in safe places.

Aside from getting your personal information organized, most of the details you gather will prove invaluable time and time again. In addition to organizing your information, the intention is to help you discover how to make serious emergency planning decisions for yourself and your family. For that reason you will find suggestions in each chapter that will give you ideas that you can discuss with your family and allow you to create your individual plans for safety.

I believe that as you go from chapter to chapter you will learn a great deal about ways to protect yourself, your family and those close to you. Then, as you complete more and more of the steps recommended throughout this book you will have learned a lot of things that will make you more confident and better prepared for all sorts of eventualities. You will be secure in being able to help yourself and your family, and in addition you will be able to use your knowledge to help in neighborhood and volunteer organizations.

As you develop your detailed personal safety and security plans you'll have actually become an effective part of the greater home-front fight to prevent crime. You will be able, if the need arises, to play a vital part, along with law enforcement, against one of the worst forms of violence in history: terrorism.

Now, with the help of the advice and material in this book, and the GettingSafer.com web site, you can immediately start to record all your details, and keep your information up-to-date and organized for yourself and your loved ones.

Here's wishing you a safe and secure future.

HOW TO USE THIS BOOK

This book, in conjunction with our website www.GettingSafer.com, is intended to be a source of information and aids that can be used in everyday situations as well as various emergencies. There is a best way to handle your first reading of the book, and if you follow these instructions, it will optimize your collection and creation of the information you need to protect yourself and loved ones.

Initially, when you work with this book, make sure you highlight in the print version or have a separate notebook in which you can write down:

- Each item or subject that needs follow-up.
- Note anything you need to research, so that you can then complete the answers to questions that apply to you.
- The forms in this book can be downloaded at GettingSafer.com Downloading is the way to start your Lifeline Personal Data System as no doubt you will have data that will need to be updated from time to time as certain facts change. The end result will give you a lot of satisfaction and your own Lifeline Personal Data System.

This book is set out so that each category is together. This format should prove helpful as you enter your information for the first time. You should also find your downloaded forms simple to update when necessary in the future.

Although many of the forms are very simple and surprisingly easy to complete, time and time again, you will discover how useful and important this data will be to you and your family (and perhaps friends too, depending upon various circumstances).

As soon as you start entering your information you will have actually taken the first step to creating your own safety and security plan! Just complete as much as you can, and as instructed above, make a note of anything that you need to research so you can then complete any unanswered questions.

No doubt you will probably have to search among old records for a lot of the details that you will want to enter, and that's okay. Just remember that once you have completed this process, you'll be able to eliminate searches for the same information over and over in the future. This time you will have everything *organized once and for all in one place!*

IN HELPING YOURSELF...YOU ARE HELPING YOUR LOVED ONES.

By making the effort, and taking the time to research and enter your information in your Lifeline Personal Data System you are being very responsible. Engaging in this entire process reveals your concern and love for your family. Developing and organizing all this detail about yourself will avoid a lot of unnecessary aggravation and searching on the part of your family members in cases of emergency, or in the event of your incapacity or death.

Just imagine if your loved ones had to search for important detailed health or financial information about you without knowing exactly where to look! Worse still, in the event of your death, nobody would know if you had any specific wishes that you would like to be carried out. It is even quite possible that some of your undiscovered assets could end up going to the state in which you lived, rather than to your heirs. With Lifeline, The Guide to Life Protection recommendations and action, you effectively can prevent this from happening.

Please Note: If you do not have sufficient space for extra data in any of the forms for your answers, simply add the extra information to the form on line. If you are using a printout, attach to the page in question with a binder clip, or indicate on the form where you have stored the additional information.

CHAPTER **One**

Personal Information

So many times as we go through life, we are required to provide personal information, and although some of it is usually readily available there are a great many facts that are not easily accessed. By gathering your personal and family information into one place you will finally be organized and better equipped to quickly provide any details needed in a crisis or if an emergency situation arises.

Complete the following questionnaire and others throughout the book with as much relevant information as possible. The forms are available on-line at www.GettingSafer.com so you can download and save all the information as part of your Lifeline Personal Data System. Remember to make a note of the questions that you are unable to answer immediately, and as soon as possible get the answers to complete your information.

PERSONAL AND FAMILY INFORMATION

Name *(first, middle, last):*
Maiden Name/Aliases:
Home Address:
Telephone: Cell Phone:
Fax: E-mail:

Birth Record:
Date & Time of Birth:
Hospital Name: City/State:

Marital Status:
Single   Married   Life Partner   Separated   Divorced   Widowed

Name of Spouse/ Partner:
Spouse/Partner's Aliases: Date of Birth:

Children's Names and Dates of Birth:
Child Name:
Birth Date & Time: Birth Record:
Hospital Name: City/State:

Child Name:
Birth Date & Time: Birth Record:
Hospital Name: City/State:

Child Name:
Birth Date & Time: Birth Record:
Hospital Name: City/State:

Prior Residences during the Past 5 Years *(Include Street, City, Zip and Date lived there):*
1.
2.
3.

Business Information:
Profession:
Company Name: Title:
Address: Telephone:
Fax: Cell Phone:
E-mail: Pager:

Social Security Number: *(Do not enter this # here). This number should be memorized. The original SS card should be stored securely in a locked file cabinet or safe deposit box.*

Drivers License Number: State:
DMV Identification Number:

Organ Donor: Yes   No   DNR: Yes   No
Specifics:

Passport Number: Expiration Date:

Student Identification Number:
Nationality:
Legal Status:
Alien Registration *(Green Card):*   Expiration Date:
Visa Type: Expiration Date:
Country of Birth:
Religion:
Your religious beliefs may become important information to include if you are ever unable to communicate your needs for foods or religious services, or if you have any special concerns about your medical care or traditions as dictated by your religion.

Mother's Maiden Name:
Father's Name:
Siblings' Names:

Military Service: Yes   No
Name Served Under:
Service Identification #:
Branch:
VA File #:

Entered Active Service:
Date: Grade/Rank: Place:

Separated From Service:
Date: Grade/Rank: Place:
Veteran:
Military Decorations:

Licenses/Certification:
Type: Number:
Type: Number:

Association Memberships:
Trade union:
Union:
Frequent Flyer/ Frequent User Programs:
Other:

Professional Organizations:
1.
2.

Service Organizations:
1.
2.

Fraternal Organizations:
1.
2.

Other:

Firearms:
Description: Model Number:
      Serial Number:
Description: Model Number:
      Serial Number:

STORAGE RECOMMENDATION: Personal Information

ENVELOPE	MAIN LOCATION	LOCATION 2	LOCATION 3
Sealed	Locked File Cabinet	Grab & Go Kit	Expanded Emergency Kit
Actual Location(s):			

Education Information
School / University
Name of Institution Presently *(Or last attended):*
Telephone Number:
Address:
Degree Achieved:
Other Schools Attended *(Include name, address, dates attended, and degree achieved for each):*
1.
2.

Highest level of Education:
Degrees:
Testing scores* (SAT, GRE, GMAT etc):
Location of originals/copies of school records, test scores and diploma (documents). You are likely to need your education documents and information from time to time, so make copies of them for safekeeping.

STORAGE RECOMMENDATION: Education Information Records

ENVELOPE	MAIN LOCATION	LOCATION 2	LOCATION 3
Open	Locked File Cabinet		
Actual Location(s):			

Code Word(s) to Identify an Approved Contact Person: _____

This is an important word(s) used to protect the safety of young children as well as seniors. It must be used carefully by family members for identification and security purposes. You may want to change the code word from time to time so there is a secure password at all times. If you do so, however, make sure that everyone who uses the word is advised of any change.

For safety reasons just enter the code word(s) on this copy. (Do not enter the contact person's name and contact information. If you change the word make sure that you keep this code word(s) updated and consistent with any information that is placed in your safety deposit box).

STORAGE RECOMMENDATION: **Code Word(s)**		
ENVELOPE	MAIN LOCATION	LOCATION 2	LOCATION 3
Sealed	Safety Deposit Box	Lock File Cabinet	
Actual Location(s):			

Favorite places, hangouts:
In the event you are missing, or you need to find a family member quickly, list places that you or any of your family would visit regularly. The places you list are those that would be checked first by family, friends or police. Be sure to update this list regularly.

NAME OF LOCATION/BUSINESS	ADDRESS	TELEPHONE

STORAGE RECOMMENDATION: **Favorite Places List**			
ENVELOPE	MAIN LOCATION	LOCATION 2	LOCATION 3
Open	Kitchen	Trusted Friend Specify	
Actual Location(s) and Contact Information for Friend:			

Carpool Information:
It is important to have names, addresses and telephone numbers of each person or child that are members of your carpool. Note children's allergies if any.

NAME		TELEPHONE

STORAGE RECOMMENDATION: Carpool Information

ENVELOPE	MAIN LOCATION	LOCATION 2	LOCATION 3
Open	Kitchen	Pocket Book or Wallet	

Actual Location(s):

Former Spouse's Information:
Full Name at Present:
Full Name at Birth:
Date and Place of Birth:
Social Security Number: *(Do not enter it here, memorize it.)*
Citizen of: ○ By Birth ○ By Naturalization
Date of Marriage: Place of Marriage:
Present Address: Telephone Number:

Names of Children Had With Spouse:
1. 2.
3. 4.

Divorced: ○ Yes ○ No Date Finalized:
Deceased: ○ Yes ○ No Date Deceased:
Location Interred:
Prenuptial Agreement: ○ Yes ○ No Location:
Details of the Agreement:

Medical History of Former Spouse *(If any children with spouse):*
Spouse and Spouse's Family (See Attached)

My Friends:

NAME	HOME TELEPHONE

CELL TELEPHONE	WORK TELEPHONE	E-MAIL ADDRESS

HOME ADDRESS
OTHER

NAME	HOME TELEPHONE

CELL TELEPHONE	WORK TELEPHONE	E-MAIL ADDRESS

HOME ADDRESS
OTHER

NAME	HOME TELEPHONE

CELL TELEPHONE	WORK TELEPHONE	E-MAIL ADDRESS

HOME ADDRESS
OTHER

NAME	HOME TELEPHONE

CELL TELEPHONE	WORK TELEPHONE	E-MAIL ADDRESS

HOME ADDRESS
OTHER

NAME	HOME TELEPHONE

CELL TELEPHONE	WORK TELEPHONE	E-MAIL ADDRESS

HOME ADDRESS
OTHER

Important Dates:
Name: Date:
○ Birthday ○ Anniversary ○ Other:
Name: Date:
○ Birthday ○ Anniversary ○ Other:
Name: Date:
○ Birthday ○ Anniversary ○ Other:
Name: Date:
○ Birthday ○ Anniversary ○ Other:
Name: Date:
○ Birthday ○ Anniversary ○ Other:
Name: Date:
○ Birthday ○ Anniversary ○ Other:
Name: Date:
○ Birthday ○ Anniversary ○ Other:

Additional Information About Your Children Under Age 18
Your Child's Route to School:
This can be a description of the route or a map so someone can reach the school from your home if you are unable to make the trip or to search for your child. Make a copy of your local street map and highlight the route from your home to the school, then attach it to this form.

Children's Play Groups *(Note allergies if any):*

CHILD	PARENT	HOME #	CELL#	ALLERGIES

STORAGE RECOMMENDATION: Children's Play Group List

ENVELOPE	MAIN LOCATION	LOCATION 2	LOCATION 3
Open	Kitchen	Trusted Friend - Specify	

Actual Location(s):

PERSONAL MEDICAL INFORMATION FOR EMERGENCIES

COMPLETE

For use in emergency, get a copy of your medical history from your doctors' office and keep it in a safe place. During a weekend or holiday your doctors' offices will probably not be accessible and you will not be able to get a copy until they open.

IDEA

DNA

Each person has a unique DNA 'fingerprint' that cannot be altered by any known treatment. DNA is different for each living being, and is rapidly becoming the primary method for identifying and distinguishing individual human beings. DNA is also used to diagnose inherited disorders; this information can be used towards treatment and for your benefit, and aids medical workers in treating individuals.

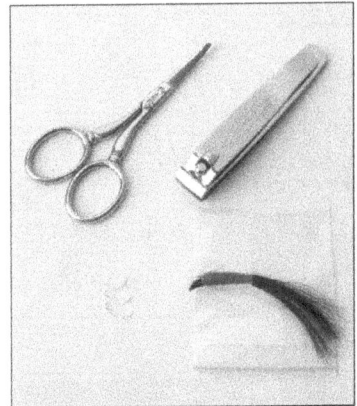

Preparing a DNA Kit is simple.

Compile the following identification items for DNA purposes, store them in a small plastic bag, and keep them in a safe place, *(preferably a safety deposit box.)* Record the location.

- Two recent photographs (not more than 2 years old)
- Hair sample
- Nail clippings sample
- Fingerprints (*Fingerprints can be made at your local police station, or see 'fingerprinting' online or in your local yellow pages.*)

STORAGE RECOMMENDATION: **DNA Records**			
ENVELOPE	MAIN LOCATION	LOCATION 2	LOCATION 3
Sealed	Safe Deposit Box	Locked File Cabinet	Expanded Emergency Kit
Actual Location(s):			

Medical Emergency Information:
This information form provides vital information in the event of a medical emergency

Name: _____ Male _____ Female _____
Height: _____ Weight: _____
Hair Color: _____ Eye Color: _____
Distinguishing marks (if any): _____

Ethnic Origin:
_____ Caucasian _____ Hispanic _____ Black _____ Native American _____ Asian _____ Middle Eastern _____ Other:
Blood Type: _____ A+ _____ A- _____ B+ _____ B- _____ O+ _____ O- _____ AB+ _____ AB-

Having a reliable and known source with your same blood type for can be a lifesaver. Although there is a supply of blood of various types available, there are reasons to consider supplying this information

In the event of a serious accident, you may need a special blood type, and this allows you to choose donors whose history you know. With enough prior notice, people can donate blood earmarked for a specific individual

Relatives and or Friends with your Blood Type:
Name: _____ Telephone Number: _____
Name: _____ Telephone Number: _____
Emergency Contact Person:
Name: _____ Telephone Number: _____

Current Medications (list all):
Name of Medication: _____ Date Began Taking: _____
Taken For What Reason: _____
Dosage and Times: _____
Prescription: _____
Prescribing Physician: _____
Other: _____

Name of Medication: _____ Date Began Taking: _____
Taken For What Reason: _____
Dosage and Times: _____
Prescription: _____
Prescribing Physician: _____
Other: _____

Name of Medication: _____ Date Began Taking: _____
Taken For What Reason: _____
Dosage and Times: _____
Prescription: _____
Prescribing Physician: _____
Other: _____

Allergies to Medicine:
Medicine: _____ Reaction: _____
Medicine: _____ Reaction: _____

Physician Information:
Name: _____
_____ Primary _____ Specialist (List Specialty)
Address: _____ Telephone: _____

Name: _____
_____ Primary _____ Specialist (List Specialty)
Address: _____ Telephone: _____

Name: _____
_____ Primary _____ Specialist (List Specialty)
Address: _____ Telephone: _____

Dentist Name: _____
Specialist (List Specialty): _____
Address: _____ Telephone: _____

INSURANCE INFORMATION

Personal Insurance Providers:
Health Insurance: _____ Telephone: _____
Group Number: _____ Policy Number: _____

Medicaid Insurance: _____ Telephone: _____
Group Number: _____ Policy Number: _____
Coverage Amount/Details: _____

Medicare Insurance: _____ Telephone: _____
Group Number: _____ Policy Number: _____
Coverage Amount/Details: _____

Medigap Insurance: _____ Telephone: _____
Group Number: _____ Policy Number: _____
Coverage Amount/Details: _____

Dental Insurance: _____ Telephone: _____
Group Number: _____ Policy Number: _____

Vision Insurance: _____ Telephone: _____
Group Number: _____ Policy Number: _____

Disability Insurance: _____ Telephone: _____
Group Number: _____ Policy Number: _____

Long-term Care Insurance: _____ Telephone: _____
Group Number: _____ Policy Number: _____

Personal Caregiver(s):
Name: _____
Address: _____ Telephone: _____
Company Name: _____ Insurance/Payment Info: _____

Release Forms *(Indicate All the Forms You Have Completed):*
Living Will _____ Yes _____ No _____ Storage Location: _____
Health Care Directive _____ Yes _____ No _____ Storage Location: _____
DNR _____ Yes _____ No _____ Storage Location: _____
Organ Donation _____ Yes _____ No
Type: _____
Location: _____
Type: _____ Location: _____

PERSONAL MEDICAL HISTORY

Mark any of the following that apply, or attach a copy of your history from your physician.

Heart:
- Stroke
- Paralysis: Partial or Full
- Shortness of Breath
- Heart Murmur
- Heart Valve Problem
- TB, Emphysema or Other Lung Disease
- Artificial Heart Valve

- Heart Disease
- Heart Attack
- Chest Pain (angina)
- High Blood Pressure Problems
- Taking Heart Medication
- Rheumatic Fever
- Pacemaker

Blood:
- Easy Bruising
- Persistent Cough/Coughing Up Blood
- Diarrhea, Constipation, Blood in Stool
- Frequent Nausea

- Abnormal Bleeding
- Blood Disease (anemia)
- Difficulty Swallowing
- Difficulty Urinating/Blood in Urine

Allergies:
Allergic to:
- Drugs - Specify:
- Foods - Specify:
- Plants - Specify:
- Other - Specify:

Taking Allergy Medication(s) *(Please specify)*: ☐ Yes ☐ No
Allergy Medication:
Schedule:
Allergy Medication:
Schedule:

Back or Joints:
- Arthritis
- Back or Neck Pain
- Joint Replacement *(e.g. total hip)*

- Arthritis/Rheumatism
- Joint Pain/Stiffness

Surgeries: ☐ Yes ☐ No
Treatment: Date:
Treatment: Date:
HOSPITALIZATIONS: ☐ Yes ☐ No
Treatment: Date:
Treatment: Date:

Blood Transfusions: ☐ Yes ☐ No
Date: Date:
Date: Date:

Diabetes. ☐ Yes ☐ No
Family History of Diabetes: ☐ Yes ☐ No
Excessive Thirst ☐ Yes ☐ No
Thirsty/Dry Mouth (for extended periods): ☐ Yes ☐ No
Frequent Urination: ☐ Yes ☐ No
Type of Diabetes: ☐ Type 1 ☐ Type 2 ☐ Type 3
Medication:

Check any of the following that apply:
- Weight Gain
- Fever/Night Sweats
- Dizziness
- Headaches

- Blurred Vision
- Seizures

- Weight Loss
- Swollen Ankles
- Ringing in Ears
- Fainting Spells, Seizures or Epilepsy
- Frequent Nose Bleeds
- Sleep Disorders

Special Diet: ☐ Yes ☐ No
Details:

Diseases and Common Chronic Conditions:
Check any of the following that apply
- Cancer
- Tuberculosis/Respiratory Disease
- HIV Positive/AIDS

- Tumor
- Herpes 1 ☐ Herpes 2
- VD (syphilis or gonorrhea)

- Intestinal Problems
- Kidney/Bladder Disease
- Hepatitis, Jaundice or Liver Trouble
- Chronic Fatigue Syndrome
- Fibromyalgia
- Osteoporosis
- Mental Illnesses: ☐ Yes ☐ No
(specify):

- Stomach Problems/Ulcers
- Thyroid or Adrenal Disease
- Alzheimer's Disease
- Depression or Anxiety Disorders
- Multiple Sclerosis
- Parkinson's Disease

Eyes:
- Eye Disease
- Glaucoma
Other:
Do you wear contact lenses?: ☐ Yes ☐ No

Alcohol and Tobacco:
Do you drink alcohol?: ☐ Yes ☐ No
If yes, how many glasses per day #
- Beer #_____ Wine #_____ Spirits #_____

Do you smoke?: ☐ Yes ☐ No
If yes, how much (per day)?:
Date of this entry:

During the past 12 months have you taken any of the following medications?
- Antibiotics or Sulfa Drugs
- High Blood Pressure Medication
- Insulin
- Aspirin
- Nitroglycerin

- Cortisone (steroids)
Other:

- Anticoagulants (i.e. Coumadin)
- Tranquilizers
- Oral Pills for Diabetes
- Medication for Constipation
- Digitalis or Drugs for Heart Trouble

Are you allergic to or have you reacted adversely to any of the following:
Check any of the following that apply:
- Barbiturates, Sedatives or Sleeping Pills
- Penicillin or Cough Medicine
Other:

- Local Anesthetics (e.g. Novocaine)
- Codeine

For Women Only:
Are you taking contraceptives or other hormones?: ☐ Yes ☐ No
If yes, Date started:
Are you pregnant?: ☐ Yes ☐ No
If so, expected delivery date:
Have any of your babies weighed more than 9 pounds?: ☐ Yes ☐ No
Have you reached menopause?: ☐ Yes ☐ No
Are you taking a Hormone Replacement?: ☐ Yes ☐ No
If so, do you have any symptoms?: ☐ Yes ☐ No

Vaccination History: *Only check the box next to the vaccinations you have received and the dates for those vaccinations.*
As a Child:

- Diphtheria /Dates:
- Tetanus /Dates:
- Acellular Pertussis /Dates:
- Pneumococcal /Dates:
- Varicella-zoster /Dates:
- Haemophilus /Dates:
- Influenza Type B /Dates:
- Inactivated Polio /Dates:
- Measles /Dates:
- Meningitis /Dates:
- Mumps /Dates:
- Rubella /Dates:
- Hepatitis A /Dates:
- Hepatitis B /Dates:
Other: Dates:
Other: Dates:

As an Adult:
Measles /Dates:
Tuberculosis (TB) /Dates:
Pneumococcal /Dates:
Varicella /Dates:
Hepatitis A /Dates:
Hepatitis B /Dates:
Influenza /Dates:
Lyme /Dates:
Rabies /Dates:
Other: _____ Dates: _____
Other: _____ Dates: _____

Serious Illnesses:
Check the box next to the illnesses you have already had and the date/age they occurred.
Chicken Pox /Dates:
Measles /Dates:
Mumps /Dates:
Rubella/German Measles /Dates:
Polio /Dates:
Other: _____ Dates: _____
Other: _____ Dates: _____

Other Medical Documents:
*You have the legal right to ask your physician for a copy of your records. It is **important** to have a current copy of your medical history and include copies of the following procedures. Keep them with this file, and store an additional copy in safe place.*
• Copy of ECG/EKG
• X-Ray Reports
• Surgical Procedures
• Operative Report Summary

Special Needs:
Handicap Requirements:
Mobility:
Medical Alert Information:
Specialty Equipment/Aids *(buttons, bracelets):*

Food/ Dietary Requirements:
Food and diet requirements can be important in many cases, such as when you are on a special diet (salt free, fat free etc.); are allergic to some foods or drinks; or wish to avoid certain foods or drinks for religious reasons.

STORAGE RECOMMENDATION: **Medical History**			
ENVELOPE	MAIN LOCATION	LOCATION 2	LOCATION 3
Sealed	Locked File Cabinet	Grab & Go Kit	Expanded Emergency Kit
Actual Location(s):			

Consider using a folded 3 x 5 card for your wallet with major diagnosis, medica-tions, serious allergies, contact names and doctor information.

Alternatively, if you carry a smart phone, emergency personnel will look for an ICE entry. This IN CASE of EMERGENCY designation should be added to your prime contact's name. That will be the person and number they will call. To enter it into your contact list simply add a second entry for the same person but put the letters ICE in front of the name.

IDEA

If you carry a smart phone, emergency personnel will look for an ICE entry. This In Case of Emergency designation should be added to your prime contacts name. This will be the person and number they will call. To put it into your contact list, simply add a second entry for the same person but put the letters ICE in front of the name so it will show under the letter 'I' in your list of contacts.

GENERATIONAL (FAMILY) MEDICAL HISTORY

COMPLETE

Try to obtain as much information as possible from your living relatives, or any other reliable sources, about any serious illness that any family member may have, or have had, in the past, as some illnesses can be hereditary and affect generation upon generation. Knowing and keeping this information handy will prove valuable to you and others in your family for disease prevention and treatment.

It is very important that any records that you are able to develop are kept for future generations. This type of information could be a vital aid at some future date. Gaining access to this type of accurate and detailed medical information will most likely help a doctor to prescribe treatment for early intervention, and perhaps prevention of, a life-threatening illness.

Hereditary Health Concerns:
Please indicate if there is a history of any of the following conditions in your family:
○ Cancer /Relationship _____
○ Heart Disease /Relationship
○ Hypertension /Relationship· _____
○ Diabetes /Relationship· _____
Other: _____
Other: _____
Other: _____

STORAGE RECOMMENDATION: **Generational Family Health History**			
ENVELOPE	MAIN LOCATION	LOCATION 2	LOCATION 3
Sealed	Locked File Cabinet	Grab & Go Kit	Expanded Emergency Kit
Actual Location(s):			

Family Medical History *(Complete for as many close relations as possible.):*

NAME		RELATIONSHIP
DATE OF BIRTH		LOCATION
DATE OF DEATH	AGE	INTERMENT LOCATION
MEDICAL CONDITIONS		CAUSE OF DEATH
OTHER		

NAME		RELATIONSHIP
DATE OF BIRTH		LOCATION
DATE OF DEATH	AGE	INTERMENT LOCATION
MEDICAL CONDITIONS		CAUSE OF DEATH
OTHER		

NAME		RELATIONSHIP
DATE OF BIRTH		LOCATION
DATE OF DEATH	AGE	INTERMENT LOCATION
MEDICAL CONDITIONS		CAUSE OF DEATH
OTHER		

NAME		RELATIONSHIP
DATE OF BIRTH		LOCATION
DATE OF DEATH	AGE	INTERMENT LOCATION
MEDICAL CONDITIONS		CAUSE OF DEATH
OTHER		

NAME		RELATIONSHIP
DATE OF BIRTH		LOCATION
DATE OF DEATH	AGE	INTERMENT LOCATION
MEDICAL CONDITIONS		CAUSE OF DEATH
OTHER		

Family Medical History *(Complete for as many close relations as possible.):*

NAME		RELATIONSHIP
DATE OF BIRTH		LOCATION
DATE OF DEATH	AGE	INTERMENT LOCATION
MEDICAL CONDITIONS		CAUSE OF DEATH
OTHER		

NAME		RELATIONSHIP
DATE OF BIRTH		LOCATION
DATE OF DEATH	AGE	INTERMENT LOCATION
MEDICAL CONDITIONS		CAUSE OF DEATH
OTHER		

NAME		RELATIONSHIP
DATE OF BIRTH		LOCATION
DATE OF DEATH	AGE	INTERMENT LOCATION
MEDICAL CONDITIONS		CAUSE OF DEATH
OTHER		

NAME		RELATIONSHIP
DATE OF BIRTH		LOCATION
DATE OF DEATH	AGE	INTERMENT LOCATION
MEDICAL CONDITIONS		CAUSE OF DEATH
OTHER		

NAME		RELATIONSHIP
DATE OF BIRTH		LOCATION
DATE OF DEATH	AGE	INTERMENT LOCATION
MEDICAL CONDITIONS		CAUSE OF DEATH
OTHER		

CHAPTER **Two**

Legal Information

It is vital to make sure you have all your legal matters in order. This is a critical exercise that must be completed no matter how much or little you possess, as your loved ones and other pertinent parties may otherwise remain unaware of the existence of some of your possessions and documents.

As you go through and provide answers in the following 'Legal Information and Documents' form related to this chapter, you will be making a record of any and all legal documents you have completed to protect yourself and your loved ones.

Some of the questions that you answer in the following pages will probably prompt ideas about getting some legal documents written, or serve as a reminder of something you have been intending to do, but have not yet done. In either case you should make a note for yourself of anything that needs your attention sooner rather than later...and make sure that you actually go about the steps to initiate any legal documents.

Check or complete the information required in all the following sections and forms. For every document, put down the lawyer's name and the address. It's possible throughout a lifetime that different attorneys will be responsible for putting together different documents for you.

The second part of this chapter will discuss wills, living trusts, estate administrations, advance healthcare directives and other critical legal information in an attempt to increase your awareness, understanding and familiarity with these matters.

Designate a specific place in your home for important documents. Documents that are recommended be kept at home could be put into a file cabinet, a fireproof safe or even a place between books.

Legal documents should be with your attorney and copies in a deposit box or home safe. Do not put a Will or healthcare documents in a safety deposit box.

Prenuptial Agreement: ○ Yes   ○ No
(A contract between two persons about to marry concerning their respective property rights upon termination of the marriage by divorce or death.)

STORAGE RECOMMENDATION: Prenuptial Agreement

ENVELOPE	MAIN LOCATION	LOCATION 2	LOCATION 3
Sealed	Your and Spouse's Attorney	Safe Deposit Box	Locked File: Home & Relative

Actual Location(s):

Power of Attorney. ○ Yes   ○ No
(A written document given by one person or party to another authorizing the latter to act for the former.)

STORAGE RECOMMENDATION: Power of Attorney

ENVELOPE	MAIN LOCATION	LOCATION 2	LOCATION 3
Sealed	Attorney	Safe Deposit Box	Locked File Cabinet: Home

Actual Location(s):

Contracts:
Type: _____   Deadline: _____
Type: _____   Deadline: _____

Promissory Notes:
Promissory Notes: _____
Debts: _____
Debts: _____

STORAGE RECOMMENDATION: Contracts, Promissory Notes and Debts

ENVELOPE	MAIN LOCATION	LOCATION 2	LOCATION 3
Sealed	Locked File Cabinet: Home	Safe Deposit Box	

Actual Location(s):

Trust: ○ Yes   ○ No
(A fiduciary relationship in which a trustee holds the title to property, from one party to another, for the benefit of another.)
Name of Trust:
Type:
Date Executed:
Name of Lawyer:
Law Firm:
Tax Identification Number:
Trustor:
Trustee:
Successor Trustees:

STORAGE RECOMMENDATION: Trusts

ENVELOPE	MAIN LOCATION	LOCATION 2	LOCATION 3
Sealed	Locked File Cabinet: Home	Safe Deposit Box	

Actual Location(s):

Inheritance Particulars:

STORAGE RECOMMENDATION: Inheritance

ENVELOPE	MAIN LOCATION	LOCATION 2	LOCATION 3
Sealed	Locked File Cabinet: Home	Safe Deposit Box	

Actual Location(s):

Real Estate:
(Check all that apply and add the location of documents.)

Home:
Address:
Mortgage Company:
Address:

LEGAL INFORMATION AND DOCUMENTS

COMPLETE

W...
I have a Will: ☐ Yes ☐ No
Date Created:
Lawyer Responsible:
Law Firm's Address:
Contact:
Last Review Date:

Executor[s]:   Alternate:
(A person or persons named in the Will to carry out the provisions in the Will)

Codicil ☐ Yes ☐ No If Yes, Date:
(A supplement to the Will with any addition, explanation, or modification of something in the Will)

Durable Power of Attorney for Healthcare: ☐ Yes ☐ No

STORAGE RECOMMENDATION: **Will**			
ENVELOPE	MAIN LOCATION	LOCATION 2	LOCATION 3
Sealed	Attorney	Copy: Locked File	
Actual Location(s):			

Guardianship:
(The person in charge of the care and responsibility for a child or senior)
Name:
Responsibilities:

STORAGE RECOMMENDATION: **Guardianship**			
ENVELOPE	MAIN LOCATION	LOCATION 2	LOCATION 3
Sealed	Guardian and Attorney	Locked File Cabinet	Safe Deposit Box
Actual Location(s):			

Other:
Add...
Gre... D...
Address:
Investment Holdings:
Address:
Lease(s):
Address:
Partnership Agreements:
Address:
Other Contracts:

STORAGE RECOMMENDATION: **Real Estate & Other Property Contracts**			
ENVELOPE	MAIN LOCATION	LOCATION 2	LOCATION 3
Sealed	Locked File Cabinet: Home	Safe Deposit Box	
Actual Location(s):			

Insurance Policies:

POLICY TYPE	NAME OF INSURED
CARRIER NAME	INSURANCE AGENT
AGENT PHONE	AGENT ADDRESS
GROUP NUMBER	POLICY NUMBER
PREMIUMS	PREMIUM DUE DATE
DOCUMENT LOCATION	COVERAGE
POLICY TYPE	NAME OF INSURED
CARRIER NAME	INSURANCE AGENT
AGENT PHONE	AGENT ADDRESS
GROUP NUMBER	POLICY NUMBER
PREMIUMS	PREMIUM DUE DATE
DOCUMENT LOCATION	COVERAGE

Insurance Policies *Continued...*

POLICY TYPE	NAME OF INSURED
CARRIER NAME	INSURANCE AGENT
AGENT PHONE	AGENT ADDRESS
GROUP NUMBER	POLICY NUMBER
PREMIUMS	PREMIUM DUE DATE
DOCUMENT LOCATION	COVERAGE
POLICY TYPE	NAME OF INSURED
CARRIER NAME	INSURANCE AGENT
AGENT PHONE	AGENT ADDRESS
GROUP NUMBER	POLICY NUMBER
PREMIUMS	PREMIUM DUE DATE
DOCUMENT LOCATION	COVERAGE
POLICY TYPE	NAME OF INSURED
CARRIER NAME	INSURANCE AGENT
AGENT PHONE	AGENT ADDRESS
GROUP NUMBER	POLICY NUMBER
PREMIUMS	PREMIUM DUE DATE
DOCUMENT LOCATION	COVERAGE

STORAGE RECOMMENDATION: **Insurance Policies**			
ENVELOPE	MAIN LOCATION	LOCATION 2	LOCATION 3
Sealed	Locked File Cabinet: Home	Safe Deposit Box	
Actual Location(s):			

Healthcare Directive: ☐ Yes ☐ No
Rel... Forms ☐ ... ☐ ...
DNR ☐ ... ☐ No
(Do not resuscitate. Used in hospitals and other health care facilities to indicate to the staff the decision of a patient's doctors and family, or of the patient via a living will, to avoid extraordinary means of prolonging life.)
Is Your Healthcare Directive on File with Physician? ☐ Yes ☐ No
Does Your Closest Relative Have a Copy of Your Healthcare Directive? ☐ Yes ☐ No

Living Will: ☐ Yes ☐ No
(A document instructing physicians, relatives, or others to refrain from the use of extraordinary measures, such as life-support equipment, to prolong one's life in the event of a terminal illness.)

Do you have a Durable Power of Attorney for Healthcare: ☐ Yes ☐ No

STORAGE RECOMMENDATION: **Healthcare Directive**			
ENVELOPE	MAIN LOCATION	LOCATION 2	LOCATION 3
Sealed	Physician	Locked File Cabinet: Home	Safe Deposit Box
Actual Location(s):			

Burial Information and Arrangements for Final Wishes:
Desired Plot Location:
Prepaid: ☐ Yes ☐ No   LOT #
Location of Receipt:
Prearranged Funeral Plan: ☐ Yes ☐ No   Prepaid: ☐ Yes ☐ No
Opening and Closing Fees: ☐ Yes ☐ No
Annual fees:
Government aid: ☐ Yes ☐ No
Persons to be contacted first in the event of your death:

Person responsible for Funeral Arrangements
Other Preferences:
Disposition of Your Remains:
Casket Type:

Funeral Service:　　Yes　　No If Yes Type:
Memor...
Open C...
Funeral Home:
Location for Service:
Religious Ceremony:
Religious Leader's Name:
- Favorite Sermons or Hymns:
- Speakers:
- Pollbearers:
- Music:
- Flowers:
- Donations:
- Service Open to All:
- Religious or Cultural Considerations:
- Special Requests:

Obituary:
Member of Memorial Society:

STORAGE RECOMMENDATION	**Burial Information**		
ENVELOPE	MAIN LOCATION	LOCATION 2	LOCATION 3
Sealed	Attorney	Locked File Cabinet, Home	
Actual Location(s):			

You should find it relatively easy to get almost any preliminary legal information you require using web sites and books, see also **www.gettingsafer.com**. However, although these methods of finding legal and other information can prove very helpful, in the end you should probably sit down with a well-recommended attorney. Once informed of your personal situation and requirements, he or she will then be able to give you expert advice and draft the type of documentation you may ultimately need.

Within our legal system, some of the titles used by lawyers for documentation can often seem daunting to a layperson. I hope that once you have read the following information you will feel more comfortable about the matters discussed, and more confident about seeking any additional individual legal information you may require.

ESTATE PLANNING

Estate planning is the creation of legal documents such as Wills, Trusts, and Durable Powers of Attorneys, for the purposes of managing your assets during a period of incapacity and distributing your assets at your death. It is a way to help prevent family disputes that can arise over amounts of money, personal assets and ways in which your property will be distributed.

Unfortunately, most of us carry any information about our wishes in our heads. We never get around to discussing our final wishes in detail with our family members. That just leaves our loved ones to do their best to sort it all out later.

As a result of our failure to plan and organize our legal and other matters, painful losses can result. Frequently, stocks, bonds, bank accounts, real estate and insurance policy benefits go unclaimed and are eventually turned over to the state government. Billions of dollars currently sit in state treasuries because the rightful property owners could not be found. Fortunately, losses like these can be avoided with a little bit of advance planning, sorting and organizing.

Basic estate planning can be relatively simple. It requires creating the following documentation and performing the following actions. By completing these steps you will be leaving behind a clear indication of your intentions.

BEWARE

Write and update your Will on a regular basis. Review the Will after any major life events but at least every 5 years. Consider your different options to distribute your property, such as trusts or living trusts.

Keep an updated list of:
• All deeds and other important documents
• Insurance policies, with name and number
• Pensions and retirement accounts
• Bank, money market and mutual fund accounts
• Items in safes, safe-deposit boxes and other locked or hidden places
• Important information about your family's history
• Location of photographs, heirlooms, valuables and other irreplaceable items
• Your preferences for funeral arrangements, and who should be notified

IDEA

As you start to organize this material, remember that it is very important to store these types of information *in more than one safe and fireproof place.* You should also discuss these new records, and their location, with those closest to you.

In addition, to help those you care about at a most difficult time, it is recommended that you write the following 2 letters with the title on the outside of each envelope:

1. Open Upon My Death:
This letter contains information about those things that need to be done immediately and also directs the reader to the location of your documents, files, contracts and policies that need to be reviewed. To assist you in this task a list of relevant headings can be found at www.GettinSafer.com

2. Open If I Am Unable To Communicate My Wishes:
This letter should contain information about your medical preferences and the names of your doctors and other medical advisors. A format for this letter with relevant headings can be found at www.GettingSafer.com

Wills

A Will is a legal document in which you clearly state how you want your property to be distributed after your death, and whom you trust to be in charge to make those distributions.

If you do not write a Will, and die intestate, then the persons who are entitled to inherit will be determined according to the State law of intestacy. Under State intestacy laws different people other than those you would have chosen could be entitled to inherit depending on the deceased persons' marital status and whether the deceased person's assets consisted of spousal or community property, or separate property.

One of the downsides or negative of a Will is that it generally requires the beneficiaries to go through a probate process before they receive their inheritances.

Probate is the court-supervised process of paying your debts and distributing your property to the people entitled to inherit. Probate procedures can drag on for months before the beneficiaries receive anything. This can be both a time-consuming and relatively expensive process, and it therefore leaves less to your heirs.

Many states have summary probate proceedings, which are faster and less burdensome, for an estate that does not exceed a specified amount, generally $20,000 to $150,000. Still, you should not rely on these summary procedures. Useful information is available at CostHelper.com/probate

Although there is no special way to write a Will, the document must show that it is intended to be your final statement of your wishes for the disposition of your property upon your death. In order for your Will to be valid, you must be aware of the nature and extent of your property, and that by signing the Will you are making a final disposition of your property. Make sure that there is no ambiguity in your Will, especially if you have made changes to it from time to time. If there is any ambiguity and your intentions are not really clear, just start over and make a new Will.

A Will becomes a matter of public record when it is submitted to a probate court, as do all the other documents associated with probate, such as complete lists and inventories of the deceased person's assets and debts. The terms of a living trust, however, need not be made public.

Most Americans haven't made even a simple Will. Depending on your age and health, however, you may not need to do much in the way of estate planning. You can learn how to write a simple form of a Will from some good self-help material (see Books at GettingSafer.com). If you are young (over 18) and unmarried, with a long life expectancy, you may not need much or any estate planning. But, at least you should have powers of attorney, one for financial management purposes and one for Healthcare and Living Will. These issues are discussed later.

If you have a lot of assets, you should write a Will. If you have a life partner but no marriage certificate, a Will is absolutely necessary, or state law will dictate where your property goes after your death. In this event your closest biological relatives will probably inherit everything.

Once you are married and have children, a Will is highly recommended. In it you can include the person that you have appointed as your children's guardian. You should also think about buying relatively inexpensive term life insurance. This type of insurance, purchased in case of an untimely death, is designed to replace your earnings, and to provide for your family.

Because the Will probably won't be located and read until several weeks after you have passed away, you should not express your death and burial preferences in it.

It is best to deal with such matters as your death and burial preferences in a separate document. In that document you can include your instructions about any personal matters, usually based on your religious preference or simply your own whims. You can designate the mortuary that will handle your burial or cremation, as well as any decisions about the following:

- Whether or not you wish to be embalmed
- The type of casket or container in which your remains will be buried or cremated.
- Details of any ceremony you want before the burial or cremation
- Names of pallbearers, if any
- How your remains will be transported to the cemetery and gravesite
- Where your remains will be buried, stored or scattered
- Details of any ceremony you want to accompany your burial, interment or scattering
- Details of any marker you want to show where your remains are buried or interred.

Most mortuaries or funeral homes are equipped to handle many of the details related to disposing of a person's remains.

The costs of some of the services you may want can vary dramatically, but since you are planning in advance, you can shop around. Just be very careful if you decide to pre-pay for any services; sometimes mortuaries go out of business, and if you have pre-paid, you may be left without recourse. Also, at some future date, if you ever move to a new location, you may not need items for which you have pre-paid, and you may find out that your prepayment funds are nonrefundable.

In any event, as part of your plan, set aside sufficient *cash (your checks can not be used after your death)* to cover expenses for the time period immediately following your death. It may take some time before legal concerns and documents are in order and until any settlements will be paid out from your estate. Make sure the cash you have set aside is in a safe place, and inform a trusted loved one or your attorney about its location.

If you die without leaving written instructions about your preferences, state law will determine who will have the right to decide how your remains will be handled. The person, who is then chosen by order of priority, will either be your spouse, child, parent, the next of kin, or a public administrator who is appointed by a court.

*Note for Storage: Safe-deposit boxes may become sealed in the event of your death.

GUARDIANSHIP

A *guardian* is a person whom you name in your will as the person you want to take care of your minor child's personal needs, including shelter, education and medical care. The guardian may also provide financial management for your child if you have not appointed a second person *(a "conservator or "guardian of the estate")* for that purpose. Remember that in the event that both you and the other parent are unavailable, and there is no will, a court will appoint someone of their own choosing without the benefit of knowing your preferences.

STORAGE RECOMMENDATION: **Guardianship**			
ENVELOPE	MAIN LOCATION	LOCATION 2	LOCATION 3
Sealed	Guardian and Attorney	Locked File Cabinet	Safe Deposit Box
Actual Location(s):			

Power of Attorney

You can create a Durable *Power of Attorney* for financial matters, which will allow the person you nominate, while you are alive, to act on your behalf in financial matters. "Durable" refers to the ability of the Power of Attorney to remain legally enforceable even after *(you)* the principal becomes incapacitated, e.g., not able to watch over and approve or disapprove of the agent's actions.

There are two basic types of Durable Power of Attorneys: those that are effective immediately upon signing of the document and those that 'spring' into effect only in the event of the incapacity of the principal. The 'springing' type is more common in family estate planning, because usually the principal is able to handle his or her own financial affairs at the time of signing, but wants to plan for the possible day when he or she can't.

Trusts

Trusts come in many shapes and sizes. Your trust is an arrangement under which one or more persons, the trustee or trustees, holds legal title to property for another person or persons, called the *beneficiary or beneficiaries.*

You can learn quite a lot about trusts by reading numerous books on the subject, or through using searches on the Internet. It is definitely best to have some ideas about what you want to achieve and then have an experienced estate planning lawyer draw up any trust documents. Even if you try to write your own documents, in most cases there will be tax ramifications, and you most probably will require professional assistance and guidance.

The most common trust used for probate avoidance is the *Revocable Living Trust.* "Revocable" means that you can change or revoke the trust during your lifetime, just like with a Will. "Living" means that you create the trust during your lifetime, as opposed to creating the trust at the time of your death, such as in a *testamentary trust*, which is created when trust language is inserted into a Will and takes effect only on your death. You can be the trustee of your own living trust, therefore keeping full control over all property held in trust.

Living Trust

The big advantage to making a living trust is that property left through the trust does not have to be handled through probate court before it reaches the people whom you want to ultimately inherit it. The person you appoint to handle the trust after your death *(the "successor trustee")* simply transfers ownership to the beneficiaries whom you named in the trust. In many cases, the whole process takes only a few weeks and there are no lawyer or court fees to pay. When all of the property has been transferred to the beneficiaries, the living trust ceases to exist.

IDEA

Making a living trust work will require some action on your part. You'll need to complete some important paperwork to transfer assets into the trust. As an example, in order to be able to leave your house through the trust, you must sign a new deed that shows that you now own the house as a trustee of your own living trust. Some states require inclusion of special language in your trust document to avoid wrinkles in those states' income tax and/or property tax laws; seek an attorney's expertise for specific information.

BEWARE

Even though you have a living trust, you will still need a Will, typically called a "pour-over will." A *pour-over Will* transfers or pours over, any property that you have not transferred to yourself as trustee during your lifetime to the successor trustee of your living trust. This successor trustee serves as the sole beneficiary of your pour-over Will. For example, if you acquire property just before you die suddenly or accidentally, you may not have had an opportunity to transfer ownership of it to your trust, and therefore it won't pass under the terms of the trust document. Using the pour-over Will, those assets can be transferred to the successor trustee of your living trust, possibly requiring a court-supervised probate proceeding as to those assets only, but nonetheless satisfying your ultimate disposition wishes.

Advance Healthcare Directive or Medical Plan

Two documents, a Living Will and a Durable Power of Attorney for Healthcare, are used to make up a medical plan. Together they are known as an "Advance Healthcare Directive" or "Medical Plan."

If you have no such healthcare documents and become incapacitated, then doctors will use their own discretion in deciding what kind of medical care you will receive. If there are any questions regarding surgery or any serious procedure doctors may, but are not required, to ask your spouse, parent or adult child for their consent.

When writing your advance healthcare directive documents you should make your wishes known regarding as many medical procedures as possible. Take into account that the most commonly-administered procedures administered to comatose or terminally ill patients are blood and blood products, cardio-pulmonary resuscitation (CPR), diagnostic tests, dialysis, drugs, respirators, and surgery. You should make your wishes known in regards to each. *Make sure the whereabouts of this document is known, as it must be found to be of use.*

STORAGE RECOMMENDATION: **Advance Healthcare Directive**			
ENVELOPE	MAIN LOCATION	LOCATION 2	LOCATION 3
Sealed	Attorney & Guardian	Locked File Cabinet*	Safe Deposit Box
Actual Location(s):			

Living Will (Healthcare Directive, or Directive to Physicians)

A *Living Will* is a legal document in which you express your wishes in advance about what extended medical treatment should be withheld or provided if you are terminally ill and become unable to communicate those wishes yourself. Once any doctor receives a properly signed and witnessed living will, it creates a contract between you and the doctor. The instructions must be honored or the doctor must transfer you to the care of another doctor who will honor your directive. Directives are used to instruct doctors to withhold life-prolonging treatments or to reinforce that you want to receive all medical treatment that is available.

Your healthcare directive becomes effective when you are diagnosed to be close to death from a terminal condition or permanently comatose. When you cannot communicate your own wishes for your medical care, either orally, in writing or through gestures, and there is a valid healthcare directive, the medical personnel attending you are notified of your written directions for your medical care. In fact this directive should be part of the medical records on your treatment board and not just on file.

You can have your directive become part of your medical record when you are admitted to a hospital or other care facility. *Remember to give copies of your completed directive to several people, including your physician, your healthcare proxy (explanation follows), and a trusted friend.*

Creating Your Living Will/Healthcare Directive

In most states, to make a valid healthcare directive you must be 18 years old and understand what the document means, what it contains and how it works. You must sign your documents, or if unable to do so, direct another person to sign them for you. Such signing must be performed in the presence of witnesses or a notary public, and sometimes both. You also need to show that you were of sound mind and of legal age when you made the documents. In some states parents are allowed to make healthcare directives for their minor children.

When you are being admitted to a hospital is not the best time to make decisions about your healthcare directive. It is much better to make those decisions when you are well and not under any pressure. So set out your healthcare directive decisions as soon as possible. You can revise them or make a new document at any time.

For advice on this matter, call or visit a senior center in your area. They should have trained healthcare staff to discuss your healthcare options with you. Also, the patient representatives at a local hospital or your regular physician are excellent sources with whom you can talk.

STORAGE RECOMMENDATION: **Living Will**			
ENVELOPE	MAIN LOCATION	LOCATION 2	LOCATION 3
Sealed	Attorney, Physician & Guardian	Locked File Cabinet*	Safe Deposit Box
Actual Location(s):			

Durable Power of Attorney for Healthcare (Healthcare Proxy)

A Durable Power of Attorney for Healthcare gives another person [your *proxy*] the authority to make medical decisions for you if you are unable to make them for yourself. The document does not state what type of treatment you want to receive, only who is empowered to make those decisions.

Your proxy should be an assertive person, but at the same time a person with whom you feel comfortable discussing your wishes, and also one whom will be able to make difficult medical decisions in line with your wishes. He or she may even have to fight with medical personnel or some family members in order to have your wishes carried out. Remember that the person you select has the right to make their own decisions concerning how they want you to be treated medically.

The person you select could be your spouse or partner, a relative or a close friend. Preferably it will be someone that lives nearby. Your proxy shouldn't be your doctor or any employee that works at a healthcare facility where you receive treatment.

Even if you do not name a healthcare proxy, it is simple, yet very important, to have your final healthcare wishes put down in writing.

Medical Information Confidentiality (HIPAA)

BEWARE

You also need to give your named successor's personal representatives access to your medical information. This has become more complicated due to the passage of the federal Health Insurance Portability and Accountability Act (HIPAA). Some states have also passed their own version of this law, which sometimes has more restrictive provisions than the federal law. This law was intended to provide a secure way for health information to be passed from one person or entity to another, and provides for stiff monetary penalties for violators. The law was not specifically targeted at estate plans, but does add a complicated twist that a complete estate plan needs to unravel.

Many estate plans provide that the appointment of successor trustees, successor agents and successor executors take effect upon the death or incapacity of a particular person. Incapacity is commonly defined as "one (or two) doctors stating in writing that the person is incapacitated." Many doctors or other health providers will be hesitant to give such writings for fear of violating HIPAA and possible state law, unless they are satisfied that they have been given the necessary medical information and release provisions.

Organ Donation

Organs and tissues are in great demand, and medical technology has made successful organ and tissue transplants easier and safer. A number of states accept any body part for donation.

The organs and tissues most commonly being transplanted are:

My commitment to share life uniform donor card

I _____ have spoken to my family about organ and tissue donation. The following have witnessed my commitment to be a donor.

I wish to donate the following:
☐ Any needed organs and tissue
☐ Only the following organs and tissue:

_____
_____

Donor _____
Signature _____ Date _____
Witness _____ Witness _____

- Bone and bone marrow
- Tendons, ligaments, and connective tissue
- Skin
- Pancreas
- Lungs.
- Corneas
- Hearts
- Livers
- Kidney

Donor cards or forms for organ donation are available from most hospitals, your county or state office, as well as from the local Department of Motor Vehicles or the National Kidney Foundation.

The official government organ donation site is: http://www.organdonor.gov

By signing and carrying a donor card, you are identified to medical personnel as a potential organ donor. Carry it with your drivers' license, and leave another original with your attorney.

Even if you do not have a signed card or any document indicating your intent to donate your organs, your next of kin can approve a donation at your death. You should also know that even if you have indicated your intent to donate your organs, medical personnel would take any objection by your next of kin into account, and usually will not proceed with the organ donation if an objection is voiced. Your best safeguard to have your organ donation wishes honored is to discuss your intentions with close friends and relatives, emphasizing your strong feelings about donating your body for research or teaching. Ideally you should have your organ donation wishes documented and witnessed by two relatives.

BEWARE

If it is your intention to donate your entire body for research you should know that if any organs have previously been removed, your donation would be refused

ESTATE ADMINISTRATION

You may have been named as the *Estate Administrator* by a friend or family member, but prior to your acceptance of the appointment as an Estate Administrator it is advisable to meet with an estate-planning attorney. In such a meeting you will discover that there can be quite of lot of things to do. You should get competent advice as to what to do if you accept the appointment. In that way, by the time you agree to accept the appointment you will know what will be involved. You will understand that you are likely to need the help of a number of different professionals from attorneys to accountants as it is definitely not a good idea to try to do everything yourself. In other words, a smart person is a person who knows when it is time to get help.

Income Taxes

If the *decedent* (the person who died) had taxable income in the year of death, then a final income tax return (IRS Form 1040) should be filed for applicable federal and state income taxes. This return is due by April 15 in the year following the year of death. Even if no income taxes are due because the decedent did not have enough income to require the filing of an income tax return, it may still be a good idea to file a final income tax return for the purpose of starting the three-year statute of limitation. The ordinary statute of limitations is the time in which the Internal Revenue Service must audit that tax year for income tax purposes. If the statute of limitations never starts running, then technically, the Internal Revenue Service can audit that tax year at any time, even thirty years later.

Estate Taxes

If the decedent's estate is large enough, then the decedent's personal representative must file a federal estate tax return (IRS Form 706). This is a very specialized tax return, and when required, is due nine months after the date of death. *There are very significant penalties and interest for not filing this return on time.*

Real Estate

Real estate owned by the decedent must be transferred to whom-ever is entitled. That person is determined by reviewing the legal documents then in force. Legal documents, such as affidavits of death, grant deeds, warranty deeds and quitclaim deeds, are commonly used to make these transfers. Many states also have property tax laws that allow the local assessor to reassess the property for property tax purposes when the owner dies. Some of these states also have exceptions, such as when the real estate passes from a parent to a child. It is important to have the property tax issues analyzed by competent tax advisors.

Starting for decedents dying in 2011, or after, if the decedent leaves a surviving spouse, it may be advantageous for the surviving spouse to voluntarily file a federal estate tax return even if the deceased spouse's estate's value is not large enough to require its filing. If the surviving spouse files a federal estate tax return, the surviving spouse can receive the deceased spouse's unused exclusion (DSUE) amount, which can help or eliminate federal taxes or federal gift taxes for the surviving spouse. A consultation with a qualified attorney is strongly suggested for these issues.

Notification of Beneficiaries

The decedent's personal representative should keep the estate beneficiaries reasonably informed on the details of the estate administration. Some states have specific notification laws, such as requiring the personal representative to give the estate beneficiaries a copy of any living trusts, or other estate planning documents that are in effect at the decedent's death, and to file the decedent's Will with the local probate court. Failure to comply with these laws could subject the personal representative to liability.

Probate

If probate is required, then an attorney should be hired to take the estate through the probate process. It is best to rely on the probate attorney's advice regarding the specifics of probating any particular estate.

Valuation of Estate Assets

The decedent's assets should be valued as of the date of death. If the decedent owned any capital assets, then those assets will generally receive a step up in tax basis at the time of the decedent's death that could result in less capital gains tax to the beneficiaries. Tax preparers upon any future sale or other disposition of those capital assets will need the updated valuations.

Accountings

The decedent's personal representative should prepare accounts for the estate. This accounting should document things such as the initial inventory of estate assets and their values, the financial impact of any sales or losses of estate assets, the amount and description of income and expenses received and incurred, and the final distribution of the assets to the estate beneficiaries.

While the details of the estate administration may appear obvious during the administration, a year or two later it is easy to have forgotten the particulars.

Agreeing to act as an executor or trustee is frequently thought of as a thankless job, therefore it is very prudent for you to proceed cautiously and document everything. Then, if there is a later claim of mistake, negligence, wrongdoing or fraud, you will want to have a record to refresh your recollection, and to use as evidence in your defense.

Protect the Assets

One of the most important responsibilities of the personal representative is to protect the estate's assets, meaning to protect the estate from loss. For example, if the decedent is heavily invested in high-risk investments, the personal representative may need to reposition the investments to a more diversified portfolio. If the decedent owned real estate, the personal representative should make sure that things such as any homeowners or other insurance policies stay in effect, and do not lapse. Additionally, the personal representative should maintain strict control of any of the decedent's automobiles, either keeping them insured, or keeping them parked somewhere safe.

How Long It Should Take to Administer an Estate

Administering an estate can take as little as one to three months, or for more complex estates, longer than three years. The timeline is estate-specific, and depends on a number of things like whether the estate must be probated, whether there is a federal estate tax return due, and whether estate assets, such as business interests or real property, are to be sold as part of the estate administration.

When dealing with estates, patience is a virtue.

CHAPTER **Three**

Financial Matters

The forms in relation to this Financial Matters topic are set out so you can record and organize all your financial information. The questions may prompt you to open some new accounts that you have probably intended to set up for a long time, but haven't as of yet. Work your way through all the questions and realize that at long last, you now have a real opportunity to get better organized financially!

After the financial data information questionnaire, the next part of this chapter will provide useful information to help you to better understand your present situation and ideas that will help you to make plans for your financial future.

To obtain information about the tax records that you need to keep, call 800-TAX-FORM, or go online to www.irs.gov/publications/p552/index.html

As you complete the questionnaire section, put a special mark beside the items that you will want to keep up-to-date as time goes on, and your financial picture changes.

Since this is an extremely important and confidential list of your financial assets and accounts, it is vital to store this list in an appropriate location.

FINANCIAL INFORMATION QUESTIONNAIRE

Bank Accounts

Bank Name 1:	Bank Name 2:
Address:	Address:
Telephone Number:	Telephone Number:
Contact Person:	Contact Person:
Name of Account:	Name of Account:
Type of Account:	Type of Account:
Checking AC #:	Checking AC #:
Saving AC #:	Saving AC #:
Other AC #:	Other AC #:
Other AC #:	Other AC #:

Security Deposit Box: Yes   No
Contents of Deposit Box List Done?   Yes   No   Date:
Location of List: Location of Key:

Credit Card Organizer:

Credit Card Type Visa/MC/Am Ex (other)	Issuing Bank	Telephone #	Card #

(Expiry dates were intentionally omitted from the above table for safety.)
Note: Over time, make sure to maintain a list of any additional credit cards.

Insurance Policies:

Homeowners'/Renters' Insurance: Yes   No
Company Name:
Agent's Name: Telephone Number:
Policy Number: Coverage Amount:
Details:

General Liability Insurance: Yes   No
Company Name:
Agent's Name: Telephone Number:
Policy Number: Coverage Amount:
Details:

Auto Insurance: Yes   No
Company Name:
Agent's Name: Telephone Number:
Policy Number: Coverage Amount:
Details:

Health Insurance Coverage: Yes   No
Company Name: Telephone Number:
Insured Person 1:   Policy Number:
Coverage Amount:
Details:

Company Name: Telephone Number:
Insured Person 2:   Policy Number:
Coverage Amount:
Details:

Medicaid/MediCal: Yes   No
Company Name: Telephone Number:
Policy Number: Coverage Amount:
Details:

Medicare: Yes   No
Company Name:
Policy Number: Coverage Amount:
Details:

Medigap Insurance: Yes   No
Company Name:
Policy Number: Coverage Amount:
Details:

Dental Insurance: Yes   No
Company Name:
Policy Number: Coverage Amount:
Details:

Vision Care Insurance: Yes   No
Company Name:
Policy Number: Coverage Amount:
Details:

Disability Insurance: Yes   No
Company Name:
Policy Number: Coverage Amount:
Details:

Long Term Care Insurance for Insured Person 1:   Yes   No
Company Name:
Agent's Name: Telephone Number:
Policy Number: Coverage Amount:
Details:

Long Term Care Insurance for Insured Person 2:   Yes   No
Company Name:
Agent's Name: Telephone Number:
Policy Number: Coverage Amount:
Details:

Life Insurance: Yes   No
Company Name:
Agent's Name: Telephone Number:
Policy Number: Coverage Amount:
Owner of Policy: Beneficiary:
Location of Policy:
Details:

Life Insurance: Yes   No
Company Name:
Agent's Name: Telephone Number:
Policy Number: Coverage Amount:
Owner of Policy: Beneficiary:
Location of Policy:
Details:

Union Insurance: Yes   No
Company Name:
Agent's Name: Telephone Number:
Policy Number: Coverage Amount:
Details:

Other Insurance: Yes   No
Company Name:
Agent's Name: Telephone Number:
Policy Number: Coverage Amount:
Details:

Other Insurance: Yes   No
Company Name:
Agent's Name: Telephone Number:
Policy Number: Coverage Amount:
Details:

Pension Plan: Yes   No
Company Name:
A/C #:   Income Amount: at age:
Beneficiary Name(s) and Contact Information:

401(k):   Yes   No
Company Name: Telephone Number:
A/C #:   Income Amount:$ at age:
Any pension loans:
Beneficiary Name(s) and Contact Information:

IRA: Yes   No
Company Name: Telephone Number:
A/C #:
Beneficiary Name(s) and Contact Information:

Spousal IRA: Yes   No
Roth IRA: Yes   No
Company Name: Telephone Number:
A/C #:
Beneficiary Name(s) and Contact Information:

SEP-IRA: Yes   No
Company Name: Telephone Number:
A/C #:
Beneficiary Name(s) and Contact Information:

403(b):   Yes   No
Company Name: Telephone Number:
A/C #:
Beneficiary Name(s) and Contact Information:

Any Loans: Yes   No

457:
Company Name: Telephone Number:
A/C #:
Beneficiary Name(s) and Contact Information:

Stock Options: Yes   No
If Yes Provide details:

Keogh Program: Yes   No
Company Name: Telephone Number:
A/C #:

Deferred Compensation Plan: Yes   No
Company:
Payout Period of Age:
Date Payout Begins: Date Payout Ends:

Profit Sharing Plan: Yes   No
Company: Plan #:

Other: Yes   No
Company Name: Policy Number:
Income Amount:
Company Name: Policy Number:
Income Amount:
Company Name: Policy Number:
Income Amount:

Financial Professionals & Advisors:

  CPA or   Accountant
Company:
Name: Telephone Number:
Fax Number: E-mail:
Address:

Stock Broker:
Company Name: Name of Broker:
Type of A/C: Account Number:
Telephone Number: Fax Number:
Email:

Broker, Real Estate:
Company Name: Name of Broker:
Telephone Number: Fax Number:
Email:

Investment Planner/Advisor:
Company Name: Advisor's Name:
Telephone Number: Fax Number:
Email:

Health Insurance Advisor:
Company Name: Advisor's Name:
Telephone Number: Fax Number:
Email:

Financial Liabilities:
Loans:
Notes Payable:
Mortgages:
Term: Rate %:
Second Mortgages:
Equity Loan:

Auto Loans:
Student Loans:
Personal Loans:

Note: Credit Cards that are usually short term. The amount that is owes is subject to constant change, and the liabilities do not have fixed or any specific end dates like other loans listed above. So just list your credit cards here so that it is easy for someone to check, in the event of your death, if there are any outstanding balances.

Credit Card Name and #:
Credit Card Name and #:
Credit Card Name and#:
Credit Card Name and#:
Other:

Personal Possessions Out on Loan:
Details:

Alimony: Yes   No
Name: Amount:
Details:

Child Support: Yes   No
Name: Amount:
Details:

Retirement Income Information:
Retirement Plan: Yes   No
Company Name: Telephone Number:
Policy Number: Income Amount:$ at age:
Location of Documents:
Beneficiary Name(s) and Contact Information:

Survivor Benefits:

Social Security Benefit: ⬡ Yes ⬡ No
Social Security Number *(last 4 digits)*: _____

Estimated Income Amount: _____

Social Security Benefit, Spouce/Partner: ⬡ Yes ⬡ No
Social Security Number *(last 4 digits)*: _____

Estimated Income Amount: _____

Annuity: ⬡ Yes ⬡ No

Company Name: _____

Policy Number: _____ Income Amount: _____

STORAGE RECOMMENDATION: **Financial Information Questionnaire**			
ENVELOPE	MAIN LOCATION	LOCATION 2	LOCATION 3
Sealed	Copy: Locked File Cabinet: Home	Copy: Safe Deposit Box	
Actual Location(s):			

SAFEGUARDING DOCUMENTS AND VALUABLES

Safety Deposit Boxes

Safe-deposit boxes can be rented for a moderate fee at most banks. Once you have access to such a box, you will have a secure place for the ownership records of your home, auto, etc., as well as personal identification documents such as birth certificates, marriage license and passports. You also may want to place small items of high value, such as jewelry in the box, as well as a copy of your complete home inventory, legal documents, trust agreements and Living Wills, powers of attorney and any other important documents. You can find a useful inventory checklist on www.GettingSafer.com [Note: Your attorney should keep any original legal documents.]

Make sure that all the documents in your box are kept *current*. Make a separate list of everything you place in your safety deposit box, and leave a copy in the box. Remember to make changes to the list as you add or remove items from the box.

The key to your deposit box should be kept in a safe location that you could reach in an emergency. Remember to note the name of the bank *as well as the location of the safety deposit box key* in your Will. You should *never* leave your original Will in your safety deposit box as there is likely to be a period of time after a death when the box is temporarily sealed. The original Will document can be left with your attorney, whose name you should give to family and friends.

Computer and other Passwords

Special codes and passwords for computers, web sites, Facebook, Twitter etc. should be kept in a secret and safe location in your home. *In addition, put these codes and passwords on a list and place a copy in a labeled envelope in your safety deposit box.* Make sure that someone knows where to find the password information in case you are no longer able to tell someone the whereabouts.

Home Safe

If you have a home safe, it is best to locate it on the ground floor where it cannot fall in the event of a fire. You should also make sure that the safe can be easily accessed if you have to exit the house in a hurry. There is a wide variety of types and sizes of home safes available, so be sure to choose a fireproof and waterproof one, as in addition to fire, water (if used to save your home) can do a lot of damage in the event of a fire.

Personal Property Inventory

An important yet often overlooked part of your assets and financial information is an inventory of the items in your home. If you already have an inventory, make sure it is current, both in terms of items and value. If you do not have a list of everything in your home, you should complete a home inventory list as soon as possible. See www.GettingSafer.com for an inventory template.

IDEA

In addition to the list itself, include photographs of any important items and any necessary professional appraisals. You can get advice from your insurance agent to help you determine the types and amounts of insurance you should have in place to protect against loss. Remember that in addition to standard coverage you can buy insurance to cover other types of losses such as flood, earthquake etc. that can occur in your part of the country.

COMPLETE

To make an inventory, go from room to room and list *all* of all your household possessions. You can find an inventory checklist at www.GettingSafer.com or you can get one from your insurance company. Everything and anything important should be listed, together with the date you acquired it, copies of receipts if possible, a photograph of the item and its current value. Where applicable, for appliances etc., include the model and serial number as part of your list. It is amazing how much value totals add up, so it is important to include all items everywhere in your home, even bed linens and clothing.

It is highly recommended that you have complete details, including photographs and/or video images of all your valuable items, such as jewelry, art and antiques.

IDEA The values of these items should be professionally updated every two to three years.

The fact that you have photographic records will prove invaluable in case of a loss. Also, in the event of a burglary, the police will have more to go on in terms of tracing any stolen items if you can supply good photos. Remember to update your inventory list whenever you add any major item. Review the list at least once a year for anything you may have forgotten to add or change.

For purposes of identification, in the event of a theft, it is recommended that you mark most items with an easy to remember ID#. *(Do not use your social security number.)* Try to mark each item in two places, one that is easy to see and another hidden from view.

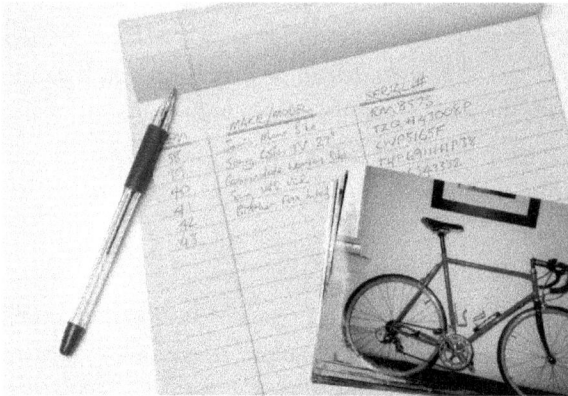

An example of inventory tools to record details of your possessions

There are a number of different methods you can use to mark items, from indelible markers to engraving tools. Your local police department may have a property identification program and they will be happy to help you get started.

Do not mark or engrave special or antique items. The best way to avoid affecting their value and still be able to provide absolute identification is to have good photographs of each item. In addition, write a detailed description of any damage or repair that is a part of the object, and attach a copy to each photograph to aid in the identification of your valuables.

If there was a fire at your home or some other disaster, your inventory list, valuations and photos with detailed descriptions will be important to help prove the value of any items that are damaged or destroyed. It will make it easier to settle your claim with your insurance company and to receive payment faster.

Make sure that copies of your inventory list are held safely either by a family member, trusted friend, or attorney, as well as in a safe-deposit box. Do not leave your only copy at home where it could be destroyed.

IDEA

There is another great advantage to having such a complete inventory list. You will find it relatively easy to indicate, on a copy that you could leave with your Will at your attorneys' office, what items you want to leave to your heirs. By designating clearly who should receive which items, you will be able to prevent any possible dispute among your heirs over the disposition of your possessions.

FINANCIAL INFORMATION FOR RETIREMENT

Build a Secure Retirement Foundation

Social Security provides a basic foundation with which to build retirement security. However, it is only a basic source of income. So if you want to have a comfortable retirement you will need to have several financial sources in addition to Social Security, such as pensions, savings and investments.

Today, only about half of all workers in America have employer-sponsored pensions, and very few people save as much as they know they should. Social Security replaces less than 40 percent of the average worker's pre-retirement earnings, and most advisors will tell you that you'll need 70 percent of your pre-retirement earnings to live comfortably. Even if you can count on a pension, you'll still need to save. If you will not have a private pension when you retire, you'll need to save more, and you must start sooner.

SOURCES OF RETIREMENT INCOME

Because there are so many potential retirement income plans the following paragraphs outline some ideas that you will be able to discuss with an accountant or financial planner. These outlines will give you some basic ideas so you can get the specific advice that will best fit your situation.

Many excellent books and web sites can help you to determine the level of assets you will need. *(See books and links at www.GettingSafer.com).* These sources will have information that can help you to learn how to calculate how much your projected income is going to be when you retire, and then you will need to match your retirement income to your expected needs. When you have completed that exercise, you will be able to calculate how much you need to accumulate in IRA's, 401(k), 403(b), etc.

If you wish to retire early, there are certain provisions in the tax law where you may not be paying penalties for withdrawing any income and/or capital when you are under age 59½.

Company Plan

Many employers provide a printout of employees' projected retirement income, as well as a variety of ways to receive this income. If you have such a plan and choose to receive the maximum amount, then your beneficiaries will not receive any benefit after your death. If you choose less than the maximum amount, your beneficiaries will receive some income after your death. Once you elect and receive benefits, you cannot change your option. Many retirees choose a lump sum rollover to an IRA so they have control over payments, investments and access to the principal if necessary. Be sure to keep your beneficiary information current with the company.

For personalized advice about your company plan, as with all major financial plans and decisions, it is best to consult a qualified advisor to determine your best strategy.

401(k) Plans

These plans are now available to both profit and non-profit organizations. They can be employer matching or employee only plans. Your employer handbook will describe what percentage the company matches (if any) and how much you are vested. The maximum tax-deductible contribution limit increases according to IRS regulation changes.

Most employers will let you choose how to invest your money; for example, whether in stock mutual funds or a fixed income plan. Many plans also have provisions where you can borrow against your account for such things as a car loan or to purchase a home. You must be careful with such loans, however, as there are penalties if loan repayment is not made regularly. Also, immediate loan repayment is required if your employment is terminated.

At retirement, you can choose to receive a monthly income or a lump sum rollover to an IRA. Be sure to keep your beneficiary information current, and if you have a living trust, consult with your attorney as to the correct wording.

457 Plans

These deferred compensation retirement plans used to be only available to government employees. As of this writing they are available to some other types of employees, and can also be used in conjunction with other pension plans to give extra benefits to management level employees. Retirement income options are similar to those mentioned above, as well as rollover to an IRA, 401(k) or 403(b) plans.

Deferred Compensation Plans

This type of plan, as the name implies, defers the receipt of income until retirement. Generally the retirement income is paid by the employer to you for a certain period of time and is fully taxable. This can therefore have an effect on the amount of Social Security income that becomes taxable. Check with your financial advisor on how much this may affect you.

Profit Sharing Plans

In this type of plan, employers set aside funds based on annual profits. The employer usually invests plan assets, and the amount of money that you will receive at retirement depends on the vesting schedule, as well as how the investments have performed. Retirement income options are similar to those mentioned above.

403(b) Plans or Tax Sheltered Annuities

These are available to employees of most non-profit organizations. They can be employer matching or employee-only plans. Maximum contributions can increase according to IRS regulations. Employers usually let you choose where and how you invest your money. You can borrow from this plan for any emergency, to buy a car etc., or to finance a personal residence. With this plan you are not required to fully pay back your loan at the time of termination of employment if the plan is not under ERISA regulations. If the loan is under an ERISA plan, then at the time of termination, you will be required to pay it off. If not paid off, the balance is subject to income tax and possible penalties if you are under 59½.Such retirement income can be deferred up to age 70½, and can even be delayed until age 75 if you are still working for the same employer.

Keogh Plans

These plans are available to the self-employed, and employees become eligible after one or two years of service. The amount that can be contributed is based upon a percentage of Schedule C income for the employer and W-2 income for the employee. The same rules apply on termination of employment as well as retirement.

SEP-IRA Plans

These plans are also available to the self-employed, with employees being eligible after one, two or three years of service. These plans have fewer reporting requirements and are easier to maintain than Keogh Plans. Thus as of this writing they have become much more popular than Keogh Plans. Contribution limits are the same as Keogh plans, and retirement income can be deferred up to age 70½.

Simple IRA's

These plans are available to companies with 100 or fewer employees who earn $5,000 or more per year. The employer can match contributions up to 3% of compensation or deposit the same percentage for all employees even if they don't contribute. Deposits to this type plan can be much greater than those allowed in a regular IRA plan. Funds can be rolled over to an IRA on termination of employment. There are increased penalties on early withdrawal during the first two years.

IRA's

This type of plan is available to employees or to the self-employed who are not covered by an employer plan. At this time, federal and state deductibility may not be the same. This means that you will need to keep track of deposits. There are deductibility limits based on Adjusted Gross Income. Non-deductible contributions can be made to IRA's. IRA's also can be converted to Roth IRA's (*see below*). Beneficiary designations are very important here, as IRA's can be "stretched" to several generations with proper planning.

Roth IRA's

Contributions to these are non-deductible. Interest and appreciation in value as well as the principal is generally not taxable on withdrawal if certain rules are followed. In general, the account must be held for five years and distribution must occur after age 59 ½. There are certain age-adjusted Gross Income limits in order to deposit to this type IRA.

Public Employees Retirement System

This pension plan is based on both employer and employee contributions. The employer retirement handbook as well as employer-sponsored seminars should cover retirement income options. You can select the option best suited to you and/or your beneficiary's needs. You will not want to roll over these funds to an IRA upon your retirement, as you will lose the funds contributed by the employer.

Annuities (Non-qualified)

A high percentage of income can be excluded from income tax using annuities. These can provide a guaranteed income for life or for a certain period that you choose. In a fixed annuity, this income will remain fixed for the period chosen. In a variable annuity, the income will fluctuate based on valuation changes. In both cases, if you "annuitize" the contract in order to have income guarantees, you will not have access to your principal. If you do not "annuitize," you can make withdrawals of income and have access to the principal. In this case it is also possible to deplete the account completely during your lifetime. Discuss the best strategy with your advisor, in addition to ownership and beneficiary designations, which could be your living trust (see Legal Information, Chapter 2).

As there are so many options available, it is advisable to seek the advice of a competent qualified financial advisor and then, if required, get a tax attorney to draw up the required legal documentation.

SOCIAL SECURITY

Your benefits from Social Security will be calculated on the earnings recorded under your Social Security number. If you ever change your name, make sure you apply and make the change of name on your Social Security card. *(There is no charge for this service.)* Children also have Social Security numbers, and parents must show the number on their tax return to claim them as dependents.

Paying Social Security Taxes

If you work, your employer withholds Social Security and Medicare taxes from your pay-check. The employer matches the amount, and sends those taxes to the Internal Revenue Service and reports your earnings to Social Security. If you are self-employed, you pay your own Social Security taxes when you file your tax return, and the IRS reports your earnings to Social Security.

Social Security "Credits"

Most people need 40 credits (10 years of work) to qualify for benefits. Lesser credits are required for younger people who qualify for disability or survivors' benefits. You earn up to 4 "credits" per year that count toward eligibility for future Social Security benefits.

Calculating Social Security Benefits

Your Social Security benefit is a percentage of your earnings averaged over most of your working life. Social Security was never intended to be your only source of retirement income. It is only intended to supplement other income you have accumulated through pension plans, savings, investments, etc.

Benefits of Social Security

There are five main benefits that Social Security can provide for you and/or your family members.
They are:

1. Retirement
   Benefits are payable at retirement age 65 (with reduced benefits available as early as age 62) if you have enough Social Security credits. Full retirement age is 66 for

anyone born before 1946. The age gradually rises until age 67 for persons born in 1960 or later. Note that a spouse can sometimes claim on the other spouse's benefit. Discuss this with Social Security.

2. Disability

   Benefits are paid at any age to anyone with enough Social Security credits who has a major physical or mental impairment that prevents them from doing "substantial" work for a year or more, or if the condition is expected to result in death.

3. **Family Benefits**

   If you are eligible for retirement or disability benefits, other members of your family might also receive benefits.

4. **Survivors**

   When you die, certain members of your family, such as your spouse, may be eligible for benefits if you earned enough Social Security credit while you were working.

5. **Medicare**

   There are two parts to Medicare: hospital insurance ("Part A") and medical insurance ("Part B"). People who are over age 65 and getting Social Security automatically qualify for Medicare, as well as people who have been receiving disability benefits for two years. Others must file an application. Part A is paid for by a portion of the Social Security taxes of people still working. This insurance helps pay for inpatient hospital care, skilled nursing care and other services. Part B is paid to cover certain items such as doctor's fees, outpatient hospital visits and other medical services and supplies. (For more on Medicare, see the Medicare section later in this chapter.)

Supplemental Security Income [SSI] Benefits

SSI makes monthly payments to people with a low income and few assets. To get SSI, you must be 65 or older or be disabled. Children as well as adults who qualify for SSI disability payments also receive assistance. Usually people who get SSI also qualify for Medicaid, food stamps and other assistance.

SSI benefits are not paid from Social Security trust funds and are not based on previous earnings.

When and How to File For Social Security or SSI

You should file for Social Security or SSI disability benefits as soon as you become too disabled to work. When the family breadwinner dies, you should immediately apply for survivors' benefits.

When you are considering retirement, talk to a Social Security representative the year before the year you plan to retire. It might be to your advantage to start your retirement benefits before you actually stop working.

Social Security: Will It Be There For You?

Absolutely! The only real question is what kind of Social Security system we will have. Social Security has been a basic part of American life for over 70 years. The Social Security law has been changed over time to meet the needs of the American people, and it will need to change again to meet future challenges.

MEDICAID

Medicaid is a jointly funded federal-state health insurance program for certain low-income and needy people. It covers approximately 40 million individuals, including children, the aged, blind and/or disabled, and people who are eligible to receive federally assisted income maintenance payments.

MEDICARE: THE BASICS

Medicare is a two-part Health Insurance Program for people 65 years of age and older, some people with disabilities under age 65, and people with End-Stage Renal Disease (permanent kidney failure requiring dialysis or a transplant). The two parts are:
- Part A: (Hospital Insurance): Most people do not have to pay for Part A.
- Part B: (Medical Insurance): Most people pay monthly for Part B.

Part A: (Hospital Insurance)
Helps Pay: Care in hospitals as an inpatient, critical access hospitals (small facilities that give limited outpatient and inpatient services to people in rural areas), skilled nursing facilities, hospice care and some home healthcare.

Cost: Most people get Part A automatically when they turn age 65. They do not have to pay a *premium* (the monthly payment) for Part A, because they or a spouse paid Medicare taxes while they were working.

If you (or your spouse) did not pay Medicare taxes while you worked and you are age 65 or older, you still may be able to buy Part A. If you are not sure if you have Part A, look on your red, white and blue Medicare card. It will show "Hospital Part A" on the lower left corner of the card. You can also call the Social Security Administration toll free at 1-800-772-1213 or your local Social Security office for more information about buying Part A. If you get benefits from the Railroad Retirement Board, call either your local RRB office or 1-800-808-0772.

Part B: (Medical Insurance)

Helps pay for: Doctors, services, outpatient hospital care, and some other medical services that Part A does not cover, such as the services of physical and occupational therapists, and some home healthcare. Part B helps pay for these covered services and supplies when they are *medically necessary*.

Cost: You pay a monthly premium for Medicare Part B. This premium is adjusted annually and as of this writing, is expected to increase over the next several years. If you did not choose Part B when you first became eligible at age 65, you will be required to pay a higher premium than if you had chosen this option as soon as eligible. Specifically, your cost of Part B may go up an extra 10% for each 12-month period that you could have had Part B but did not sign up for it, except in special cases. You will have to pay this extra 10% for the rest of your life.

Open Enrollment Period

Enrolling in part B is up to you. You can sign up for Part B anytime during a seven-month period that begins three months before you turn 65. Visit your local Social Security office, or call the Social Security Administration at 1-800-772-1213 to sign up.

If you choose Part B, the premium is usually taken out of your monthly Social Security, Railroad Retirement, or Civil Service Retirement payment. If you do not get any of the above payments, Medicare sends you a bill for your part B premium every 3 months. You should get your Medicare premium bill by the 10th of each month. If you do not get your bill by the 10th, call the Social Security Administration at 1-800-772-1213 or your local Social Security office. The website for Social Security is at www.ssa.gov

For more information: Call your Medicare Carrier about bills and services or 1-800-633-4227 to speak with a Medicare representative. Additionally you can access their web site at www.medicare.gov

MEDIGAP INSURANCE

Even with Medicare coverage, a serious illness or injury can cause financial havoc because Medicare does not cover all medical bills. As a result many Medicare recipients buy some kind of private health coverage, called *Medigap insurance*, to help cover the gaps in Medicare.

If you enroll in Medicare Part B when you turn 65, for the next six months federal law forbids insurance companies from denying you eligibility for Medigap policies. This six-month period is called the "open enrollment period." After the open enrollment period you could be refused coverage.

Before you buy a Medigap insurance policy, carefully consider the services that are covered by the insurance company, the amount of benefits and the monthly cost of the policy. Check how much the premiums may rise in the future. Make sure the company will not discontinue offering this type of insurance to new applicants, and if they do, whether you will be allowed to keep the policy even if you are willing to pay the premiums.

FINANCIAL PRECAUTIONS

It is unfortunate but true that there are many people who would love to steal some or all of your assets any way they can. You need to be very careful and avoid the most common mistakes that can lead you into becoming a victim.

IDEA

First, *always try and limit the amount of cash you carry.* Unlike credit cards and travelers checks that have security measures to protect you, the user, there is no way you can reclaim lost cash. Always know which credit cards you carry in your wallet. Keep all your account numbers and the credit company contact numbers written down in places you can quickly access, such as at home and in your wallet. An easy way to keep track of the contents of your wallet is to make copies of both sides of your cards and keep the copies in a safe and easy-to-reach place. Then, if a card or your wallet is lost or stolen, you can immediately contact your credit company, close your existing account and minimize your liability.

Credit Card Theft: Protection

Many of us unfortunately know firsthand the feeling of panic when we realize that our wallet has either been lost or stolen. Despite our best attempts to protect ourselves from thieves and our own carelessness, we may find ourselves scrambling to cancel our credit cards and doing everything we can frantically think of to prevent further loss.

While there is little we can do to recoup the cash and wallet after it has disappeared, there are precautions and measures we can take to limit the extent of loss after the discovery.

As soon as you discover that your wallet or credit card is missing, do not waste time looking for it. Instead, call the credit card company immediately, and (a) Report the lost card; (b) Cancel your card and; (c) Ask to have a new card sent. Then call the police in the jurisdiction in which the card was stolen and report your loss. These actions act as proof to the credit companies to show that you were being diligent and could be of help with an investigation.

Identity Theft

While financial loss can be costly and upsetting, identity fraud can be terrifying. Much of the information that a criminal needs to hurt you can be found in your wallet. Access to your name, address and date of birth combined with your Social Security number can be catastrophic. This is because your Social Security number is the important key that is used to verify your identity. If someone obtains your Social Security number they can open up new accounts in your name or change your mailing address. If that happens, it can take many years, and it can seem like forever, to clear your name.

NEVER carry your Social Security Card or your birth certificate in your wallet. Just memorize your Social Security number.

Unfortunately since your Social Security number is used and requested so frequently nowadays, the chances that it may fall into the wrong hands have greatly increased. Think about it: you are asked to enter your number on applications for everything from bonus cards at supermarkets to various rental forms, student identification cards to health insurance forms. It is not very difficult for someone to look over your shoulder as you fill out an application and steal the information. So be wary of providing the number to anyone, or at least be very careful when you complete any applications. Whenever possible use some other identification information, such as your driver's license number or a utility bill, and try to avoid using your Social Security number.

If you believe that your Social Security number has been used without your permission or knowledge, report the theft of your number to Social Security as well as the police and your credit card companies. Once those reports are made, it alerts the credit reporting agencies that a future user is not really you and any credit is denied. (Social Security contact information below). You should also contact Identity Theft Data Clearinghouse, 600 Pennsylvania Avenue, NW, Washington D.C. 20219. Telephone: 877-ID-THEFT.

FRAUD ALERT

In addition to trying to prevent financial loss, you need to take precautions to protect yourself from fraud.

If you are aware that your wallet or a credit card is missing, or your Social Security number has been misused, it is extremely important to immediately call all three national credit-reporting organizations. You should also place a fraud alert on your name and Social Security number. (*Contact information below*).

A *fraud alert* is a message that is added to your credit file. Credit grantors then know that they must call you, the applicant, and verify that you are the person actually applying for new credit. Once the fraud alert is added to your file, it is illegal for a credit granter to grant credit without confirming you actually want it. If they do not get your confirmation, they are responsible for all future losses associated with the opening of that account.

To be effective, it is important that you contact all three-credit reporting companies because different credit grantors report to different credit report companies.

Fraud Reporting:
The fraud alert telephone numbers for the credit reporting companies are:
*   Equifax: 1-800-525-6285.
*   Experian (formerly TRW): 1-888-379-3742.
*   Trans Union: 1-800-680-7289.
*   Social Security Administration (fraud line): 1-800-269-0271. Fax: 410-597-0118 Mail: SSA Fraud Hotline, PO Box 17785. Baltimore MD 21235

Reporting a theft to a credit card company only cancels that particular account and stops your responsibility for charges. Fraud alert prevents thieves from opening new accounts under your name.

You also need to know that each credit agency may have different time periods that they apply to your account for fraud protection, and that these periods can range from 6 months to 7 years. Prior to the protection expiration, you should receive a reminder that you need to re-request the protection. The process is very simple and can be completed over the phone in a few minutes. In addition to notifying credit providers, a fraud alert removes your name from a list of pre-approved credit offers and marketers. You can opt to have your name removed from the marketer's list without the Fraud Alert, but once the fraud alert is enacted, you are automatically removed from the marketer's list.

The advantage of putting a fraud alert on your account is that it protects you from having anyone opening any new account under your name. The negative is that it will be more difficult for you to get instant credit because you have removed yourself from the pre-approved credit list, and, as mentioned earlier, any credit provider has to contact you to verify that you are really the applicant. One way to speed up the process is to provide the credit reporting companies, in a department store for instance, with your cell phone number so they can contact you even if you are out and about. Otherwise be sure to suggest a time when you will be available to receive their call.

Note: If you ever want to verify all of your credit history, you will need to contact all three of the above-cited companies to obtain a complete picture. This full verification is especially useful to do before you apply for a real estate mortgage or refinancing.

Credit Rating

Try to minimize the number of unnecessary credit cards you have under your name. The more cards you own, the greater the risk of something going bad and the more points you carry on your credit rating. If you have ever signed up for a credit card and never used it and never canceled the account, then it is likely that the account is alive and well on your credit report. *It is important to know about all the accounts that you do have, and to close any accounts that you don't use.* A personal credit report can prove very revealing: From it you can learn what accounts are still open, and you can also learn who buys your credit information.

Negative Points on Your Credit Report

Despite what many people think, a personal request for a copy of your credit report does not mean that you will earn negative points towards your credit report. There are, however, a number of things that will cause negative points. Some examples would be applying for a new credit card, or when you allow your credit card to be used by the dealer to get you qualified while you are test-driving a car, or your bank requests your credit information for such things as refinancing your home or property. Other examples would be applying for any type of insurance, or applying to have new utilities installed.

As long as you pay all your bills on time you should be able to maintain a good credit rating. However, sometimes the wrong information may end up in your report. For that reason, you should check your credit report at least once a year.

A web site with a lot of helpful and detailed credit scoring information is: www.creditscoreguide.org

MAIL THEFT

IDEA — The loads of junk mail you receive can be very frustrating, and the temptation to simply throw it away without looking at it is extremely tempting. However, to do so would be like providing a crook with a surprise birthday party! Hidden in all that paper may be countless pre-approved credit offers. All someone needs is to get hold of the information in those offers! Once they have it, they can accept the offer, change the mailing address and go on a shopping trip with your compliments.

To prevent a crook from taking that dream vacation to Hawaii at your expense, begin by shredding *(or at least tearing up)* all mail from credit card companies such as pre-approved credit cards and "checks" for your existing credit card. Never simply throw this information away unopened. You also should shred or tear any piece of mail that you receive if it contains account, credit, loan or other confidential information. You can prevent your credit information from being used for pre-approved credit offers by contacting the three nationwide consumer-reporting agencies *(see "Fraud Alert" for contact information)* and telling them you do not want your information being made accessible for that purpose.

BEWARE — Another target of mail thieves is your regular monthly mail. You must develop the habit to open all of your bills as soon as you receive them and check the statements carefully. Keep track of the dates of any bills and checks that you expect to receive. If they do not arrive on time, make inquiries and find out if they were mailed to you. This precaution is especially important for senior citizens to take. Another scam is where crooks used to go through elderly people's mail on days that their social security checks were supposed to arrive, and they steal them from their mailbox. With direct deposit this cannot happen, but you need to check your account to verify receipt of payments.

As do many people, you probably hold onto your paid bills, credit statements and bank statements. These receipts and documents contain a lot of information that a thief would like to be able to access, so keep them in a secure place, preferably under lock and key.

If possible, it is best to receive your regular pay and income checks through direct deposit. If you are able to use that method none of your incoming checks can be stolen. Direct deposit is a secure way of receiving your funds in a timely and efficient manner.

IDEA — When it comes to your own outgoing mail it is best to place your envelopes in the mail boxes provided by the U.S. Postal Service. Do not place them in your own letterbox for collection by the mail person, as a thief can easily take the envelopes instead.

MAIL TAMPERING

Due to potential mail tampering, the CDC (Center for Disease Control) recommends that you never sniff or hold any mail near your nose. The United States Postal Service has a list of things that should be checked to help identify suspicious mail. You can print a copy of the USPS suspicious mail poster at this part of the US Postal Service web site: www.usps.com/posters/pos84.pdf or visit your local post office for a copy.

Some of the things that are shown in the poster that would be a cause for concern would be envelopes or packages marked 'Personal,' 'Confidential' or 'Do not X-ray', especially if you do not know the sender. Check your mail and packages in particular to see if there is excess postage, wrong spellings, a strange (or no) return address and or an incomplete or wrong title. Be extremely cautious if there is any powdery substance or any discoloration to the packaging, such as oily stains or even any unusual or excessive outer packaging.

GENERAL FINANCIAL PRECAUTIONS

More steps you can take to protect your credit include being careful when receiving telephone sales calls. Never buy anything over the phone, unless you have initiated the call and know the other party. Keep all receipts of credit card purchases, ATM transactions, gasoline purchases and debit card transactions; store them in a secure place and compare the receipts with your monthly statement. If you share accounts with anyone else, make sure you compare financial activities regularly and confirm anything suspicious with your partner. Don't just assume it was your partner who conducted an unrecognized transaction.

When you receive a sales receipt, you will see that most merchants block out part of the account numbers on receipts; however, this is not always the case with credit and debit card transactions. Do not leave these lying around.

Memorize and never share your Personal Identification Number(s) PIN with anyone. Do not write it down and be cautious when using a PIN number because someone may overhear you or see you entering the number.

Be extremely protective and cautious with your debit cards. They do not require a PIN number, and unlike a credit card, debit cards directly access your personal finances.

If you move, be sure to notify all of your creditors and financial institutions of your new address, phone numbers, etc. If your change of address is not acknowledged from each within a month of moving, call and investigate the situation. Even if you have changed your address through the post office, ask the new occupant of your old address to forward mail to your new address. You never want any of your mail to go astray.

CHAPTER **Four**

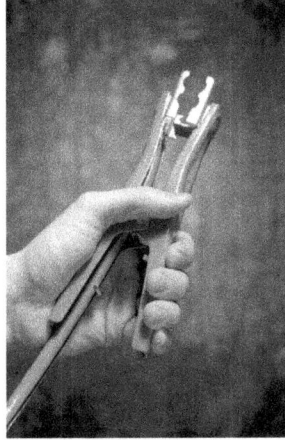

Vehicle Ownership

The vehicle identification information that you enter in this section can apply to any type of vehicle you own, whether it is an automobile, truck, plane, boat or cycle.

Take a few minutes and gather all the ownership and license documents of the vehicle(s) in question first so you can complete this form fully. You'll then have all the important details in one place, easily accessible either for your own needs or for someone whom you have designated as your spokesperson in the event of a serious accident that leaves you unable to communicate.

If you have more than one vehicle, don't forget to make some blank copies of the questionnaire first, and then complete one form for each vehicle. The forms at www.GettingSafer.com can be downloaded and updated from time to time.

Following the vehicle information form, this chapter has useful information about how to stay safe when you are driving. There is also a section about the many ways you can help prolong the life of your vehicle. These suggestions will help you to save money, maintain the best value of your vehicle and also provide a safer means of transport.

VEHICLE INFORMATION

Complete the following:

Name:
Driver's License Number:
State:

Renewal Date:
Expiration date:

Driver's Insurance Information:
Name of Company:
Policy Number:
Mailing Address:

Agent Name:

Vehicle (Automobile or other type of transport):
Make:
Year of Manufacture:
License Plate Number:
Vehicle Identification Number (VIN) Information:
Registration Information:
Date of Purchase:
Any special identification:

Model:
Color:

Price:

Ownership Title (see registration or certificate of ownership):
Name of Owner:
Company Name:
Leasing Company:
Location of Certificate of Ownership:
Warranty Information:

Specifics:
Extended Service Contract: ○ Yes ○ No
Auto Club: ○ Yes ○ No
Name:
Telephone Number:

Membership Number:
Emergency Call Number:

STORAGE RECOMMENDATION: **Vehicle Information**			
ENVELOPE	MAIN LOCATION	LOCATION 2	LOCATION 3
Sealed	Copy: Locked File Cabinet: Home	Copy: Safe Deposit Box	
Actual Location(s):			

AUTOMOBILE SAFETY

In addition to observing the rules of the road and the laws that must be obeyed when driving, you should use the following advice and basic safety information to help keep you, your passengers and other road users safe. Take the time to read through the following sections carefully and make notes of any safety suggestions that you do not yet practice. Try and incorporate these 'new to you' safety suggestions into your daily life as soon as possible.

AUTOMOBILES AND YOUR PERSONAL SAFETY

You always need to be alert and act defensively whenever you are either approaching your car, parking, dealing with breakdowns or when stopped by the police. There are a number of safety precautions and important recommendations below, and you will find more information on the Internet as well as from AAA, your local police and in books on this subject. Take the time to learn as much as possible about the many ways you can protect yourself, and ways to stay safe.

- Always lock your car doors after entering or leaving your car.
- Keep your car doors locked and the windows rolled up *no matter how safe the neighborhood looks.*
- Park your car in well-lit and safe areas, preferably where other people park.
- Have your car keys in your hand before you approach your car. You do not want to be distracted by fumbling for them.
- Walk with purpose and be vigilant at all times.
- Look around while approaching the car and before getting in, check the back seat and under the car for anyone hiding from your direct view.

The following precautions are especially important to take in unsafe areas:

- Whenever possible, try to avoid driving alone at night.
- If you think that you are being followed, drive to a police/sheriff's station or a public, well-lit place where other people are present.
- If your car breaks down, open the hood, attach a white cloth to the antenna and put on the emergency flashing lights. Then, stay inside your locked car, provided it is in a safe place out of the flow of traffic so it cannot be hit. If someone stops, roll the window down slightly, and ask him or her to call the police or a tow truck service.
- If you have to stop for the police or highway patrol at any time, slow down and indicate that you are aware they are stopping you. Pull over as soon as possible in a safe, well-lit location. Make sure your doors are locked, and merely crack your window to slide out the requested information unless requested otherwise. It's always important to be very careful that it's actually the police who are stopping you. If you are unsure about their identity, have them verify their identity by having another police car come by.
- It is recommended that you have a cell phone for emergencies. However, do not use it while driving, as cell phones serve as a major distraction and are the cause of too many accidents. Never text when driving. Some states have already made it illegal for drivers to use hand-held cell phones.
- When coming to a stop, leave enough space between cars. Leave sufficient room so that in case you sense trouble, you can maneuver your car and get away.
- Don't stop on the road to assist a motorist; instead, call for assistance for them.

IDEA

- Carry a cell phone/camera or keep a disposable camera in the glove compartment. It can be very useful at times, especially when there is an accident.
- Always make sure that your gas tank is half full. Don't wait until you're driving on fumes. You could be delayed in traffic and not be able to get to a gas station in time.
- Drive safely and follow all laws, including the use of turn signals.
- Always leave a safe distance between your car and the one in front. The correct distance will depend upon your speed and the road conditions. Just remember that whenever you hit a car from behind, no matter the circumstances, it will be your fault.
- Do not antagonize other drivers, even if you were not at fault; the result might be road rage.

DRIVING SAFELY

In America almost half of all accidental deaths are automobile-related, and the major causes of these deaths are speeding and distractions while driving.

IDEA

To avoid speeding, develop the habit of allowing yourself sufficient time to get to your destination. Make allowances for the time of day, weather conditions, special events, etc. It may not be easy to do this all the time, but it is worth making the effort. If you are running a little late, it is safer to call ahead and let someone know, rather than speed and perhaps not get to your destination at all.

Aside from reducing the speed at which you drive, there many other safety precautions you can take to make your road travel safer.

- Never drive when you are too tired; if necessary, find a safe location to get some sleep, and only then continue driving.
- Avoid aggressive drivers on the road and never tailgate.
- Make sure that you and your passengers always use seat belts and are buckled up properly.
- It is often tempting to get through the lights at an intersection before they turn red, but it is also one of the places when numerous accidents occur. If you have allowed time for your journey, do not allow yourself to be tempted to race through any intersections. Your life is more important than driving time.

DISTRACTIONS

As a driver you have a serious responsibility. Driving safely requires your *full* attention. You are responsible for your own safety as well as the safety of others. Whenever you have passengers, they should understand that they are responsible for not distracting you so that you can fully concentrate on your driving. Children must be told how to behave in a car and that by doing so they can help you to drive safely. Always make sure that all children are secured in the proper seats before you start on a drive, and provide them with books, games or DVD's to keep them occupied. If they need some attention, stop the car in a safe area and take care of their needs.

Never attempt to turn around or pass things to passengers in the rear of the car; if you do so, your attention will be diverted from the road, and it only takes a split second for a serious accident to occur. Common distractions that can result in an accident include such things as adjusting your radio, changing a tape or trying to reach something on the passenger seat or in the glove compartment. Let someone else change the radio station or the CD. If there's no one else, wait until you're stopped at a light or parked. Until then, stay focused on driving.

Texting, dialing or talking on a cell phone greatly reduces your level of concentration on your driving. In fact, the latest research in the UK has shown that speaking on the phone now causes more auto accidents in Britain than alcohol! So if you need to make a call, pull over to a safe spot and stop the car completely before using your cell phone. If you receive a call, let it ring, and when you stop in a safe place pick up your voice-mail. Remember that in many states it is now illegal to talk on phone while driving unless the phone is hands-free and in some cases not even then.

Some drivers try to perform all sorts of unsafe activities in their car. Grooming, eating and drinking, smoking, and reading maps or advertisements will cause a driver to avert his or her attention. Plan ahead and allow time to take care of all your needs.

Remember, just a split second can mean the difference between life and death… yours or your loved ones!

IF YOU HAVE BEEN INVOLVED IN AN ACCIDENT

The following is a list of recommendations to keep in mind if you are involved in an auto accident.
• Turn off the engine immediately.

- Attend to any superficial injuries, and call for medical help if necessary. Do not move anybody who is injured until medical help arrives.

BEWARE
- Call the police if anyone is injured.
- Documents, unless required by the police or your own insurance representatives, should never be signed at the scene.
- You will need to provide proof of insurance, which must always be in your car.

- Do not discuss who is at fault. Allow your insurance company to handle the matter.
- Obtain the facts. Write down any important information while you are still at the site of the accident.
- Make a note of the names, license plate numbers, makes and models of the cars, telephone numbers, drivers' license numbers and insurance information of all the drivers involved in the accident.
- Get the names of any passengers and the names and phone numbers of any witnesses.
- Note any specific damages to all vehicles involved, and use your cell phone camera or your disposable camera, packed away in your glove compartment, to take pictures of any damage.

IDEA
- Call your insurance company to report the accident. By law, it is required that any accident must be reported to the DMV within 10 days where the cost of repair exceeds $500 (the amount varies by state) in damage, or if an injury occurs. Most insurance companies, once you contact them, will make the report to DMV on your behalf.

- Do not discuss responsibility or anything concerning the accident with anyone other than your insurance agency's authorized representative or your own legal counsel.
- If contacted afterwards by the other parties involved in the accident, only give them your policy or claim number, and ask them to contact your insurance representative.

AUTOMOBILE THEFT PROTECTION

Most cars are stolen because so many people make them too easy to steal! So when you get out of your car, never leave it unlocked, and never leave the windows open or the keys in the ignition.

Do not leave a spare key in your car or hidden on the car; keep it with you.

BEWARE

Do not keep your house and car keys on a key ring that you would leave with your car either at the mechanic's or with the valet. A thief could easily make a copy of your key, find your home address on the documents in your glove compartment and burglarize you before you even get home.

Do not leave your garage door opener in the car when your car is being serviced or repaired. Take it with you.

IDEA

If you are locked out of your car, call AAA if you are a member or a locksmith. Locksmiths are reliable and are accountable through security checks, fingerprinting and licensing. The police will not usually respond to this type of call unless it is a real emergency, such as a child locked inside your car.

Some keys have manufacturer's codes engraved on them. These are the codes for your specific door lock. If a thief gets that number, they could go to a key maker and say they need that key. Qualified locksmiths will look for proof of ownership or they will not make a key of this type.

Make sure that your glove compartment is always locked and that no envelopes or papers with your home address are left lying around in your car.

Your purse, valuables or shopping bags should never be left in plain sight. They should be placed in the trunk. However, be very cautious when putting anything in the trunk because as you do so you are not able to see if someone is approaching you from behind.

- If possible, park in well-lit public areas.
- Use a steering wheel lock; they deter most car thieves.
- Do not leave the original pink slip (ownership document) in the car.

MAINTENANCE

As you go through this section, make your own list of any items that may need attention, and have them checked out or taken care of as soon as possible. Regular auto tune-ups can reduce the overall cost of repairs, extend the life of your car and make it a safer vehicle to drive. The following is a list of typical auto maintenance concerns:

- Battery Replacement
- Belts & Hoses Replacement
- Brake Fluid
- Cooling System Service
- Filter Changes
- Fuel Injection Cleaning
- Oil and Lube Service

- Tire Replacement and Installation
- Tire Rotation
- Transmission Flush
- Tune Up
- Wheel Alignment
- Wheel Balancing
- Wiper Blade Replacement

You may be able to take care of most of the general upkeep yourself, and rely on a trustworthy mechanic to look after the more difficult maintenance items.

The following is a list of items that require maintenance and a suggested timetable. (Check the owner's manual for any variations)

Air filter: Check *every other month.*
Action: Replace when it is dirty or as part of a tune-up.

Antifreeze/coolant level: Check *weekly.*
Action: Fill to level marking with 50/50 solution of antifreeze and water

Battery: Check: *with every oil change.*
Action: Replace as needed.

Belts and hoses: Check *monthly*
Action: Replace worn, glazed or frayed belts

Brake fluid: Check *monthly*
Action: If needed, add the approved type of fluid and check for possible leaks throughout the system. Do not overfill.

Engine oil: Check *every other fill-up.*
Action: If it is low, add oil. Change the oil and oil filters every 3 months or 3,000 miles.

Exhaust clamps and supports: Check *for holes in muffler or pipes.*
Action: Replace rusted or damaged parts. Have emission checked at least once per year for compliance with local laws.

Lights: Check *at least once a month.* Have someone look at your brake and reverse lights and let you know they are working properly. If one of the signal lights fails you will notice a fast flashing light when you try to indicate a turn.

Action: As soon as possible, replace any failed lights. Maintain and keep all lights in clean and working order, including brake lights, turn signals and emergency flashers. Keep spare bulbs and fuses in your vehicle.

Power steering fluid level: Check *monthly.*

Action: Add fluid and inspect the pump and hoses for leaks.

Signs of oil seepage on shock absorbers: Check *regularly.*
Action: Worn or leaking shocks should be replaced in pairs.

Tires: Check *regularly.*
Action: Check for cuts, bulges and excessive tread ware. Keep a record of tire rotation. Having the correct air pressure will save money on gas.

Transmission fluid: Check *monthly.*
Action: Check while engine is warm and running, and the parking brake is on. Do not overfill.

Windshield washer fluid: Check *every other time you fill with gas in bad weather conditions and you are using the washers frequently.*
Action: If needed, fill the reservoir.

Windshield wiper blades: Check *whenever you clean your windshield and it does not clean completely.*
Action: Replace with the correct type and size at least once per year in a mild climate and twice a year in bad weather regions or whenever they are worn or brittle.

IN VEHICLE EMERGENCY KIT

The following are recommended items that should be kept in your vehicle's emergency kit. They are all items that will prove very useful in an emergency situation or an accident. Some items only apply to regional weather conditions such as snow or freezing weather. Use the list as a guide, and include or eliminate those items that are related to your particular situation and needs. If in doubt about your need for any of the items, err on the side of safety and pack them in the kit.

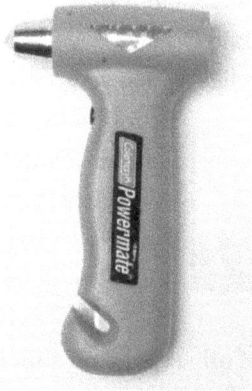

Emergency glass breaker and seat-belt cutter- an essential part of a vehicle emergency kit.

Select from the following list of items for your In-Vehicle Emergency Kit:

- Emergency medical kit (*available from The Red Cross as well as most drug stores.*)
- Small amount of money, including some change.
- Disposable camera
- Cloth or a roll of paper towels
- Booster cables
- Jack (*usually supplied with car; also make sure you know how to use it.*)
- Flashlight and batteries
- Window-washing solvent
- Warning devices (flares or triangles)
- Bright-colored or white cloth (*to attach to antenna to signal that you need assistance*)
- Pen and paper
- Road atlas
- Emergency glass breaker/seat-belt cutter
- Window scrapers
- Material for hazardous road conditions, such as a small bag of abrasive material such as sand, gravel, salt, or kitty litter, or traction mats
- Chains
- Shovel
- Water suitable for drinking or if your car overheats (*change at least every six months*)
- Non-perishable food such as energy bars (check expiry or "best used by" dates)

When you are making up your vehicle emergency kit, remember to note any expiration dates on the items. Then make a list of those items that need to be replaced and the appropriate dates. Please see www.GettingSafer.com for links to smart-phone applications to automate expiration date reminders.

Now that you have read the guidelines and suggestions in this chapter, make good use of the information and we all know that careful and considerate driving can and will have a major impact on others using the road.

It is my hope that you will enjoy many years of safe driving. Also, see Automobile Concerns in Winter, Chapter 8.

CHAPTER **Five**

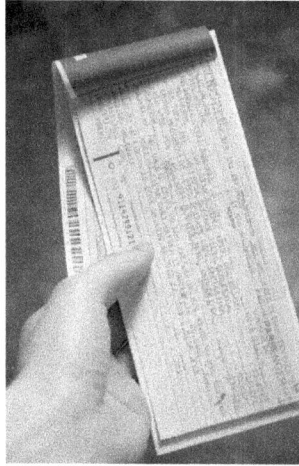

Travel Safely: Vacations or Business

Until recently, traveling either for business or vacations was relatively easy and usually enjoyable. Now, however, we are at a stage where travel of virtually any kind can be unpleasant and, at times, potentially risky because of the chance of terror-related activity.

So many people are traveling now that there are frequently lines at every turn. Before 9/11 there were some forms of security but usually only for hand baggage and routine metal detectors at airports. Now there is personal scrutiny and document screening in addition to baggage checks. Even passing through the metal detectors has become more complicated, as passengers are frequently asked to remove their shoes and belts as they are screened. This has led to increased delays and longer check-in times at airports. Nowadays there are even checks at sensitive road junctions and bridges from time to time. Despite all this, however, when you want to get from one place to another, whether for family visits, vacations or business, you just need to make your plans…and get on with your life!

With safety concerns in mind, it is certainly prudent to make detailed plans whenever you are going to travel.

Let someone you trust know that you are going to be away, where you will be and how you can be contacted. If there will not be anyone at home you should cancel your mail or arrange for someone to collect it for you. They could also be the one to open and close your drapes and make sure your home does not look unoccupied. You may need to arrange for garden care in your absence. For additional safety, unplug all appliances including any TV, toaster, iron, washing machine, etc. If you have an electric garage door opener, unplug it.

Once you have made all the proper arrangements you can relax and concentrate either on your business trip or your vacation knowing everything at home is taken care of.

For each trip, a Travel Information Form available at www.GettingSafer.com should be completed and given either to a trusted family member, a friend or a work colleague. They should keep it in a safe place in case of an emergency.

Complete all the appropriate sections on the form whenever you are planning a trip. If you prefer, simply make a list of the items that apply to your own needs, and then draft your own forms.

This chapter dealing with Travel Safety includes information and tips that will help to make your trips for business or vacation safer and easier to plan.

Note: Each person traveling should complete relevant sections of this 'Travel Information Form' and enter their applicable individual information.

TRAVEL SAFETY TIPS

It has always been prudent to make careful preparations for any journey, whether it is for vacation or business. In these troublesome times it makes even more sense to make detailed travel arrangements and plans and know how to take precautions so you will be safe in a variety of circumstances.

The following suggestions are things you can do that will help increase your safety and help to lower the level of stress that you might otherwise experience when traveling:

- When packing, only take items that are really necessary for the trip.
- If necessary, because of your health welfare, bring a copy of your appropriate medical records. Your physician will advise you on this matter.
- Do not pack all your medications in your luggage. Carry those most critical for your care for a day or two in your hand baggage. However, remember to be extremely careful about what items you place in your hand baggage *(see Baggage Restrictions, later in this chapter, for a specific listing of prohibited items)*.
- Expect that security personnel will probably search your bags and may choose to examine some of your items very carefully. Do not allow this to stress you unnecessarily. Remember that they are simply trying to keep you and your fellow passengers safe. Don't make jokes or comments; security is a serious business, and you can get into serious trouble if you do so.
- You may be asked to turn on your laptop computer and any other electronic devices you are carrying with you, so make sure these items are easily accessible.
- Every piece of your luggage should have identification tags with your name and contact information. The tags should be placed on the outside of your baggage, ideally on a tag that folds over or has a covering that hides the information from casual observers. Put an additional tag inside each bag.
- Remember to lock your luggage for general travel.
- For airline travel checked baggage *must* be unlocked, due to security requirements at airports. This is a requirement so that prior to being placed on the aircraft it can be examined by security personnel.
- As a traveler, limit yourself to the fewest credit cards you may really need. Make two photocopies of everything in your wallet. Keep one set of copies in a sealed envelope in your own suitcase and either give the other set of copies to a travel companion, or leave them at home.

- Try not to make yourself conspicuous when traveling. Usually people that stand out as tourists are the first to be targeted for harassment or theft.
- No matter where you are, listen to your intuition, and if you think that something is either out of place or does not look right, bring it to the attention of the local authorities.

- Each person traveling abroad should have a notarized copy of their passport that is kept on their person in a sealed plastic covering, another copy in their hand baggage and one that is left with a contact or at home.

- Carry important documents, such as your passport and tickets, concealed, on your person. Special wallets or belts for these items can be purchased from most travel shops.

- Whenever possible, deposit your original passport in your hotel's safe, and only carry a notarized copy of your passport with you.

- If you give your bags to either a porter or bellman, *always* get a receipt.

- When you register at your hotel do so quietly.
- When you answer your hotel room phone do not give your name.
- Carry only small amounts of cash that you are likely to need.
- Never show how much money you are carrying and only take it out when you are in a safe and private place.

- Use credit cards or travelers checks rather than cash when possible. You could consider http://www.smartcreditchoices.com/educationcenter to help select the best card for your needs.

- Be on the lookout for pickpockets, and especially while you are in crowded places. Pickpockets have many tricks that they use to confuse and distract you and ultimately separate you from your possessions.

- When shopping, *always* make sure you keep one arm and hand free for personal security reasons and protection. Do not try to carry too many packages.

- Tourists are prime targets. If someone approaches you and you feel threatened, hold onto your belongings tightly, look them directly in the eye and loudly yell "Police!" Show them that you mean business and not be an easy victim. Try to move away from any unsavory-looking people as quickly as possible.

- If you believe your life may be in danger, give the thief whatever he or she wants. Your life, and that of those who may be accompanying you, is more important than your possessions.
- Always be alert and aware of your surroundings wherever you go.

- If you use public transport stay awake, and if possible, sit near the driver.
- Only get into a taxi if the driver is alone. Never allow any other pick-ups on your journey.
- If you are alone and renting a car, always get an escort to walk you to your car. If there is no escort available, use valet service if it is available. You do not want to be walking around alone in a strange parking lot.
- Take extra precautions when traveling, since you are not in your own familiar town. Be aware of anyone acting conspicuously or in an unusual manner.
- If you are exercising, whether walking or jogging, never wear earphones to listen to music. You will not be able to hear someone approaching.
- Do not accept packages or gifts from strangers, and never leave bags or luggage unattended anywhere.
- If you see unattended packages anywhere, report the location and description to the authorities.
- Do not go into dangerous-looking, unlit or unpopulated areas. If you find that you have unexpectedly wandered into a place in which you feel uncomfortable, get out immediately.
- Carry an ID card in your purse or wallet showing medications, allergies and an emergency contact telephone number.

AIRLINE TRAVEL SAFETY

Due to the heightened levels of security since 9/11, strict new regulations have been implemented concerning check-in times at airports and the types of items that are allowed on flights. It is important that everyone adheres to all the current policies, so if you are uncertain as to the specific requirements for a flight, check on line, contact the individual airline or airport ahead of time for the most accurate information. Always make sure that you allow sufficient time when arriving at the airport for complete security checks.

Don't be disconcerted by the fact that you may see more law enforcement personnel and possibly FAA canine patrols at the airports.

For all flights, each passenger must have at least one form of photo ID. Some airlines or airports may require two forms of identification.

It is preferable to reconfirm your flight directly with the airline 24 to 48 hours prior to departure. In some countries confirmations are required, so check with your airline or travel agent about specific airports and countries to which you are traveling.

Some airports have eliminated curbside check-in, and implemented special security restrictions for parking, unloading and picking up passengers. Make sure you know in advance which regulations could affect your travel.

When you have checked in for your flight, proceed directly to your gate, so that you are sure to hear important information or changes that might be announced.

Never leave your bags unattended or with a stranger.

Never accept, hold or even watch any item from a stranger or carry any package without knowing the contents and the sender.

If you hear anything unusual, or notice anything out of place, trust your intuition and alert the airport authorities. They will determine whether the incident you are reporting is serious or not.

Try to eat about every four hours. This will prevent you from getting too far away from your regular eating pattern, and will help you feel better. On long flights do not take too much caffeine, but perhaps bring something nutritious, like nuts and fruit, for the journey.

When you arrive at your destination, proceed immediately to baggage claim and retrieve your luggage. You do not want to give anyone the opportunity to either take your bags or tamper with them.

BAGGAGE RESTRICTIONS

Airlines are now very strict about what passengers are legally permitted to carry in their luggage. The restrictions are designed to enhance safety, and should be complied with. Any offender may risk penalties and, in some instances, imprisonment. Some of the items that are forbidden may seem harmless, but in the wrong hands or environment they could prove to be very dangerous. If you are unsure whether the items that you wish to pack in your luggage or ship by air are restricted, contact your airline representative for more information. As changes are made from time to time, for up to date luggage restrictions see www.tsa.gov/traveller-information/prohibited-items

Do not try to pack or try to carry in your baggage:
- Fireworks — Signal flares, sparklers or any type of explosives.
- Flammable liquids or solids — Fuel, paints, lighter refills or matches.
- Household chemicals — Drain cleaners or any solvents.
- Pressure containers — Spray cans, butane fuel, scuba tanks, propane tanks, CO_2 cartridges or self-inflating rafts.

- Undeclared Weapons — Firearms, ammunition, gunpowder, mace and tear gas or pepper spray.
- Sharp Objects— Knives, scissors, box cutters, nail clippers or any sharp metal object.
- Other hazardous materials — Dry ice, gasoline-powered tools, wet-cell batteries, camping equipment with fuel, radioactive materials, or poisonous or infectious substances.

Exceptions to the aforementioned restrictions may be allowed if the items are required for personal care, medical reasons or sport. The following are some examples:

- Personal care items that contain hazardous materials (e.g., flammable aerosols such as hairspray) totaling less than 75 ounces may be carried on board. Contents of each container may not exceed 16 fluid ounces.
- Matches and lighters may only be carried on your person. "Strike-anywhere" matches, lighters with flammable liquid reservoirs and lighter fluid are still forbidden.
- Firearms and ammunition are not allowed as carry-on on any aircraft. Weapons and small ammunition that have been declared during check-in, and unloaded and stored in a locked container, may be allowed in your checked luggage.
- Electric wheelchairs, medical assistance equipment, and infant equipment must be transported in accordance with individual airline requirements. The items may have to be dismantled or the power source removed.

Most of the suggestions that apply to airline safety also apply to cruise and train travel as well.

SEA CRUISE TRAVEL

Security is now extremely strict with all cruise lines. This applies to all cruise-line personnel, employees, merchants and vendors, so everyone working with the cruise lines is subject to full security and screening.

There are also strict security measures for travelers. The procedures employed can mean a longer time to park, check-in and pass through security checks.

Since embarkation and debarkation may also take longer to accommodate the more stringent security checks, you should allow plenty of time when you are arranging for any connecting travel.

Strict enforcement and scrutiny of identification as well as nationality and travel documents is commonplace nowadays. When you make a reservation with your travel agent you should carefully check the identification requirements, or contact the cruise line for specifics.

Give yourself sufficient time in case you need to get some additional documents after your questions are answered.

Acceptable documentation for US citizens: A valid passport, or a birth certificate original or certified copy. In addition, a photo-ID *(such as a driver license)* issued by a state federal or local government agency is required. Children under 16 do not require a picture ID

Documentation for Non US citizens: A valid passport and visa in addition to Alien Registration Green card if living in the US. Some Canadian or Mexican citizens may travel with alternative documentation depending upon their alien status in the US. For customs and immigration purposes, guests must have a passport visa and other travel documents based upon their nationality and country of residence.

Make sure you have identification and travel documents, your medication, cash and jewelry in your hand baggage. This carry-on luggage may be searched. It is a good idea to make a list of all the items in your checked baggage and carry it with you.

IDEA

For virtually every cruise, bring rubber-soled shoes for walking the decks for your comfort and safety. For other ideas about appropriate clothes to bring, ask your travel agent or the cruise line.

For the safety of all on board, today's cruise lines have the most comprehensive and proactive health and sanitary protocols developed by the CDC in the travel and tourism industry. However, you do need to be cautious about eating and drinking when you leave the ship to visit ports of call. .

Since safety and security is such a high priority on cruise lines, even at sea there are telephones and the Internet, as well as satellite communication. So there is usually a method available for staying in touch with family, friends and business associates.

Cancellation policies vary so check with your cruise line directly. A useful web site for cruise line information is www.cruising.org which is the web site for Cruise Lines International Association

TRAIN TRAVEL

Many people travel by train as they think it is a safer than an airplane. Others choose this form of travel to avoid the long delays caused by security at airports.

Unfortunately, whatever form of transport you are going to use, you must be extra- vigilant and immediately report anything to authorities that appears out of place or unusual. Your report could be lifesaving.

Due to security concerns, train travel has also been subjected to new safety measures. This means that baggage allowances and the type of baggage allowed on board a train is somewhat restricted, and subject to inspection.

All baggage must be labeled with your name and address. This information does not need to be visible, but it must be available to authorized personnel if requested.

Carry-on baggage is restricted to size and weight limits. For specific baggage requirements, check when you are making reservations or call 1-800-USA-RAIL for specific baggage and storage availability on the train you wish to travel.

Recognize that train companies reserve the right to refuse those who do not observe the train company's guidelines.

For general passenger safety measures there are a number of things you can do:

- Arrive at the station early and do not rush to your train.
- Be very careful when boarding or leaving the train.
- Never exit a moving train.
- Use handrails whenever moving about the train.
- Always wear shoes when you are moving about the train.
- Never leave children unattended.
- Review any safety instructions or ask the conductor.
- Remember to walk; do not run.

HOTEL SAFETY TIPS

Depending upon your destination, check with your travel agent to see if your hotel is equipped with smoke detectors. They are not installed in every hotel in the world. If your hotel is not equipped with smoke detectors, pack a battery-operated one in your luggage for use when you arrive.

As soon as you arrive at your destination and get to your room, check all the locks on your doors and windows. If they are not secure, immediately ask for another room or for someone to repair them before you accept the room.

Locate the fire escape, emergency exits and elevators nearest to your room, and memorize their locations. Pace the distance and count the number of doors between your room and the emergency exits in case you have to reach them when there is smoke.

In the event of emergency, use the fire escape stairs, never the elevator.

Take your room key with you in case you cannot escape and need to get back to your room. This is better than being isolated in a corridor.

Don't smoke in bed (this applies when you are at home, too).

Always report any suspicious people in the halls or rooms to management.

BEWARE

Never let someone into your room unless you know them. If someone claims to be a hotel representative or worker, i.e. room service or maintenance, and wants access to your room, call the front desk to verify their purpose and the name of the individual before you let them into your room.

Do not ignore unusual or suspicious phone calls. Report them to the front desk.

Never show anyone your room key with the name of your hotel and room number.

Never tell anyone your room number. If someone needs to contact you, they can ask for you by name, and then be connected to your room telephone number.

Be cautious when returning to your room; always make sure that you are not being followed.

If you are concerned that someone is following you, quickly return to the hotel lobby and ask an official employee to escort you to your room.

Never leave valuables in your room. Use the hotel safety deposit box whenever one is available, or carry your valuables with you.

VEHICLE RENTAL AND PERSONAL PROPERTY SAFETY

Carry your wallet or purse and checkbook with you. Never leave them in your car.

IDEA

Do not advertise that you are a visitor by leaving maps, travel brochures or any valuable items visible in your car. Make sure you place everything either in the glove compartment or trunk before arriving at your destination.

Whenever you park your car, day or night, remove your bags and other valuables. If you need to keep them in the car, place them in the trunk before you reach your destination.

If your car breaks down, turn on your flashing lights and raise the hood. Wait in the car or in a safe place. Do not stand outside where you can be hit by a passing car. Instead, stay safely inside the car until help arrives.

If you become lost and find yourself in an area that does not look safe, do not stop. Unless you can safely use your cell phone, continue driving until you find an open business in a safe looking neighborhood and then call your hotel.

TRAVEL INSURANCE

Many people, whether they are first-time or well-experienced travelers, inquire about buying traveler's insurance to protect their interests on international and national trips. There are many different insurance plans and options available, covering everything from trip cancellation and lost luggage to emergency medical needs.

Because there are so many insurance options, it is important when shopping for coverage that you discuss the specific type you need for each trip with an experienced travel insurance representative. Since this form of insurance can be quite expensive and the policies can have a variety of exceptions, you need to understand all the details, and be fully informed, before you buy.

Types of Travel Insurance

Travel Insurance: This can reimburse you for monetary losses resulting from delayed, canceled or interrupted trips, lost, stolen or damaged luggage, damaged rental cars, and also dental and medical emergencies.

Flight Insurance: This compensates for loss of life or limb during an actual flight.

Trip Cancellation Insurance: This refunds your money only for "covered" reasons such as medical emergencies, cruise or tour bankruptcy, severe weather, jury duty, terrorist activity and others. Refunds will not be given because of business interference or a change of mind.

Purchasing Insurance

Travel insurance can be purchased any time before you begin your trip, but some exceptions exist.

One such example of an exception is with pre-existing health conditions. Those are described as non-controlled (requiring changes in medication or treatment) illnesses or injuries that existed 60 days prior to, and including, your coverage period. The costs of incurred treatment while travelling are only covered if the insurance is bought within 7 days of your first down payment for your journey, and if the cost of the trip is less than $10,000 per person.

There are many travel policies offered by insurance carriers. They can be purchased either on the web, from your travel agent, or from some banks, as well as from any travel insurance company's agents and brokers. Remember that since the benefits and the premiums can vary greatly, allow sufficient time to do your research first, and also the time to speak with any of the representatives from the insurance sources you have selected about your different options before you make a commitment.

ALTERNATIVE TRAVEL INSURANCE COVERAGE

You may already have some credit cards, a homeowner's policy, even medical coverage or some other insurance that may provide limited coverage for some components of your travels. However, if you are going to rely on any of these types of insurance, you need to have a clear understanding of what you are covered for and the claims process. These alternative forms of coverage usually do not cover or have trip cancellation or interruption, treatment at a foreign hospital or emergency medical transportation. Make sure you check on the benefits offered before you purchase your tickets with a specific credit card.

If you follow the suggestions in this chapter when taking a particular trip, you should feel much better prepared, more relaxed, and able to look forward to a terrific vacation or a successful business trip.

Have a great time and return home safely!

CHAPTER **Six**

It's Your Home: Make It Safe!

We all like to think that our home is a safe place. And in most respects, it probably is. Yet while home is certainly a place where we probably spend a great deal of our time, it is also where way too many accidents can occur.

This chapter sets out to help you understand and identify potential hazards in your home and offer ideas and suggestions on ways to eliminate them so that you and your family can be safer.

No doubt you are aware of some things that need attention in your home. Of course you've intended to take care of them, but somehow you have never quite gotten to them. This is your big opportunity to make a really comprehensive and serious 'things to do' list.

Millions of disabling accidents and tens of thousands of avoidable deaths occur in homes every year. So, take steps to protect everyone in your household and don't become a statistic.

To make your home as safe as possible means that you need to crime-proof your home as well as make it as accident-free as possible. These important elements in your overall home safety plan are addressed in this chapter.

As a first step, for babysitters or others, start by completing the following 'Home Location' form. In the event of an emergency, you'll need to provide this information to police or other personnel, so make sure to keep a copy of this small completed form beside each phone.

```
HOME LOCATION FORM                                          COMPLETE

Name:
Address: _____
Nearest Cross Streets: _____

Home Phone Number: _____
Where you can be reached if not available by phone or out of town: ____

_____
Cellular Phone Number: _____
Alternate Contact/Other: _____
Special Instructions: _____

Local Police/Sheriff Office: _____
```

CRIME-PROOF YOUR HOME

Aside from all the potential physical hazards in and around most homes that can usually be corrected, there are other things that, if ignored, can affect your safety, such as home security.

You can actually achieve a great deal by taking some preventive measures about the house. When you make your home more secure, you experience a greater peace of mind through knowing that you and your family are better protected. Also, an added advantage to having a security system installed is that you may be able to get a reduction in premium you pay for your home insurance. So, before you choose and install any system, discuss this possibility of a lower premium aspect with your insurance agent.

Burglary is unfortunately one of the more serious problems faced by all homeowners. It is a sad fact that 1 in 10 homes are burglarized every year, and almost everyone will have something of value stolen from them during their lifetime.

Strange as it may seem, burglars actually enter most homes through an open door or window, simply because residents make it very easy for them to get in and out quickly. Most thieves are just looking for cash, jewelry, watches and small items of value. They want the types of things they can grab quickly, take out of the house easily and sell with no problem.

The best way you can prevent a burglary is almost too obvious: Reduce or eliminate any opportunities for a criminal to get into your home. *Just make your home an undesirable target for criminals by making yourself and your possessions harder to get to.*

The following lists those things you can do to help prevent your home becoming one of the burglary statistics.

- Be alert to any unusual or suspicious behavior in your neighborhood, especially during daylight hours. Most home break-ins and burglaries occur during the day when residents are out at work.

IDEA
  - Call the police immediately if anything on your street looks suspicious. Before you forget any details, write down a description of any persons, license plate numbers of vehicles and anything else that you feel is pertinent.
  - Make sure that there is no easy unwelcome access into your home. This means you *must* keep your garage door fully closed and locked at all times, even if you are at home or sleeping.

IDEA
  - Install strong locks on all outer doors as well as on your garage door and the door that connects the garage to the house.

BEWARE
  - Strangers using a code-grabber can capture the radio signal that opens your garage and in this way can open older model automatic garage doors. [Newer model automatic garage doors usually come equipped with a scrambler already installed.] To thwart such easy access, buy a device to scramble your code at an electronics store.
  - Close and lock all your doors *even when you are home*; someone could enter through the front door while you are in the backyard, or through a side door while you are upstairs. Don't think that just because you are somewhere on your property that a thief will not enter. Besides, thieves may choose to enter because they may not even realize you are on the premises!

- Ask someone in your neighborhood that stays at home during the day to act as a "look out." Do the same for them when you are around.

IDEA
  - Break-ins at night usually occur at houses that are dark and have an unlived-in look. Motion detection lighting is a great deterrent, so install adequate exterior lighting with motion sensors if possible.
  - Using lights that are on timers can be a deterrent because they make it appear that someone is home. However,

if you are away for any length of time, use the type of timer that allows the lights to go on and off at different times rather than the light-activated type. Those come on at dusk and stay on until morning and probably will not deter a burglar.

- To protect both yourself and your property, you can give added protection to your home by putting up a secure fence. Also, such things as video cameras, alarm systems, motion detectors and dogs are also excellent deterrents. Just choose what works best for you and your budget.

- All basement and first floor windows should have strong locks or bars, but make sure that in case of fire they can be opened easily from the inside. A simple way to inexpensively secure windows throughout your home is to drill a hole and insert a nail or screw into the track. This limits the space between the glass frame and the track and prevents the window from being pushed up or opened from the outside. Ask the police crime prevention expert, a home improvement store or other security expert in your area for more details.

- Exterior doors should have heavy-duty deadbolts, strong hinges that are on the inside of the door and well-secured long strike plates that make locks and doors much more difficult for a burglar to pick or to kick in. Make sure that dead bolts can be opened quickly in the event of fire or other emergency.

- Wide-angle peepholes and windows should provide a clear view so you are able to clearly see the area surrounding all doors that lead to the outside.

- Any glass near the exterior doors to your home should be a security type. Check with your local home improvement store for more specifics.

- Always ask for identification before you open the door for strangers or before letting any worker into your home. If an unsolicited worker approaches you offering their services, ask for references. Make sure you check them.

- If a stranger rings your bell and asks to use your phone, have them wait outside and make the call for them. Do not let them inside your home; they may harm you or be casing the place for a robbery.

- Make sure that the landscaping around your property does not provide hiding places or a way into your property. Remove tree branches that someone could use to climb and enter your property.

- Safely store and lock away any equipment that someone could use to enter your home, such as ladders.

- Mark or engrave personal property items with an identification code or number in case any are stolen.

- When you move into a new home, change the locks or at least re-key immediately. Anyone could have made a copy. Do the same if you have given your key to someone you no longer trust or if you have misplaced a key, even if the key has been returned to you.
- Store large amounts of cash for emergencies and your valuables in a secure place. Keep their location and any security combination numbers secret, and put the information in your safe-deposit box.
- Be careful about where you write down your security codes and to whom you provide them. See chapter one for security code storage recommendations.
- It is preferable to have a security alarm system, and in many cases it can help to reduce your home insurance premium.
- If you have an alarm system, give your cell phone and any other telephone numbers to your security company so they can reach you if you are away on business or vacation.
- Equip each bedroom with a telephone and a working flashlight. Make sure that there is a list of emergency phone numbers posted next to every phone.
- Know the location of the police or sheriff offices in your area. You will find a list of them in the community/local government blue pages in the front of the phone book or search on the Internet under: local government, emergency services or public agencies.

BEWARE
- Doggy-doors that are too big can be dangerous—a small adult or child could easily crawl through to enter your home very easily. Replace any larger doors with smaller, less accessible doors.

IF YOU ARE GOING AWAY ON BUSINESS OR A VACATION

- Ask a neighbor to look after your home when you are away, and do the same for them.
- Tell a trusted neighbor if your house will be unoccupied for an extended time and how to reach you in an emergency.

IDEA
- Inform the police if you are going to be away for any length of time, and ask if they will include your house on their route.
- If you will be away for more than a couple of days, arrange to have your mail and newspaper removed. This should be done as often as possible so there is no evidence that might suggest your home is unoccupied. Alternatively, stop your

BEWARE

newspaper delivery and also request that the post office hold your mail until your return, at which point you can collect all your mail from the post office.
• If applicable, make arrangements to have snow removed so your home is not noticeably vacant. No footprints can be very telling.
• When going away on vacation, disconnect the automatic garage door opener.

HIGH RISE APARTMENTS

High rise apartments with a full-time door man or front desk clerk are generally considered safer than other types of multi-family housing. But they too have their own security issues. For example, there should be only one point of entry so it can be watched easily since the doorman cannot be everywhere at one time. Vigilance in the lobby is important. So if you see someone or anything suspicious report it to security or management. If the front desk staff is lenient and allows people to enter too easily it is time to complain.

If there is no doorman, front doors to your apartment building should be closed and locked at all times. Never allow anyone to enter the building after you. It is not being rude to protect your home; it is just a sure way to be safe. If someone wants to enter your building, inform security so they can deal with the situation.

Never indiscriminately buzz people into your building, even when you are expecting visitors. Make sure they are the only ones you allow to enter by checking their identity first. It is a good idea to have a code word for family and friends.

One of the advantages of a high rise building is that it is very easy to introduce yourself to your neighbors on your floor and team up with them and others in your building to form a cooperative crime watch group.

BEWARE

Never leave a note on your door or at the door buzzer to indicate that you are away or out. The wrong people could see the note and take the opportunity to burglarize your home.

Cancel mail when you are out of town. If you trust your doorman or the staff, ask them to accept packages for you when you are away.

Use time-activated lights to give the appearance that someone is at home.

Never arrange to have furniture of any large items delivered when you are not home. You never want to have messages attached to your door or packages left on your doorstep.

If you and your neighbors can band together to look out for each other's safety, then a high rise building can be one of the safest places to live. Everyone just needs to remember it is in everyone's best interest to co-operate with each other on security issues.

IF YOU ARE A VICTIM OR PRESENT DURING A ROBBERY

IDEA

Police often give out the following advice to prevent harm from coming to any victim during a robbery. Read this information carefully, and discuss it with your family so everyone knows what they can do if a robbery takes place.

Act calm and do exactly whatever the robber tells you to do. It is not worth putting yourself in danger over a few possessions.

BEWARE

Keep all your movements slow and smooth, and tell the robber when you are going to move and to where. You want to avoid startling the robber and prevent the situation from escalating into a more dangerous one.

Inform them if there is anyone else in the building or if you expect anyone.

For everyone's safety, cooperate. Robbers are easily excited and provoked; they may lash out if they feel cornered.

Only activate an emergency alarm if it can be done *secretly*.

Try to pay close attention to the robber so that you can provide a good description to authorities. Since a robbery usually lasts less than two minutes, pay particular attention to the face, clothing and unusual mannerisms or markings, as well as the direction in which they left and the mode of transportation used, including license, make and color of any vehicle involved.

After the robber leaves, immediately call 911. Lock all doors and do not let anyone into the crime scene until the police arrive. While waiting for them, write down everything that you can remember about the robbery and the robber, and do not discuss what happened with others until the police have taken all statements. Such quick and thoughtful reactions may help the police apprehend the criminal. *(See Appendix C for a guide to appropriately use the emergency 911 phone number.)*

Preserve the crime scene by not touching anything or walking in an area the robber may have been.

If there are any witnesses, ask them to remain until the police arrive, or have them write down their contact information. Before they leave, ask to verify their information by looking at their driver's license or identification card.

PLAN FOR THE WORST: EVACUATION

Preparations and Procedures

This is a part of your overall safety planning process that I hope you will never have to put into action. However, in order to be safe it is important, if not imperative, that you develop a plan and practice it so that you will be familiar with what to do in the event that you have to evacuate your home.

There are many reasons why you might have to evacuate your home, such as in the case of a fire or a natural disaster. Whatever the reason, there is no doubt that you'll be able to cope much better if you have a pre-arranged and practiced evacuation plan.

For everyone's safety you must *practice* what you have planned to do *at least twice a year.* By doing so, everyone in your household becomes familiar with what to do, and comes to recognize that the plan really *will* work in an emergency!

It is quite possible that a baby-sitter could be the person that might need to conduct the evacuation from your home, so make sure that there is always someone competent in charge, and that they are familiar with "your plan" and what they should do. So, get ready and make a start. Realize that there is a lot of work involved in developing a really good evacuation plan, but with a workable evacuation plan you are likely to save lives, especially in the event of a real emergency when evacuation is the best, or only, option.

One of the first things you need to do is to draw a simplified plan of your home.

HOME LAYOUT PLAN

The following illustration is a sample of the type of drawing you should develop as part of your evacuation plan. By the time you have finished this plan, you will know your home better than you ever thought possible. Do plans for each floor of you home – basement, ground, first, and second if applicable.

1. Electrical panel
2. Utility shutoff
3. Exit doors
4. Exit windows
5. Non exit
6. Fire extinguisher(s)
7. Smoke detector(s)
8. Carbon monoxide detector(s)
9. Sealable safe room

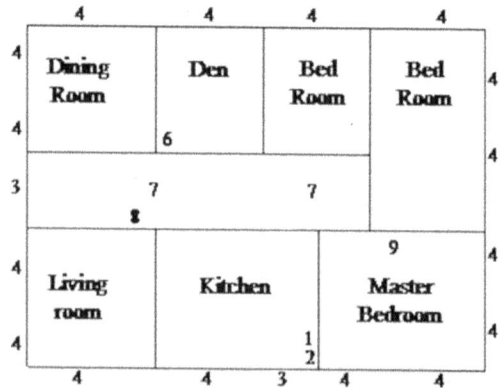

Ground Floor
(Sample Plan Diagram)

Your plan can be as simple as the sample plan illustrated here or more detailed. The most important aspect is that anyone who is in your home is familiar with all of the above elements and has practiced an evacuation.

Your layout drawing should show the locations of any stairs, all the windows, internal doors and exits, and the purpose of each room, such as kitchen, bedroom etc. Remember to add into your drawing the locations of items such as fire extinguisher(s), carbon monoxide detectors, smoke alarms, escape ladders, etc. Also indicate where each of the utilities is located.

For added safety, write out instructions on how to turn off the gas, electricity and water, and leave the instructions beside each turnoff valve, together with the proper tools. Keep a copy of these instructions with the drawing of your home.

Now indicate two potential exit routes from each room in the house, so that someone can still escape the area in the event that one route becomes blocked or is impassable due to fire or fallen debris. But remember: in order for the exercise of planning and drawing to be of use in your overall plan, you *must* arrange to have practice evacuation runs.

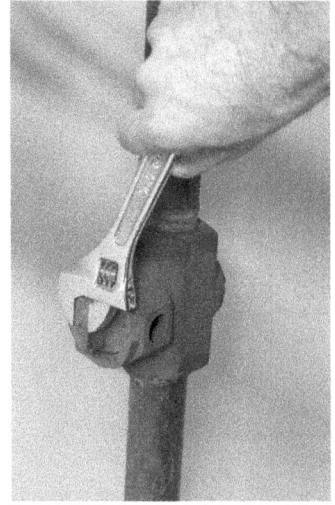

Know where to locate and how tooperate your utility shut-off.

EMERGENCY EVACUATION PLANNING

As soon as you start to develop your emergency evacuation plan, get everyone in your household involved. Get their help in making the plan and in developing lists of all the things that apply to you and your family situation. In addition, each person should make a list of the things they would like to take in the event of an evacuation. Once this is done, review the lists to be certain the items listed are rational choices, and then figure out a plan that works for everyone.

Next, make up a Grab 'n Go emergency kit that you should place near your pre-planned emergency exit from your home. (The suggested contents for this and other kits are detailed in Chapter 9 that addresses 'terrorism'.)

Note: During times of disaster and damage to the home, people suddenly realize the value of family and other photographs. Such items are often irreplaceable. Yet photographs are one of the easiest and most inexpensive things to select and copy before a disaster strikes! Get those photos copied now, and put them in your emergency kit. This way, nobody has to risk their life trying to collect precious photos at the last minute.

In addition to photos, you need to have any other selected items, i.e., some non-perishable foods, water and some money, ready to go at a moment's notice. Decide where you are going to place these things and in what type of container. Leave these items next to your Grab 'n Go emergency kit.

Another part of your plan involves organizing and copying any important legal and financial documents that should be placed with your attorney or in your safety deposit box.

Remember that the emergency lists in this book suggest a broad range of options for supplies. In each case, decide which items are going to be of most value to you, bearing in mind your specific location. Also consider the likely length of time you will need to rely on using your own supplies before you will reach help, or help might reach you. You can customize and download these lists from www.GettingSafer.com once you are a registered user.

EMERGENCY CONTACT AND MEETING PLACES

Even though it may be difficult at times, always leave information about how you can be reached. You never know when an emergency might occur, so it is important that each person in your household can be contacted when they are away from home. In this day and age, with cell phones and pagers, it is relatively easy to be able to stay in touch.

The next part of your overall plan will involve making arrangements for emergency meeting places, and knowing whom to call to let them know about your situation. You should arrange to have a designated meeting place in front of your home, as well as one a short distance away, along with others near school and work. It would be prudent to also arrange a meeting place far from home, even out of state, just in case there is contamination within a few miles of your home. Then, if you have made these arrangements, everyone involved in your plans will be familiar with what they should do and will not waste time or be confused. They will know where they should go and where to meet.

GENERAL NEIGHBORHOOD EMERGENCY

In the event of a general emergency you might be prohibited from leaving or entering an area, or it could be difficult to travel large distances. In this type of situation the authorities in your neighborhood will probably set up shelters. You and your neighbors will be informed via email, phone, radio and TV about what to do by police or other personnel. In addition, the authorities will probably use public announcement systems, as well as go door to door informing each resident individually about their options.

Neighborhood Map

To improve your chances of getting away safely in the event of a widespread emergency, develop and draw a map of your neighborhood and write out a plan that includes information about any local public transport such as buses, trains, taxi or car services that may be available. Even if you have a car you may not be able to reach it. If you have access to a computer and are connected to the Internet you can obtain a great deal of information on this topic, and also create a variety of maps showing alternative routes out of your neighborhood. Since power may not be available in times of emergency, all of your planning *must* be done in advance. . Don't rely on your smart-phone as cell towers can be adversely affected and could make the phones virtually useless. Waiting until you need a plan or a map may be too late.

It cannot be stressed enough that everyone in your household needs to be familiar with and practice all the elements of your escape plan at least twice a year. These practice runs will not take very long…but they could save lives.

TELEPHONE/ EMERGENCY LISTS

There is no doubt that having access to personalized emergency telephone lists is vital when time is short. You should also keep an updated copy of your list in your 'Grab 'n Go' emergency kit so you will have it with you in the event of an evacuation.

Neighbor's Contact #'s:

NEIGHBOR 1		HOME TELEPHONE	
CELL TELEPHONE	WORK TELEPHONE		OTHER
NEIGHBOR 2		HOME TELEPHONE	
CELL TELEPHONE	WORK TELEPHONE		OTHER
NEIGHBOR 3		HOME TELEPHONE	
CELL TELEPHONE	WORK TELEPHONE		OTHER

Out-of-Town Emergency Contact #'s:

NAME 1		HOME TELEPHONE	
CELL TELEPHONE	WORK TELEPHONE		OTHER
NAME 2		HOME TELEPHONE	
CELL TELEPHONE	WORK TELEPHONE		OTHER

School Emergency Contact #'s:

SCHOOL NAME, CHILD 1	TELEPHONE
ADDRESS	
SCHOOL NAME, CHILD 2	TELEPHONE
ADDRESS	

EMERGENCY CONTACTS FORM FOR CHILDREN OR SENIORS

This is another style of emergency list you can make. This is a list that is specially designed for children or seniors. It is formatted in large font to make it easy to read and it has pictures of specific people and their types of services, such as fire or police. The pictures make it easy for young children or seniors to match the picture with the number and use of the information.

If there are young children or seniors that could benefit from such a list put a copy near each phone, or perhaps on the inside of a cupboard door. Make sure everyone knows where the lists are located, and that they can be easily read.

Take the time to teach your children when and how to make an emergency call. There are many instances when the quick action of a child has saved an otherwise disastrous situation, so this is an extremely important exercise for you and your children. In addition, they need to understand what will happen after an emergency call is made, and what to expect.

IDEA

Note: *If you have access to a computer and the Internet, go to www.ready.gov/kids/ games. This site offers lessons to help children prepare for emergencies.*

CONTACT	TELEPHONE NUMBER
Local Police	
Local Fire Department	
Ambulance	
Mommy	
Daddy	

STORAGE RECOMMENDATION: **Emergency Contacts For Children and Seniors**

ENVELOPE	MAIN LOCATION	LOCATION 2	LOCATION 3
Open	Kitchen Wall	Grab & Go Kit	Expanded Emergency Kit
Actual Location(s):			

HOME MAINENANCE CONTACTS LIST

This is a list that can be extremely handy time and time again. It will save time whenever anyone needs to contact any of the services you use. It is easy to forget who your initial contact was unless you have the information written down. Besides, the list is useful for someone other than yourself who may need to contact these services if you are at work or out of town. Get this customizable list at www.gettingsafer.com then you can add any additional categories and contact information that may be needed.

HOME MAINTENANCE CONTACTS LIST — Sample Form

Category	Company	Contact Name	Phone #
Alarm/Security Company			
Appliance Repair			
Cable TV Service			
Carpet Cleaning Company			
Chimney Sweep			
Cleaning Service			
Computer Technician			
Domestic Help			
Electrician			
Electric Company			
Exterminator			
Gas and Electric Company			
Handyman, general			
Heating/Air Conditioning			
Heating Oil Supplier			
Internet Service			
Landscape Service			
Mechanic			
Painter			
Pest Control			
Plumber			
Roof Repair			
Snow Remover			
Swimming Pool			
Telephone Company			
Utility Company			
Water Company			
Window Cleaning			
Other			

WARRANTIES LIST — Sample Form

Item	Model #	Serial #	Purchase Date	Warranty Expiration	Other
Air Conditioner 1					
Air Conditioner 2					
Air Conditioner 3					
Blender					
Camera					
CD Player					
Computer					
Dishwasher					
Dryer					
DVD Player					
Fax Machine					
Food Processor					
Freezer					
Furnace					
Hood					
Humidifier					
Lawn Mower					
Leaf Blower					
Microwave					
Oven					
Printer					
Radio					
Range					
Refrigerator					
Scanner					
Stereo System					
Telephone System					
Toaster Oven					
Trash Compactor					
TV 1					
TV 2					
TV 3					
Vacuum					
VCR					
Video Camera					
Washing Machine					

HOME HAZARDS

Identifying Hazards

Some of the most innocent-looking things in your home can be hazardous or deadly if they are left alone, used incorrectly or put in the wrong hands. Take a fresh look at everything in your home that might be a danger, and particularly take the time to read the labels on all containers and bottles, whether they are detergents, cleaning materials or medicines.

Keep in mind that special hazards exist for young children and elderly persons who are part of your family unit or who may be visiting. After your initial inspection and taking care of possible problems, go through your home carefully at least once a year looking for any potential hazards and removing them from easy access. This exercise will help make your home safer for yourself and your loved ones.

General Safety Measures

To Prevent Accidents:

- Check and secure any items in your home that can shift or fall.
- Do not hang heavy items such as pictures and mirrors over beds or places where people sit.

- Brace overhead light fixtures. Make sure that any ceiling fan is securely attached and out of the reach of someone's head or hand.
- Place large or heavy objects on the floor or on lower shelves.
- Install clips, latches, or other locking devices on cabinet doors.

  - Anchor water heater, large appliances, bookcases, other tall or heavy furniture, shelves, mirrors, and pictures to wall studs.
  - Fit the water heater with a flexible gas supply line, to allow for some movement.
  - Provide strong support and flexible connections on gas appliances.

- Repair any deep cracks in ceilings or foundations.

SAFETY DEVICES AND EQUIPMENT

In addition to removing or reducing physical hazards it is important to realize that some accidents can still happen even while you are out of your home or in bed asleep. For these reasons, it is prudent, and sometimes required by law, to have adequate safety equipment installed.

Smoke Detectors:

Smoke detectors will more than double your chance of surviving a fire by their ability to detect smoke and combustion gasses in the air. It is best to sleep with the bedroom door closed, as toxic smoke can spread quickly, and once the smoke alarm has sounded you will have some extra moments to get out before the smoke reaches *you.*

Install at least one smoke detector on every level of your home, especially near or ideally outside of each bedroom. Test the smoke detectors every month, and replace all the batteries at least once a year.

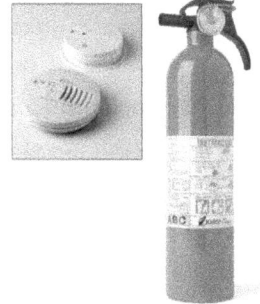

Fire Extinguishers:

You need to have at least one fire extinguisher, an (A-B-C type) in your home. Ideally place one in the kitchen and one on each floor of your home. Maintain and recharge fire extinguishers according to the manufacturer's instructions. Show all your family members, as well as anyone you would leave in charge of your home, the location, and how to use it.

Fire Ladders:

Home escape ladders come in two standard lengths: 15 feet for most two-story bedrooms and 25 feet for three-story buildings. Above that, and for high rise buildings, there are fire escapes already built into the design. One of the more important features to get with a home fire escape is *standoffs*. Standoffs are protrusions that help to steady and hold the ladder away from the side of the house so you can climb down easier than if the ladder is lying against the wall.

Portable ladders are usually made from aluminum or heavy plastic chains with rigid rungs. These ladders are kept rolled up in a box in the bedroom. For use, unroll and hook the top of the ladder to the windowsill and drop the rest out of the window. Make sure the ladder fits the window for which it is intended and most importantly, test it and practice climbing out. First practice from a first floor and make sure everyone in your home knows and practices how to use these escape ladders.

Roll-up ladders can be found in the Yellow pages under safety equipment. Suppliers of fire equipment may also sell home escape ladders. Alternatively, call around to hardware stores or look on the Internet.

CARBON MONOXIDE

Carbon monoxide (CO) has no smell, taste or color. So that is why carbon monoxide detectors placed correctly are vitally important. CO is produced by the incomplete combustion of gas, oil, coal and wood used in boilers, engines, oil burners, gas fires, water heaters, solid fuel appliances and open fires. Dangerous amounts of CO can build up as a result of poor installation, poor maintenance or failure or damage to an appliance that is being used.

Once there is any build up of CO anyone in the area is likely to develop a slight headache. As the CO increases the headache becomes more severe and is followed by nausea, dizziness, convulsions and then unconsciousness. CO enters the blood stream by normal breathing, and this puts the functions of the heart, brain and all other vital functions of the body at risk.

Anyone with heart or respiratory problems, infants and children, expectant mothers and pets are likely to become affected by CO poisoning much more quickly than others.

To Prevent Accidents:
* Service all appliances that burn fossil fuels regularly.
* In homes with good insulation and double-glazing it is even more important to have good ventilation. When rooms are poorly ventilated, any CO produced cannot escape.

- Because there is no smell, taste or color CO alarms are the only way to know if CO is present before tragedy strikes.
- Have proper CO detectors installed that give both a visual and a sound warning as soon as there is any build up of CO to dangerous levels.
- Install one carbon monoxide detector on each level of the home. In homes with more than one floor it is very important to have a CO detector alarm on each level.

CHEMICAL HAZARDS

To Prevent Accidents:
- Store flammable liquids such as gasoline, acetone, benzene, lacquer and paint thinners in approved safety cans, preferably well away from the home. Close their lids tightly, and place any of these types of products and containers in a well-ventilated area. To prevent spills, secure the containers so they cannot fall.

- If flammable materials must be stored in the home, use a storage-can with a UL (Underwriter's Laboratories) or (FM) Factory Mutual approved label.

BEWARE Remove and keep flammable materials away from heat sources, open flames, gas appliances and children.
- Keep combustible liquids such as paint thinner, kerosene, charcoal lighter fluid and turpentine away from heat sources.
- Store oily waste and polishing rags in covered metal cans.
- Instruct family members never to use gasoline, benzene or other flammable fluids for starting fires or cleaning indoors.

COOKING AND KITCHEN HAZARDS

Most accidental fires that occur in homes start in the kitchen. In fact, cooking accidents are the leading cause of fires that result in injury to homeowners.

Other than fire, serious accidents in the kitchen are caused by scalding and steam. Scalding is the # 1 burn injury to children under 4, and seniors are at **IDEA** high risk too.

Burn accidents are most likely to occur if someone is in a hurry, angry or under pressure. Try to relax or wait a moment or two if you are working with anything very hot.

Also, make sure you are protected when removing hot or steaming foods from your microwave. Even tap water at 140° will cause a third-degree burn in just 5 seconds, so adjust your water heater temperature to 120° to 125°. Coffee, tea and soups, as well as hot tap water over 120° can cause severe burns. Make sure to never hold a child when you are drinking a hot liquid.

To Prevent Accidents:

- Keep the stove area clean and clear of combustibles. These are things that can catch fire and burn easily, such as bags from the supermarket, or containers from products just used or finished, like sugar, cereal and cookie boxes. Make sure you always keep all these types of things well away from the range and oven.

IDEA

- Cook on the back burners as much as possible, and keep the handles of pots and pans turned inward and away from the front of the range.
- If a fire starts in a frying pan or a saucepan, the best way to stop the fire is to put a lid over the burning material to cut off the air supply. If that does not work, immediately call 911 and only then use a fire extinguisher. Be very careful if you are tempted to try to move a flaming pan, as the movement can cause the fire to spread. Salt or baking soda can be used to smother and extinguish a small kitchen fire.

BEWARE

- *Never* pour water on grease fires.
- The kitchen is *the most important place in the home for a fire extinguisher.* Make sure you have one that is appropriate for grease fires and for electrical fires, an ABC type. However, having an extinguisher is no good unless everyone living in your home understands when and how to use it.

ELECTRICAL HAZARDS

IDEA

To Prevent Accidents:
- Replace any frayed or cracked wiring, extension and appliance cords, loose prongs and plugs.
- Never overload outlets or extension cords.
- If you must use an extension cord, use a cord that's rated for the electrical load you desire
- Make sure there is only one plug per outlet,

Overloaded power strips can be hazardous.

and that multiple socket cube-taps converting a single socket into 2 to 5 sockets are kept to a minimum.

- Remove any wiring and electrical cords that run under rugs or over nails, heaters, pipes, or high traffic areas.
- Cover exposed outlets and wiring.
- If you have a child, place safety plug covers on exposed outlets.
- Immediately repair or replace appliances that overheat, short out, smoke or spark.
- If a circuit breaker keeps disconnecting, have it inspected by a professional.
- Only purchase appliances and electrical devices that have a label indicating that they have been inspected by a testing laboratory such as (UL) Underwriter's Laboratories or (FM) Factory Mutual.

FIRE HAZARDS

To Prevent Accidents Indoors:
- Never smoke in bed. Smoking is the leading cause of household fires that result in fatalities.
- Refrain from smoking when you are tired or when you have had a lot to drink.
- Clear out old rags, papers, mattresses, broken furniture and any other combustible materials from your home that are no longer needed.
- Move clothes, curtains, rags and paper goods away from electrical equipment, gas appliances or flammable materials.
- Use fire-retardant or not highly flammable materials and furnishings whenever possible.
- Clean the lint trap in the clothes dryer with every load.
- Clean the stove/range vent hood to prevent grease build-up.
- Keep heaters and candles away from curtains and furniture.
- Never leave a lit candle unattended, even if you will be away only for a minute.
- Keep matches and lighters away from children.
- Place portable heaters on a level surface, away from high traffic areas. *(Purchase portable heaters that are equipped with automatic shut-off switches, and avoid the use of extension cords.)*
- It is unlawful to have a propane cylinder inside whether it has any propane or not.

To Prevent Accidents Outdoors:
- Remove fire hazard material such as dried grass cuttings, tree trimmings and weeds from your property.
- Clean and repair chimneys, flue pipes, vent connectors, and gas vents.

- Only use a barbecue outdoors. In addition, it is unlawful to operate a BBQ within 10 feet of a combustible wall or window whether it is open or closed.
- When lighting a BBQ have the lid open and the match burning before you turn on the propane.
- Charcoal should be soaked with lighting fluid for about 5 minutes before being lit. Never use kerosene, gasoline or naphtha to light a BBQ.
- Never move a BBQ when it is lit.
- If taking your BBQ indoors for storage, remove the propane cylinder and leave it outside.

HEATING DEVICES HAZARDS

Heating devices such as portable heaters, wood stoves and fireplaces require special operation and maintenance.

To Prevent Accidents:

- Buy only approved heaters and follow the manufacturers' directions for their correct use.
- Use portable heaters in well-ventilated rooms only.
- Never refill heaters when they are still in use.
- Refuel kerosene heaters outdoors only.
- Have chimneys and wood stoves cleaned annually.

POISONOUS HAZARDS

To Prevent Accidents:

- All household chemicals and medicines should be kept in their original bottles or boxes. Then, if you need to speak with Poison Control, you will be able to read the labels and give them the important information they will need.
- To avoid confusion, never store any chemicals or medicines in the same place as food and drink. Accidents occur when someone swallows poison thinking that it is something else.
- Keep all household chemicals and medicines in locked cabinets that are out of reach of little children. Make sure that all the containers are clearly labeled.
- Make sure that "child-proof" caps are always tightly closed.
- Information about how to dispose of medications that you no longer need go to this web site: www.fda.gov/forConsumers/consumerUpdates/ucm10163.htm

- Keep all chemicals found in the garage or around the house in locked cabinets.
- Do not use different types of chemicals together, as some fumes can mix and become toxic.
- Know the names of the plants in your home, and make sure they are safe. Some plants can be very dangerous and even fatal.
- Keep dangerous plants away from children and pets. It is best to remove all toxic plants like poinsettias from your home or property if you have small children or curious animals.
- Remember that if something is hazardous to human beings, it is most likely going to be hazardous for animals as well. However, there are some plants that may be safe for humans but can be dangerous for pets. (See Chapter 11, Pets)
- Teach your children never to put any part of a plant (berry, stem or leaf) in their mouth.
- Store all planting seeds and bulbs away from children and pets because they may be poisonous.
- When using herbal medicines or mixtures, remember that herbs are almost entirely unregulated for safety uniformity of contents and contamination. FDA approval is not required for packaging or marketing claims.
- Because the first aid directions on general product labels may be wrong or out of date, do not blindly follow them. Call the Poison Control Center for advice instead 1.800.222.1222

UTILITIES HAZARDS

To Prevent Accidents:

Contact your local utility companies for instructions on how to turn the utilities off.
- Teach your family members when and how to turn utilities off.
- Leave a copy of the instructions in a clear plastic cover near the shut-off location.
- You do not want to be searching, so attach a shut-off wrench or specialty tool to a pipe or near to any gas or water shut-off valves.
- Paint shut-off valves with white or fluorescent paint to increase visibility.
- Locate the main electric fuse or circuit breaker box, water service shutoff, and natural gas main shut-off. Show their locations on your Home Layout Evacuation Plan.
- Clear the area around shut-off switches to provide easy access.

PERSONAL INJURY HAZARDS

Tripping or falling frequently causes personal injuries that could be prevented. Age does tend to play a role in the type of fall. Because of changes in vision and balance, coupled with other medical and physical conditions, older adults tend to trip and fall more often. Infants are more likely to fall from furniture.

Seniors' Safety Concerns:
- Check vision and hearing regularly for any changes.
- Know the side effects of medications that could lead to loss of balance and or coordination.
- Limit the amount of alcohol (if any) that you drink.
- Wear rubber-soled and low-heeled shoes that fit properly and also support the feet. Avoid loose-fitting slippers that can be the cause of accidents.
- Remove from all walking areas anything that a person can trip over.
- Remove small rugs, or use double-sided tape under small rugs to prevent slipping.
- Always keep stairs clear of clutter.
- Have handrails and lights installed on all staircases.
- Maintain the temperature in your home at a comfortable level to avoid anyone becoming too dizzy from extreme cold or heat.
- Keep frequently used items in reach, so that a step stool is unnecessary.
- Have handlebars installed next to toilets and bathtubs or showers.
- Use non-slip mats in bathtubs and showers.
- Improve the lighting in the home.
- Remove any electrical cords from the floor in walking areas.
- Be extra careful on wet or icy sidewalks.
- Exercise regularly to maintain bone strength and flexibility.

CHILDREN'S SAFETY

Furniture Hazards: To Prevent Accidents:
- Never leave a baby unsupervised on any furniture -- beds, tables, sofas, cribs with the guardrails down, or changing tables - even if they have never rolled over; a baby can do so unexpectedly.
- Only choose baby products that meet required safety standards. Look for special safety features and make use of all straps and safety features.
- Install temporary padding on sharp corners.

Window Hazards

Windows that are open as little as five inches can be a real danger to children under the age of 10 as they could get their head into that space and get caught. Falls from windows tend to cause severe or fatal injuries, and even a closed window can be dangerous, as falling through glass can be extremely harmful.

To Prevent Accidents:

- Install window guards on all windows above the first floor.
- If you must open windows for ventilation, make sure your child cannot reach the open window.
- Set rules with your child about playing near windows.
- Any furniture that children can climb on must be moved away from windows.
- Do not rely on insect screens to keep children from falling out of windows.

Stair Hazards

To Prevent Accidents:

- Use approved safety gates to keep babies and toddlers from falling down stairs. Make sure they are properly installed.
- Avoid accordion gates in which children can become trapped.
- Keep stairs clear of clutter.
- Make sure there is adequate lighting on stairways.

Playground Hazards:

Playgrounds are wonderful places where children can meet friends, play and exercise. Yet some playgrounds can also pose safety hazards. Faulty playground equipment, equipment that should only be used by specific age groups and/or careless behavior leads to many injuries and a number of fatalities of children ages 14 and under each year.

To Prevent Accidents:

- Adults should always supervise children during trips to the playground.
- Make sure the playground equipment is age-appropriate.
- Surfaces under and around the playground equipment should be soft enough to absorb falls and large enough to cover fall-zones. Recommended surfaces include wood chips or mulch, sand, pea gravel, synthetic turf, rubber and rubber-like materials.
- Play areas with concrete, blacktop and hard-packed grass surfaces are considered unsafe.
- Make sure all the play equipment has been specifically designed and approved for playground use.

Baby Walker Hazards:

Baby walkers cause more injuries than any other nursery product. Most children that sustain injuries from baby walkers are between the ages of 5 and 15 months. And in fact, baby walkers *increase* the risk of falling down stairs! 76% of baby walker-related injuries are caused by falls down stairs (76%), with 12% caused by the walker tipping over.

Baby walkers also can give small children access to hot or poisonous substances on tables and stoves that would otherwise be out of reach.

To Prevent Accidents:

- Choose alternatives to baby walkers that are safer: stationary "walkers" which allow the child to rotate and bounce, play pens, and approved high chairs.

Water Hazards:

Contrary to what you might believe, most children drown at home, not at the beach or at public pools. Young children can drown in as little as two inches of water.

To Prevent Accidents:

- Be extra careful. Never leave children alone in the bathtub, near buckets that hold any kind of fluid, toilets or pools of any kind.
- If you are alone with a child and the phone rings, either take the child with you or let your answering machine take the call.
- Completely surround all home pools of any type or size, or any open water source, with a fence and a self-closing gate.
- Children that are in or near a pool or any water must be watched at all times. It only takes a few minutes of being under water for serious brain damage or death to occur while a parent or guardian is distracted,

Bike/Scooter/Skating Safety

To Prevent Accidents:

- Children should always wear helmets, kneepads and other protective gear when skating or riding bicycles or scooters. The safety gear may not prevent bumps, scrapes, bruises or broken bones, but it will help protect children from life-threatening injuries and brain damage.
- Children on scooters should not wear wrist guards, which tend to limit the range-of-motion. They need to be able to maneuver out of tight spots.
- When riding a bicycle, scooter or skateboard, children should understand the rules of traffic and wear brightly-colored clothes so they are highly visible.

Children and Auto Safety Hazards

To Prevent Accidents:

- Never leave a child alone in a car at any time or under any circumstances. During the summer months or hot weather, a few minutes alone in the car, even with the windows rolled down, can prove fatal.

- Remember that it doesn't matter whether or not you're a good driver, you can't control other drivers or prevent a crash. Driving carefully and using the proper child safety seats correctly installed may help save you and your child's life.

- Children 12 and under should always ride in the back seat and wear a seat belt. An airbag in the front seat may help save an adult's life, but it may prove fatal for a baby or child.

- Infant seats should be rear-facing seats that are designed to hold infants until they are 1 year old and weigh 20 pounds.

- Children over 1 years of age who weigh between 20 and 40 pounds should be in a forward-facing child seat.

- Place children between ages 4 and 8 (weighing about 40 to 80 pounds) in a booster seat that will help to properly position the lap and shoulder belt over their hips and chest. They will not be adequately protected in a crash if they use the lap and shoulder belts designed for taller adults. *(Note: Usually children over 8 will correctly fit a lap/shoulder belt.)*

Now that you have gone through this chapter you are much better informed about potential hazards. Hopefully you have made a list of the things that need repair or some attention. If you did not make a list, go over the sections that are relevant to you and start today. There is no time like the present.

CHAPTER **Seven**

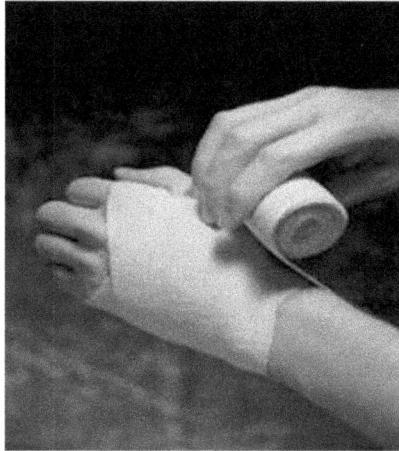

Basic First Aid and Home Emergencies

In the event of a real general emergency in your neighborhood, it may not be possible to access medical advice if the phone lines or cell towers are down. You may not even be able to get to a hospital. In that type of situation you will have to rely on whatever information and help you can get wherever you are. For that reason it is recommended that you keep an elementary list of health problems and the ways to treat them in your emergency kit. Such a list is included in this chapter. With that information at hand you would be able to deal with minor accident or medical conditions until you are able to get professional care.

This chapter will help you to become more familiar with many health-related matters that can be dealt with at home. In other cases, depending upon the symptoms, medical care may be preferable or even urgently necessary. Whenever that is the case, call 911 first.

There are many times when minor accidents or illnesses occur at home and it is best to know what to do. Each of the health problems in this chapter are briefly explained along with their symptoms and treatment.

Of course, almost every home has some products that can assist in medical care, even if it is only aspirin or Band-Aids. But, no matter what you have now, review the potential

Medicine Cabinet Items list in this book, and then make your own selection based on the number and ages of people in your home

THE MEDICINE CABINET

Almost every home has a supply of various pills and medicines that are kept in a medicine cabinet. Usually the medicine cabinet is in a bathroom, although that may not be the best place to keep medicines and medical supplies. The heat and humidity caused by steam from showers and baths can cause the medicines to weaken or deteriorate. Instead, try to store them in a box or cabinet in cool, dark and dry place such as the top of a linen closet. Remember that *all medications should be in a locked container or cabinet that is out of the reach of children*. In addition,

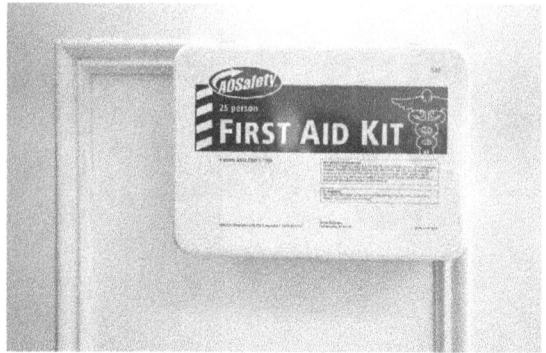

Inside your wardrobe is an ideal place for your First Aid and Medicine KIt

always make sure that all the childproof caps on the medicines are correctly sealed.

In order to avoid any confusion, medicines and supplies should be kept in their original containers; that way, you will know what the correct dosage should be and the correct expiration date.

Empty the medicine cabinet once a year and clean it with disinfectant. At the same time, go through the items and medicines and discard any products that are no longer required as well as outdated or damaged containers. Check all expiration dates, even those on first aid kits. Realize that some items may need to be disposed of in a special way. Old mercury thermometers that are now banned, should be placed in a tightly sealed jar and disposed of during your city's 'Household Hazardous' waste pick-up day. Visit www.nist.gov/pml/mercury.cfm for information about alternatives to mercury thermometers.

Restock supplies, and update the type of supplies you will store, according to your changing needs.

Even if you already have the following numbers on other lists, keep <u>primary care physician</u>, <u>emergency physician</u>, <u>local hospital emergency room</u>, <u>pharmacy</u> and <u>poison control</u> telephone numbers near to or taped in the medicine cabinet as well. Also, include a list of family allergies and health conditions.

Concerns for Children

It is always important to follow the dosage instructions printed on all medication packaging, especially the dosage for children, as they usually require a much smaller dose than adults do.

Never tell children that medicines are candy, as they may think that any medicine they come across is candy, and help themselves to an overdose of medicine.

BEWARE

You should be aware that any products that contain iron are extremely dangerous, and iron tablets are a leading cause of accidental deaths of children. Iron poisoning accounts for approximately 30% of the pediatric deaths from medications even though it is a requirement that iron-containing vitamins or medications be packaged in child-resistant packaging.

Aspirin should *not* be given to children under 12 years of age. There is a link between aspirin and Reyes Syndrome, a rare disorder that affects the liver and brain and can be fatal. Your doctor should be able to recommend a suitable "non-aspirin aspirin" substitute that does not contain salicylate and is available

BEWARE

from most pharmacies. The following site has some very important and useful information: http://www.keepkidshealthy.com/medicine_cabinet/aspirin_salicylates.html

Always keep any medications and vitamins, even those in sealed containers, out of the reach of children. Never discard these products by flushing them down the toilet or leaving them in a wastebasket where a child could find them.

Medicine Cabinet Items

This following list of items is far more extensive than you are likely to need in your home medicine cabinet. Simply use the list as a guide to choose the items you need based on a discussion with your physician and pharmacy. Check the items you intend to keep, and make your own personalized list. See www.gettingsafer.com to make your customized Medicine Cabinet list that you can save or print.

In *all* cases, follow the directions supplied with a product or on a container.

- Acetaminophen *(i.e. Tylenol®) (adult and children's strength)*
- Activated Charcoal *(absorbs poisons)*
- Adhesive Tape
- Adhesive Tape, Hypoallergenic
- Alcohol, Isopropyl *(skin cleansing)*

- Alcohol Wipes
- Analgesic Cream
- Antacid Liquids
- Antacid Tablets
- Antibiotic Ointment
- Anti-diarrhea Medicine

- Antihistamine (*allergy relief*)
- Antiseptic, Povidine (*iodine solution and gel*)
- Aspirin (*adult and children's strength*)
- Bandages, Adhesive (*a variety pack*)
- Bandages, Butterfly
- Bandages, Triangular
- Bulb Syringe (*Nasal Aspirator*)
- Calamine Lotion
- Candle and Matches
- Cotton Balls (sterilized)
- Cotton Swabs
- Cough Suppressant (*Antitusives*)
- Decongestant
- Dosage Spoon
- Elastic Bandage 3" (*i.e., Ace Bandage*)
- Enema Equipment
- Eye Cup (*or small plastic cup to bathe eye*)
- Eye Dropper
- Eye Wash, Sterile
- Flashlight

- Foot Powder (*for athlete's foot*)
- Gauze Pads, 4" x 4", Sterile
- Gauze Roll

- Hydrocortisone Cream
- Hydrogen Peroxide
- Ibuprofen Fever Reducer (*for children and adults*)
- Infant Tylenol (use with a dropper only, not a spoon)
- Children's Tylenol®
- Latex Gloves, Disposable
- Laxative
- Pads, Sterile and Non-Stick
- Paper Cups
- Pen and Pencil
- Petroleum Jelly
- Rubbing Alcohol
- Safety Pins
- Scissors
- Silva Base Cream (for burns)
- Sling
- Soap
- Sunscreen (*SPF 15 or higher*)
- Thermometer, digital (*oral, rectal*)

- Tongue depressors
- Tweezers
- Vitamin A & D ointment for burns.

QUICK FIND INDEX OF HEALTH PROBLEMS

BASIC FIRST AID TREATMENT FOR MEDICAL EMERGENCIES AND MINOR CONDITIONS

When to Seek Immediate Help

Whenever any health condition appears extremely serious, *immediately call 911 and/or go to your local emergency room.* If medical help is not immediately available, conditions that are more serious may have to be treated at home until the person receiving aid can be transferred to the local emergency room.

For any of the following conditions or when there is a change in the status of an existing illness or there are new or acute symptoms that could be potentially serious.

Call 911 immediately

- Unconsciousness
- Difficulty breathing
- Choking that persists
- Change in speech
- Change in mental status
- Coughing blood
- Paralysis
- Vomiting (unexpected)

- Rectal bleeding
- Change in vision
- Chest pain
- Severe pain
- Severe wound
- Severe burn
- Very high or low body temperature
- Suspected bone fracture

Fortunately, with basic first aid treatment, many minor conditions can be completely and successfully treated at home. But there can be times when some more serious conditions have to be treated at home until professional, medical or authorized personnel can offer expertise and aid.

Even when you need to see the doctor, the information in this chapter is likely to prove useful. In many cases it will help you to better understand and be better able to explain your symptoms and allay your fears about possible treatment.

The content of this chapter is set out to provide overall health care information and should not be used as the only source for the treatment of any of the topics discussed. Rather, it is intended to provide an impetus for you to seek further detailed and on-going training to become proficient in dealing with emergencies that unfortunately happen from time to time.

TREATMENT OF MEDICAL EMERGENCIES AND MINOR HEALTH CONDITIONS:

Allergy and Anaphylaxis

Allergy is defined as a "harmful, with increased susceptibility to a specific substance". The more common types of reactions are allergic rhinitis, asthma, skin allergies and hives. However, the most severe form of allergic reaction is anaphylactic shock.

Anaphylactic shock causes swelling of body tissues (including the throat), cramps and a sudden drop in blood pressure. It can result in death. Anaphylaxis most often occurs in persons particularly sensitive to such things as penicillin, stinging insects and shellfish or nuts (especially peanuts, but also walnut, cashew or Brazil nuts), latex or medications.

First aid activation is associated with recognizing an anaphylactic reaction and the appropriate treatment recommendations.

Symptoms and Recognition of Anaphylaxis:
- Skin: Hives, swelling, itch, warmth, redness, rash.
- Breathing: Wheezing, a shortness of breath or tightness at the throat, a hoarse voice, tightness in the chest or trouble swallowing.
- Stomach: Pain, cramps, nausea, vomiting, diarrhea, itchy mouth/throat.
- Circulation: Pale or bluish color, a weak pulse, dizziness, light-headedness, low blood pressure, fainting or shock.
- Other: Anxiety, itchy/watery/red eyes, or headache.

Treatment:
- Call 911. Seek immediate medical attention.
- Check to see if the person is carrying special medication to inhale, swallow, or inject (*Epi-Pen*) in order to counter the effects of the allergic attack.
- If the person is unconscious or not breathing, perform cardiopulmonary resuscitation (CPR).

Bleeding, Minor

A minor cut or scrape (see Cuts and Scrapes section) at home, work or play can often occur. Bleeding is considered minor if the bleeding is slow and not spurting.

Treatment:

- To stop minor bleeding, apply direct pressure to the bleeding area with a gauze pad, any other dressing or any clean soft material or even your hand if nothing else is available. Apply steady, hard pressure on the wound.
- If the bleeding continues, continue to apply pressure to the bandaged or covered wound. Do not remove the original dressing. Instead add an additional dressing; a double thickness may be required.
- If the wound or dressing shows continual bleeding after 15 minutes, seek medical advice.
- To help reduce blood flow, elevate the bleeding area if possible.
- When the bleeding has stopped, carefully remove the dressing and clean the wound (*see Cuts and Scrapes*).

Bleeding, Major

- Bleeding is considered severe if there is evidence that the bleeding is profuse; has a pumping, or spurting nature; cannot be promptly controlled with the pressure methods; or if the individual is in a shock-like state.

Treatment:

- Use the same pressure methods and applications as in the Minor Bleeding section, above.
- If there is no evidence that the bleeding is slowing, call 911 or emergency services. Continue applying pressure for at least 45 minutes while waiting for assistance.
- Avoid using a tourniquet unless you are familiar with this method, or are receiving medical instruction.

Bumps and Bruises:

Bumps and bruises often occur accidentally by hitting something or when someone bumps into you and causes a fall. This can happen almost anywhere and anytime, and especially happens to children, and frequently, seniors.

Treatment:

- Avoid massaging the bump or bruise, as this will make the injury worse.
- Apply an ice pack for 20 minutes, but do not apply any ice directly on the injury. Instead, wrap the ice in a towel or, alternatively, use frozen vegetable packages or any

other frozen items wrapped in a clean towel or a plastic bag. These items make great ice packs.

- Elevate the injured area if possible.
- Give acetaminophen or ibuprofen for pain as directed by a doctor. *Never* give aspirin since it may prolong bleeding into or under the tissue.
- Do not pop blood blisters if they occur. They will go away spontaneously within a week or two.
- A doctor should evaluate multiple unexplained bruises.

Burns

Skin burns (The Basics) Patient information:
Written by the doctors and editors at UpToDate visit www.uptodate.com

Skin Burns Overview – Skin burn injuries are common with over one million burn injuries occurring every year in the United States. Skin burns can result from exposure to several possible sources, including hot water or steam, hot objects or flames, chemicals, electricity, or overexposure to the sun.

What are the symptoms of a skin burn? — The symptoms depend on how bad your skin burn is. However, the classification of a burn can change over the first few days. So, a burn that may appear superficial initially, then become deeper over time. If unsure how deep the skin is burned contact a health provider.

Here are the up-to-date terms doctors use to describe different types of burns:

- Superficial skin burn (used to be called a "first-degree burn"): The burn is only on the top layer of your skin. Your skin will be dry, red, and painful. When you press the burn, it turns white. Superficial skin burns heal in 3 to 6 days without leaving a scar.
- Superficial partial-thickness burn (used to be called a "second-degree burn"): The burn is on the top 2 layers of your skin, but does not go deep into the second layer. Your skin will hurt with a light touch or if the air temperature changes. The skin will be red and leak fluid, and you might get blisters. The burn will turn white when you press it. Superficial partial-thickness burns take 7 to 21 days to heal, and the area of skin that was burned might be darker or lighter than it used to be. The burn might or might not leave a scar.
- Deep partial-thickness burn (used to be called a "third-degree burn"): This kind of burn also affects the top 2 layers of skin, but is deeper than a superficial partial-thickness burn. The burn will hurt when you press it hard, but it will not turn white.

You will get blisters. This kind of burn takes more than 21 days to heal, and will probably leave a scar.

- Full-thickness burn (used to be called a "fourth-degree burn"): Full-thickness burns include all the layers of the skin and often affect the fat and muscle underneath. The burn does not usually hurt, and the burned skin can be white, gray, or black. The skin feels dry. Your doctor will treat this kind of burn with surgery. You might also need to stay in the hospital for a time and take medicines.

Should I see a doctor or nurse?

See your doctor or nurse right away if you are not sure how bad your burn is or if the burn:

- Involves your face, hands, feet, or genitals
- Is on or near a joint, such as your knee or shoulder
- Goes all the way around a part of your body (such as your arm or leg)
- Is bigger than 3 inches across or goes deep into the skin
- Causes a fever of at least 100.4°F or shows other signs of infection. Infected skin gets more and more red, is painful, and might leak pus.
- Goes deeper than the top layer of skin AND you have not had a tetanus shot in more than 5 years

People younger than 5 years or older than 70 years with any kind of skin burn should also see their doctor. In fact, anyone who has trouble fighting infection, for example, because they have cancer or HIV, should see a doctor if the burn goes deeper than a superficial burn.

Is there anything I can do on my own to feel better?

If your burn is not too severe, you can take the following steps:

- Clean the burn: Take any clothes off of the area and wash it with cool water and plain soap. If your clothes stick to the burn, go to the emergency room.
- Cool the burn: After you have cleaned the skin, you can put a cool cloth on it or soak your skin in cool water. Do not use ice to cool the burn.
- Prevent infection: If the burn goes deeper than the top layer of skin, you are at risk of infection. To help prevent infection, you can use aloe vera gel or cream, or an antibiotic cream. If your burn forms blisters, cover it with a clean, non-stick bandage and change the bandage once or twice a day. Do not pop the blisters, because that can lead to infection.
- Treat pain: If the burn hurts, try raising the burned part of your body to a level above your heart. For instance, if you burned your foot, try lying down and propping your

foot up on pillows. This slows blood flow to the area and can prevent swelling and ease pain. You can also take over-the-counter pain medicine, such as acetaminophen (sample brand name: Tylenol) or ibuprofen (sample brand names: Advil, Motrin).

- Do not scratch the burn: Scratching can increase the risk of infection.

How is a skin burn treated?

If the burn does not need a doctor's care right away, the first step is to try the things you can do on your own. If you have a more serious burn, your doctor might give you a stronger medicine for pain or apply special bandages. For a severe burn, your doctor might suggest surgery to repair the area that was burned. He or she might also prescribe medicines to prevent infection.

Can skin burns be prevented?

You can reduce the chances that you or your children will get burned by:

- Keeping candles, matches, and lighters away from children
- Keeping any hot objects away from the edge of the table or stove (examples include foods or liquids, or the handles of pots and pans)
- Using a humidifier with cool mist, not warm mist or steam
- Keeping children away from hot stoves, fireplaces, and ovens
- Having a smoke detector on each floor of your home
- Dressing your children in clothes that do not catch fire easily—especially at night. Clothes made from cotton are a good choice.
- Setting your hot-water heater no higher than 120°F
- Covering car seats and seat belts with a cloth if the car is sitting in the sun on a hot day
- Using sunscreen if you are going to be in the sun

Treatment of Minor Burns: Superficial burn

Clean the burn daily with mild soapy water or saline. If available, silver sulfadiazine (Silvadene) should be applied to the burn area daily. (Don't use this on the face, in pregnant patients or those with sulfa allergies.) Bacitracin® ointment is an acceptable alternative. Avoid caustic agents such as hydrogen peroxide. Povidone-iodine (Betadine®) is not recommended as it might delay healing. Keep any dressings clean and change them every 1 to 2 days. Suspect an *infection* if there is an increase in pain, redness, swelling, or any fluid draining from the burn, signs of swollen regional lymph nodes or red streaks spreading from the burn. If you see these symptoms, call a doctor immediately.

- Other than for a minimal burn, the burn victim should receive tetanus shots if not already immunized within the past five years.

Treatment of Major Burns:

Get help as soon as possible. Trained medical personnel in a medical center should treat all major burns.

The following Treatment of Major Burns applies to:

- Any Superficial partial-thickness burn or Deep partial-thickness burns the extent of which you are unsure.
- All Full-thickness burns, severe or extensive; airway burns – from smoke inhalation. Electrical or chemical burns or a person in a shock-like state.

Treatment of Major Burns: When it is impossible to move or get to a Medical Center.

The following recommendations are preliminary measures to be utilized when it is not possible to immediately transfer a burn victim to medical experts.

- If someone, or their clothing, is on fire, douse them with water and wrap them in a thick cloth like a wool or cotton coat, rug or blanket. Try and avoid using anything synthetic because it may melt.
- Only remove clothing around the burn area if it comes off easily. However, make certain that the victim's clothing is still not on fire or smoldering.
- Check for vital signs if the victim is not breathing. If the airway is blocked, clear the airway and begin rescue breathing and CPR.
- If the victim's breathing is fine, then cover the burn with a sterile bandage or a cool, clean piece of cloth. Do not use anything rough like a blanket or towel, and do not apply any ointments.
- Never apply grease, cream, ointment, ice, adhesive bandages, fluffy cotton or anything rough to the injured area. These types of dressings may prevent proper healing.
- If the victim's fingers or toes are burned, separate them very carefully, if possible, and wrap them individually with dry, sterile, non-adhesive dressings.
- In severe burn cases, do *not* apply cold compresses or submerge the victim in cold water. This may result in shock.
- Elevate the burned area above the heart level if possible, and protect it from pressure and friction.
- Prevent shock by laying the victim flat and covering them with something to help keep them warm. Elevate the feet 12 inches. However, do not elevate if there is possible trauma to the neck, head, back and leg or if the victim is uncomfortable.
- If there is an airway burn, do not place anything under the victim's head. A propped head may close the airway.
- Monitor the victim's vital signs until medical help arrives.

- Prevent contamination and infection by not breathing on, coughing or touching the burn.
- Avoid scraping or disturbing blistered or dead skin, unless instructed to do so by trained personnel.

Choking

Choking is the body's response in attempting to remove a foreign object (such as food) from the airway, the passage between the oral cavity (mouth) and the lungs. If this region is blocked, the air we breathe (that contains oxygen) cannot get to the lungs. Without an oxygen supply the brain begins to die within 4 to 6 minutes. Thus rapidly administered first aid for choking can save a life. Solid foods, such as nuts or meat, are often the source of the problem. Choking is more likely to occur when one is chewing and talking at the same time. Since children will take almost anything in their mouth that fits, they can choke on all sorts of things in addition to food items.

Education is a good strategy to prevent FBA, foreign body aspiration in children. Although educational efforts may change safety-related knowledge and behavior, direct evidence that educational counseling results in lower injury rates is lacking. Nonetheless, the American Academy of Pediatrics recommends that anticipatory guidance to prevent choking/FBA be provided to caregivers beginning when the child is six months of age. At this age, children begin to develop the fine motor dexterity to pick up small objects and put them into their mouths. Important aspects of anticipatory guidance include the following:

- Marbles, small rubber balls, and latex balloons should be mentioned specifically, since aspiration of these items may be fatal
- Hard and/or round foods should not be offered to children younger than four years of age; these include (but are not limited to), hot dogs, sausages, chunks of meat, grapes, raisins, apple chunks, nuts, peanuts, popcorn, watermelon seeds, raw carrots, hard candy
- Infants should be fed solid food only by adults, and only when the infant is sitting upright; all meals for young children should be supervised by an adult
- Children should be taught to chew their food well; shouting, talking, playing, running, crying, and laughing while eating should be discouraged.
- Chewable medications should be given only after the age of three years (when molars are present)
- Coins and other small items should not be given to young children as rewards
- The practice of using the mouth to hold school supplies or other small objects should be discouraged

- Avoid toys with small parts, and keep other small household items out of reach of infants and young children
- Follow the age recommendations on toy packages
- Be aware of older children's actions as they may give younger siblings dangerous objects
- Parents, teachers, child care providers, and others who care for children should be encouraged to take a course in Basic Life Support and choking first aid

A choking person's airway may be completely or partially blocked. A complete obstruction is life threatening. A partial obstruction can also be life threatening if the person's ability to breathe in and out becomes poor, thereby reducing oxygen flow into the lungs and delivery to the brain. It is best to treat any significant obstruction as a complete obstruction.

Symptoms:
- Gagging, gasping, wheezing
- Sense of panic and fear
- Face may turn purple and the eyes may bulge
- Grabbing the throat by the hand (the universal sign for choking); if you see this, call 911
- Noisy breathing, or high-pitched crowing sounds
- Coughing, which may become weak and ineffective
- Loss of consciousness or convulsions (due to lack of oxygen)

Treatment:
    If you encounter a <u>conscious</u>, choking individual that is coughing, encourage continued coughing. If the victim is unable to cough, speak, or breathe, send someone to call 911
- First, lean the person forward and give 5 back blows with heel of your hand.
- Then give 5 quick abdominal thrusts using the Heimlich maneuver by placing the thumb-side of your fist against the middle of the victim's abdomen, just above the navel. Grab your fist with the other hand.
- Repeat the 5 back blows and then the 5 abdominal thrusts until the object the person is choking on is forced out and person breathes or coughs on his or her own.
- If the choking adult is <u>unconscious</u>, attempt to locate and remove the foreign body in the back of the mouth with a sweeping finger motion.
- Be extra careful and do NOT try to grasp or poke the object lodged in the victim's throat as it might push it further down.

- Do NOT interfere with the victim if they are coughing forcefully and are able to breathe in and out or cry.
- Do NOT start CPR unless the victim has stopped breathing and the airway is clear.
- Performance of the HEIMLICH MANEUVER alone in an attempt to remove the foreign body is no longer recommended due to the increased likelihood of injury.

Heimlich maneuver:

The Heimlich maneuver is considered an effective way to help remove something stuck in an adult's or older child's throat, but only if used in conjunction with back blows. A different technique is used for small children and infants, and is detailed later in this section.

The maneuver is not difficult to perform, nor does it require great strength, but it can help to save a person's life. You can even use it on yourself and save your own life!

Once you see it demonstrated it is quite easy to learn the Heimlich maneuver very quickly. Make a call to your local Red Cross to ask where and when you can attend a demonstration.

Technique:
- Stand behind the victim and wrap your arms around their waist (or around the lower chest if they are obese or pregnant).
- Make a fist. Then place the thumb side of your fist in the middle of the victim's abdomen - just above the navel and below the tip of their breastbone (or the middle of the breastbone if the victim is obese or pregnant).
- Grasp that fist with your other hand.
- Keep your elbows out and press your fist into the victim's abdomen inward and upward with quick, distinct thrusts.
- Continue these abdominal thrusts every few seconds until the object is dislodged, help arrives, or the victim loses consciousness.
- If the victim loses consciousness, give first aid for an unconscious person.
- If the victim develops convulsions or seizures, give first aid for this problem.

What to Do if the Victim Continues Choking
Treatment:
- If the victim continues to choke or is unconscious, call 911 and your healthcare provider.
- If you are not alone, have one person call the local emergency number while the other person starts the first aid treatment or CPR.
- If you are alone with the victim, shout for help. If you are trained in CPR, call 911 and then administer CPR.

Other Considerations for Choking and Foreign Bodies

- Even if you successfully dislodge the obstruction and the victim seems fine, complications could arise from the incident and from the first aid measures taken. Therefore, keep the victim still and call the doctor for further instructions.
- Sometimes some of the foreign body that caused the choking may enter the lung rather than being completely expelled. While the victim may appear to improve and breathe normally, in a few days some suggestions/ indications of a foreign body in the lung, such as wheezing, persistent cough and pneumonia might appear. *If this occurs, seek medical help immediately.*

If You are the one Choking and You are Alone:

Since time is likely to be short when you might need this procedure, it is best to have practiced the following treatment several times just in case you ever need to apply the real thing some day.

Treatment:

- Call 911.
- Even though you can't speak, most 911 calls go through systems that can trace you to your address.
- When you do not speak, that type of 911 is treated as a "silent call" and the safety dispatch center checks to find out if you are, or are not, a deaf person. They will then ask you to indicate by pressing 1, 2 or 3 what type of emergency service you require. You will be asked to press 1 for police, 2 for fire or 3 for ambulance.
- Since the service being sent to help you knows that you are incapacitated, upon their arrival, if they cannot gain easy access they will force entry into a building to find you.
- Leave the phone off the hook once you have placed your call, and perform one of the methods below. You have a little bit less than two minutes before you pass out. Because your life may be at stake, you need to force yourself to administer this following painful technique on yourself:
- Using your own hands, make a fist with one hand and place it thumb-first against your abdomen, below the ribs and above the belly button.
- Cover that fist with your other hand, and pull your fist inwards and upwards sharply, quickly and forcefully. Repeat until the object pops out.
- If the method mentioned above does not dislodge the object, use something with a straight edge, such as a chair back, countertop, or an edge of a table, railing or another straight and firm item. Bend forward over it, and press your abdomen against

it firmly, or run into the object. Attempt to meet the edge at the spot just above your belly button. Repeat with as much force as possible until you dislodge the object.

Choking: Heimlich maneuver in Infants
Symptoms:
- Inability to breathe or cry
- High-pitched noises
- Ineffective cough
- Face begins to turn blue

Treatment:
  - Lay the infant face down along your forearm with the child's chest in your hand and the jaw between your thumb and index finger. Use your thigh or lap for support. Keep the infant's head lower than his or her body.
  - Give 5 quick, forceful blows between the child's shoulder blades with the palm of your other hand.
  - Turn the infant over to be face-up on your other arm. Again, use your thigh or lap for support. Keep the infants' head lower than the body.
  - Place 2 fingers on the middle of his or her breastbone just below the nipples.
  - Give 5 thrusts down, depressing the breast ½" to 1" each time. Each thrust is a separate attempt to clear the baby's airway by forcing air out through the windpipe.
  - *Continue this series of 5 back blows and 5 chest thrusts until the object is dislodged or the baby loses consciousness.*
  - If the back blows and the Heimlich maneuver combination are not successful and the infant has lost consciousness or is not breathing, place the baby with his or her back on a hard surface, keeping the back in a straight line and firmly supporting the head and neck. Ex: pose the child's chest.
    - Open the infant's mouth with your thumb and index finger, placing your thumb over the tongue. If the foreign object is visible and loose, remove it.
    - Lift the infant's chin while tilting the head back to move the tongue away from the windpipe. If a spinal injury is suspected, pull the jaw forward without moving the head or neck. Don't let the mouth close.
    - Place your ear close to the infant's mouth and watch for chest movement. For 3-5 seconds, look, listen and feel for breathing. If the infant is not breathing, use the following rescue breathing method for infants.

Rescue Breathing Method for Infants [Same as CPR for Infants]:
- Open the airway by tilting the head and lifting the chin. *Do not tilt the head back too far.*
- If the baby is not breathing, give 2 small mouth-to-mouth breaths. Do so by covering the infant's mouth and nose with your mouth. Each breath should last for 1½ to 2 seconds. The infant's chest should rise with each breath.
- If there is no evidence of circulation [coughing, moving, breathing), start gentle compressions, *only* about ½" to 1" deep, by positioning your 3rd and 4th fingers in the center of the chest half an inch below the nipples. The compression rate should be approximately 100 per minute, or close to two compressions per second.
- Continue CPR, administering one breath for each 5 compressions. After 1 minute of repeated cycles, call 911. Then continue the CPR efforts. Check for the return of breathing every 2 minutes.
- If the baby begins to have convulsions or seizures, refer to first aid for that condition (see Convulsion, First Aid).

Choking: When an Adult or a Child Over One Year of Age Becomes Unconscious
Symptoms:
- Inability to breath or cry
- High-pitched noises
- Ineffective cough
- Face begins to turn blue
- Unconscious
- Not breathing
- Inability to move air into the lungs with mouth-to-mouth resuscitation

Evaluation and Initial Treatment:
- Roll the victim onto their back on a hard surface, keeping their back on a straight line and firmly supporting their head and neck. Expose the victim's chest.
- Open the victim's mouth with your thumb and index finger, placing your thumb over their tongue and your index finger under their chin. If the choking object is visible and loose, remove it with your fingers directly, or with a sweeping movement of the fingers in the mouth.
- Lift the victim's chin while tilting the head back to move the tongue away from the windpipe. If a spinal injury is suspected, pull the jaw forward without moving the head or neck. Don't let the mouth close.

o   Place your ear close to the victim's mouth and look for chest movement. Listen and feel for breathing.

o   If the victim is breathing, continue with the ongoing first aid for whatever other basic injury has occurred.

o   If the victim is not breathing, begin rescue breathing.

Rescue Breathing Method for Adults and Older Children

- Holding the head steady, close the victim's nostrils by pinching them with your thumb and index finger, and cover the victim's mouth tightly with your mouth. Give 2 slow, full breaths for 2 seconds each, with a pause between your breaths.

- If the victim's chest does not rise, reposition the head and airway and give 2 more breaths.

- If the victim's chest still doesn't rise, begin abdominal thrusts, as follows. Kneel at the victim's feet or astride the thighs (or to the side if the victim is obese or pregnant). Place the heel of your hand in the middle of the abdomen just above the navel, well below the tip of their breastbone. (If the victim is obese or pregnant, place the heel of your hand in the middle of the victim's breastbone. Do not place your hand on the ribs or on the tip of the breastbone.) Place your other hand on top of the first hand.

- Give 6 to 10 quick thrusts, compressing the victim's chest about 2 inches and pressing your hands inward and upward. Do not press to either side. Each thrust is a separate attempt to clear the victim's airway by forcing air out through the windpipe

- Open the victim's mouth with your thumb and index finger. If an object is visible and loose, remove it. Observe the victim's breathing. If a young child (1-8 years) stops breathing, begin CPR. After 1 minute of CPR, call EMS/911. If an adult or older child is unresponsive, call EMS/911 immediately.

- In an older child or adult, if the object is not dislodged, give 2 breaths, then 6 to 10 abdominal thrusts, and check for the object. Repeat this sequence until the object is dislodged or a total of 5 minutes has elapsed since the onset of this event. If unsuccessful, check for circulation if knowledgeable. If there is no improvement in the victim's condition, start chest compressions.

- Check for circulation, if you are trained for pulses. Otherwise, the signs of circulation are coughing, breathing, moving. If absent, begin chest compression.

- For Chest compression for children (1-8 years) and adults (over 8 years), see Chest Compression as part of the CPR section later in this chapter.

- If the victim starts having seizures or convulsions, give first aid for this problem (see Seizures/Convulsions).

Convulsions: see Seizures/Convulsions

Cuts or Scrapes:

This category refers to minor injuries that can usually be treated at home. Even with small cuts and scrapes, proper care of the wound is necessary to prevent infections and complications (see Bleeding, Minor).

Treatment:

- Rinse the injury with clear water. Avoid putting soap directly on the wound, as it can be irritating. The area around the wound can be cleaned with soap and water using a soft washcloth. If any dirt remains in the wound, attempt to carefully remove with a tweezers that has been cleaned in isopropyl alcohol.
- Avoid "kissing a cut" to make it "all better," since this can result in an infection.
- Apply an antibacterial ointment (like Bacitracin, Neosporin, or Polysporin) to reduce local infection if you do not plan to show the injury to a doctor.
- If the cut is in an area of the body that can become dirty easily or will be irritated by clothing, cover it with an adhesive bandage. Change the dressing daily. Otherwise, small wounds can be left without covering, since most small cuts or scrapes will usually stop bleeding within a few minutes.
- In some cases, firm but gentle pressure using a piece of gauze, clean cloth or tissue may be required for 20 to 30 minutes. This will generally prove effective. If the bleeding persists, apply another layer of gauze or cloth on top of the first layer and continue applying firm pressure. To reduce bleeding on an arm or leg, raise the extremity above the heart level. If there is continued bleeding or spurting blood, seek medical assistance.

If the cut is from an animal bite, apply the same wound care as described above. Have the bite examined by trained medical personnel. Tell the doctor how and where the injury occurred, as it may have to be reported.

All puncture wounds should be watched carefully for any signs of infection such as pain, swelling, drainage, redness or tenderness. These signs of infection can occur weeks or even months after the puncture. If the cut is a puncture wound that occurred through a shoe, i.e. stepping on a nail, a doctor should evaluate the wound immediately.

Take the patient to a doctor to have the cut evaluated for stitches if:

- The edges of the cut are separated.
- The cut is longer than ¼ inch.
- Fat is protruding from the cut.

Lastly, check to be sure that the injured person has had a current tetanus shot.

Dehydration

Dehydration is caused when the body loses water content and essential body salts. Occasionally, drugs such as diuretics, which deplete body fluids, and electrolytes can cause dehydration, and can result in dangerous side effects such as diarrhea, vomiting, fever or a heat-related disorder. Children and persons over the age of 60 are particularly susceptible to dehydration.

Symptoms:
- Thirst
- Less-frequent or scant urination
- Dry skin
- Fatigue
- Light-headedness
- Dizziness
- Confusion
- Dry mouth and mucus membranes
- Rapid pulse
- Rapid breathing

In children, additional symptoms may include: no tears when crying, no wet diapers for more than 3 hours, sunken abdomen, eyes, and/or cheeks, high fever, listlessness, irritability and skin that does not flatten when pinched and released.

Treatment:
- If caught early, dehydration can often be treated at home under a physician's guidance. This is especially important in the case of children.
- *Mild dehydration*: Simple re-hydration is recommended by drinking fluids. Many sports drinks on the market effectively restore body fluids, electrolytes (essential chemicals) and salt balance.
- *Moderate dehydration*: Intravenous fluids may be required, although if caught early enough, simple re-hydration may be effective.
- *Severe dehydration*: Should be treated as a medical emergency, so that hospitalization, along with intravenous fluids, is necessary. Immediate action should be taken. Call 911 or medical personnel as soon as possible.

Prevention:

- Drink plenty of fluids, especially when working or playing in the sun.
- Make sure you are taking in more fluid than you are losing.
- Try to schedule physical outdoor activities for the cooler parts of the day.
- Drink appropriate sports drinks to help maintain electrolyte balance.
- For infants and young children, solutions like Pedialyte® will help maintain electrolyte balance during illness or in case of heat exposure.
- Do not try to make fluid and salt solutions at home for children. If you live in a hot climate, you may want to keep some supplies of sports drinks on hand.

Dental Injuries

Treatment: Babies and Young Children:

- If there has been a knock to the mouth, baby teeth may or may not be knocked loose. Even if biting is not affected, see the dentist.
- If any baby teeth are knocked out, although they are not usually replanted, see the dentist.

Treatment: Older Children and Adults:

- In the event of a broken, displaced or knocked-out tooth, or if a tooth has a large piece broken off, call your dentist or go to an emergency center immediately.
- If a knocked-out tooth is replanted within an hour or, preferably, within 30 minutes, there is a better chance it will survive.
- Do not attempt to reinsert the tooth yourself unless you are following the direction of a dentist or doctor.
- If instructed to do so, pick up the tooth by the crown (the part that shows in the mouth), and not by the root. Gently rinse the tooth with water as the tooth should be kept as germ-free as possible. Immediately insert the tooth gently back into the socket and bite down gently on the tooth, or hold it in place with sterile gauze until you get to the emergency provider.
- Alternatively, to keep the tooth moist, hold the tooth in the side of your mouth or just place the tooth for transport in a paper cup or zip-lock bag filled with either cool milk, the victim's saliva, saline, water or a commercially-available tooth "rescue" kit.
- If the tooth does not *easily* fit back into the socket, do not force it. Apply firm pressure with gauze or a towel for approximately 10 minutes to control bleeding, and have your dentist or emergency care provider reinsert it for you.

Drug Use and Overdose

Drugs can be used to relieve pain, obtain pleasure or alter reality. Unfortunately, drug use can lead to abuse, and sometimes addiction. Here are two of the most common kinds of drug usage, defined:

Drug abuse: This is the use of a legal or illegal substance either in large doses or in frequent doses that results in physical, mental or social harm.

Drug addiction: This is the loss of control over drug use.

The outward signs of drug usage vary, and could be any of the following, such as:

- Changes in looks or attitude
- Changes in behavior that affects work or relationships
- Abrupt or bad temper
- Money problems
- Drug dependence and an inability to stop taking
- Lying about drug use

Symptoms:

- Abnormal pupil size. For example, dilated pupils (enlarged), pinpoint pupils (very small) or non-reactive pupils (pupils that do not change when exposed to light).
- Nausea and vomiting
- Sweating
- Agitation
- Convulsions
- Tremors
- Staggering or unsteady gait
- Difficulty breathing – rapid, shallow, decreased or labored breathing
- Drowsiness
- Unconsciousness
- Hallucinations
- Terror
- Delusional or paranoid behavior
- Violent behavior
- Death

Treatment:

- If someone is having difficulty breathing, having a seizure, seems drowsy, is unconscious, seems like their life is in danger, or has overdosed on drugs, call either 911 or the Poison Control Center at 1-800-222-1222
- Drugs can cause violent and unpredictable behavior. *Do not put yourself in any danger.* If you do not think you can handle the victim, immediately call for professional help.
- If a person is having a seizure or convulsions or in shock, follow instructions for that condition.
- If possible, find out what kinds of and how much drugs the victim took. Collect any drug containers, any remaining drugs and samples of the victim's vomit; this information may be vital in treating the victim.
- Check the victim's vital signs (pulse and blood pressure if you are trained, and their respiration). If the airway is clear and you do not detect breathing or a strong pulse, perform CPR immediately.
- Monitor all vital signs until help arrives.

Electric Shock

Symptoms:

Before losing consciousness, the victim may complain of:

- Lightheadedness
- Weakness
- Nausea
- Pale and clammy skin
- Muscle spasms and pain

Treatment:

- First, *always* remember to remove the victim from the source of electricity before you touch them. Either turn-off the master switch to disconnect the power, or use a nonmetal, dry object such as a stick to pull the wire or electrical source away from the person's body.
- If the victim, who is still conscious and removed from the electrical source, begins to feel faint, have them lean forward and lower their head between the knees (in an attempt to improve blood flow to the brain).

If the victim is unconscious:

- If the unconscious victim is not breathing, begin rescue breathing immediately. A victim whose heart has stopped needs CPR.
- If the person is unconscious, but is breathing and has a heartbeat, place them in a comfortable recovery position and monitor their breathing and heart rate until medical help arrives.
- Whether the victim is conscious or unconscious, try to keep the victim lying down, with the head lowered and the legs elevated. In many cases, the victim will regain consciousness shortly after being placed in this position.
- Loosen any tight clothing
- Apply cool, damp cloths to the face and neck

If the victim regains consciousness:

- Do not let the person get up until you can get them to answer questions such as: Who are you? Where are you? Do you know what day it is? You need to be sure they have completely recovered.
- Discuss their condition with trained medical personnel to determine if any further treatment or evaluation is needed.

Eye Injuries

Every day thousands of eye accidents occur that could be prevented with the use of protective eyewear. Don't allow yourself or your loved ones to become a statistic.

Of approximately 1 million eye injuries that occur each year, 43% of occur in the home. About 40,000 sports-related eye injuries occur in the United States annually. Using the appropriate protective eyewear could prevent about 90% of sports-related eye injuries.

Eye injury may damage tissues near the eye as well as the eyeball itself. Injuries to the eyeball are generally very serious and frequently can cause blindness. In any situation when there is an injury of any type to the eyeball, seek medical help *immediately.*

Recreational and sports-related eye injuries are very common, so it is ideal if children and adolescents wear appropriate eye protection for *all* sports and recreational activities.

The highest number of sports-related accidents to the eyes occurs in basketball, then baseball, swimming pool sports, racquetball, tennis, football and badminton.

You can obtain more information about these kinds of accidents from many sources and particularly from Prevent Blindness America at 1-800-331-2020 and www.preventblindness. org. Their address is 211 West Wacker Drive, Suite 1700. Chicago, Ill 60606 This volunteer eye health and safety organization has affiliates throughout the country.

Another good source of information is the American Academy of Ophthalmology, see www.aao.org. The AAO Headquarters address is 655 Beach St., San Francisco, CA 94109 and their telephone is 415-561-8533.

Treatment:
- Avoid rubbing the injured eye as this may cause additional eye damage.
- If possible, in order to protect and shield the eye, press the bottom of a clean foam cup or something similar against the bones surrounding the eye (brow, cheek and bridge of nose).
- Do not apply any ointment or medication to the eye, as it may not be sterile and could interfere with an eye doctor's examination.
- If there are cuts or punctures to the eye, protect the eye with a covering without pressure, and seek medical help.

Chemical burn or injury:
- Flush the eye with clean water and seek emergency treatment.

Blow to the eye:
- Apply a cold compress to reduce pain and swelling. If the eye becomes "black" or the vision is not normal, contact emergency assistance.

Sand or debris in the eye:
- Flush the eye with eyewash. If the foreign object is not removed, seek emergency help.

Avoid giving aspirin, ibuprofen or other anti-inflammatory drugs as they could thin the blood and increase any bleeding that might be present. Pain that is severe may require prescription medications.

Prevention:
The leading causes of eye injuries include household chemicals, workshop and yard debris, battery acid, sports accidents, fireworks, inappropriate toys and games used without adequate supervision and over-exposure to ultraviolet radiation.

Ultraviolet light from the sun and UV light emitted from welding arcs and tanning beds can damage your eyes. Excessive exposure to sunlight that is reflected off sand, water or pavement can burn the eye's surface.

Be sure to wear the right protective eyewear in the workshop, garden, sports activities, workplace or home, and avoid personal fireworks.

Wear only certified eye protection goggles when playing such activities as paintball.

Heart Attack//Chest Pain

If not treated, a heart attack may be fatal. In most, but not all cases the body will send warning signs that indicate a heart attack.

A heart attack *(in technical terms, a "myocardial infarction")* can result when one of the main arteries of the heart that supplies blood and oxygen to the heart muscle becomes blocked. This blockage results in a lack of oxygen and causes that affected area of the heart muscle to be damaged.

Symptoms (Warning signs of a heart attack):
- Uncomfortable pressure, fullness, squeezing, pain, or discomfort in the center of the chest that lasts for more than two minutes. The discomfort may be more to the left or right of the chest than in the center. The pain is usually persistent but may go away and return.
- The discomfort *(pain)* may spread to, or also be felt in, the shoulders, arms, wrists, back, neck or jaw.
- Any or all of the following symptoms may be experienced.
  - Sweating
  - Shortness of breath
  - Nausea, vomiting
  - Palpitations
  - Chest discomfort that is accompanied by lightheadedness, fainting, dizziness, weakness, fatigue, or paleness.

Treatment:
- If you or someone in your presence exhibits any of the above warning signs, act immediately and call 911. If you are experiencing the pain yourself, do not make the mistake of driving yourself to the doctor's or an emergency room; an accident may occur that may prove fatal to you or others.
- Immediately chew and swallow an adult aspirin. Aspirin may reduce the tendency for the blood to clot in the heart (coronary) artery, and reduce the likelihood of a complete blockage of the blood flow within that artery.

- In the event that you feel you are going to pass out, begin to cough continuously as this may interrupt a bad heart rhythm and might help to prevent passing out.
- If you are with a person that is not responsive, call 911, then start CPR (see the following) if you are trained. If you are not trained and are able to reach 911, they can instruct you over the phone.

CPR = Cardiopulmonary Resuscitation
- CPR is a procedure that attempts to restore and maintain the supply of oxygen to the brain by applying chest compression to a victim where this function has been impaired. Mouth-to-mouth breathing is an attempt to put your breath (that contains oxygen) into the patient's lungs and in turn into their blood-steam. Chest compressions squeeze the non-functioning heart between the breastbone and spinal area to provide a pumping action that moves the blood that distributes the oxygen to the important body tissues, especially the brain. Even if you're well trained and confident in your ability, begin with chest compressions instead of first checking the airway and doing rescue breathing. Start CPR with 30 chest compressions before checking the airway and giving rescue breaths.

CPR is also known as BLS (Basic Life Support). CPR or the BLS procedure should be started within 4 minutes of heart collapse if at all possible. (After a lapse of four minutes, the brain is very likely to suffer a degree of irreversible damage due to the lack of oxygen.)

CPR/BLS (Basic Life Support) priorities

The two most important procedures that can determine a victim's chance of survival are the early application of CPR and, if necessary, electrical defibrillation of the heart.

Survival is best achieved by starting the CPR procedure as soon as possible. Immediately contact those emergency services that can administer defibrillation using an automatic external defibrillator (AED).

In CPR, it is the actual chest compression more than mouth-to-mouth breathing that is vital in restoring function. Ideally, everyone should learn this hands only compression technique, and update their skills in performing CPR, every 2 to 3 years.

Treatment:
- Determine unresponsiveness by gently shaking the patient and asking loudly, "Are you OK?" However, try not to shake the patient's head or neck area if an injury to that area is suspected.

- If the patient does not respond, call 911, and notify the emergency medical system before starting CPR. Exceptions would be in cases involving adult victims of submersion, trauma, and drug intoxication, or infants when you should provide CPR first and then call 911.
- Position the patient. Place the victim on a firm, flat surface. If necessary, try to move them from a face down to a face-up position by rolling the body as a whole. Make sure to keep the head, neck and body stable so that the entire body is moved at the same time.
- Open the victim's airway. The mouth needs to be open. If there is no obvious neck injury, lift the chin and tilt the head backward with both hands. Check for foreign bodies in the mouth and throat area and clear with a finger-sweeping motion. If dentures are in place, do not remove them.
- Check that the victim is breathing. This can be done by listening for breath sounds, feeling for air motion on your cheek and ear, and looking for motion of the chest.

__Note__: If the patient's chest rises it suggests that the ventilation strength is adequate. If the chest is not rising, carefully reposition the head and try with the 2 breaths again. If this still is not successful, recheck for foreign bodies in the mouth. If the victim still fails to respond to your attempts at respiration, carefully perform the Heimlich maneuver and remove any object that has entered the mouth.

The signal to begin chest compressions is the absence of signs of circulation, such as normal breathing, normal coughing and spontaneous movement. Unless you are specially trained, do not try to check for a pulse or start mouth to mouth..

Chest Compressions Procedure:
- Make sure that the victim is on his or her back on a firm surface.
- Place one hand on the lower end of the breastbone and the heel of the other hand on top of that hand.
- Position your shoulders directly above your hands and keep your elbows in a locked position.
- Attempt to depress the victim's breastbone 1½ to 2" with each compression. The compression rate should be 100 per minute, and there should be 15 compressions in each cycle. The pushing down and letting up phase of each cycle should be equal in duration; don't jab down and relax.
- After each set of 15 consecutive compressions, administer 2 ventilations or breaths.

- If someone experienced is assisting you, have him or her check to see if the patient's neck or groin pulses respond to the compressions. (No longer recommended for lay rescuers).

Note*: The ratio (chest compressions to breaths) given is that for one-person and two-person CPR. In both one and two person CPR, there is a pause in chest pumping as mouth to mouth ventilation is administered. In two person CPR one person should be responsible for administering the breaths; the other, for the compressions.*

In both instances stop the procedure for 5 seconds every few minutes to check whether the patient is breathing on their own and any evidence of circulation is present.

The following advice on CPR is by Mayo Clinic Staff
http://www.mayoclinic.org/first-aid/first-aid-cpr/basics/ART-20056600

CPR for Infants Less than One Year of Age:

Cardiopulmonary resuscitation (CPR) is a lifesaving technique useful in many emergencies, including heart attack or near drowning, in which someone's breathing or heartbeat has stopped. The American Heart Association recommends that everyone — untrained bystanders and medical personnel alike — begin CPR with chest compressions.

It's far better to do something than to do nothing at all if you're fearful that your knowledge or abilities aren't 100% complete. Remember, the difference between your doing something and doing nothing could be someone's life.

The Mayo Clinic information continues with the following:

Here's advice from the American Heart Association:

- **Untrained.** If you're not trained in CPR, then provide hands-only CPR. That means uninterrupted chest compressions of about 100 a minute until paramedics arrive (described in more detail below). You don't need to try rescue breathing.
- **Trained, and ready to go**. If you're well trained and confident in your ability, begin with chest compressions instead of first checking the airway and doing rescue breathing, Start CPR with 30 chest compressions before checking the airway and giving rescue breaths.
- **Trained, but rusty.** If you've previously received CPR training but you're not confident in your abilities, then just do chest compressions at a rate of about 100 a minute. (Details described below.)

The above advice applies to adults, children and infants needing CPR, but not newborns.

CPR can keep oxygenated blood flowing to the brain and other vital organs until more definitive medical treatment can restore a normal heart rhythm.

When the heart stops, the lack of oxygenated blood can cause brain damage in only a few minutes. A person may die within eight to 10 minutes.

To learn CPR properly, take an accredited first-aid training course, including CPR and how to use an automatic external defibrillator (AED).

Before you begin

Before starting CPR, check:

- Is the person conscious or unconscious?
- If the person appears unconscious, tap or shake his or her shoulder and ask loudly, "Are you OK?"
- If the person doesn't respond and two people are available, one should call 911 or the local emergency number and one should begin CPR. If you are alone and have immediate access to a telephone, call 911 before beginning CPR — unless you think the person has become unresponsive because of suffocation (such as from drowning). In this special case, begin CPR for one minute and then call 911 or the local emergency number.
- If an automatic external defibrillator AED is immediately available, deliver one shock if instructed by the device, then begin CPR.

Remember to spell C-A-B

The American Heart Association uses the acronym of CAB — circulation, airway, breathing — to help people remember the order to perform the steps of CPR.

C = Circulation: Restore blood circulation with chest compressions

1. Put the person on his or her back on a firm surface.
2. Kneel next to the person's neck and shoulders.
3. Place the heel of one hand over the center of the person's chest, between the nipples. Place your other hand on top of the first hand. Keep your elbows straight and position your shoulders directly above your hands.
4. Use your upper body weight (not just your arms) as you push straight down on (compress) the chest at least 2 inches (approximately 5 centimeters). Push hard at a rate of about 100 compressions a minute.
5. If you haven't been trained in CPR, continue chest compressions until there are signs of movement or until emergency medical personnel take over. If you have been trained in CPR, go on to checking the airway and rescue breathing.

A= Airway: Clear the airway

1. If you're trained in CPR and you've performed 30 chest compressions, open the person's airway using the head-tilt, chin-lift maneuver. Put your palm on the person's forehead and gently tilt the head back. Then with the other hand, gently lift the chin forward to open the airway.
2. Check for normal breathing, taking no more than five or 10 seconds. Look for chest motion, listen for normal breath sounds, and feel for the person's breath on your cheek and ear. Gasping is not considered to be normal breathing. If the person isn't breathing normally and you are trained in CPR, begin mouth-to-mouth breathing. If you believe the person is unconscious from a heart attack and you haven't been trained in emergency procedures, skip mouth-to-mouth rescue breathing and continue chest compressions.

B=Breathing: Breathe for the person

Rescue breathing can be mouth-to-mouth breathing or mouth-to-nose breathing if the mouth is seriously injured or can't be opened.

1. With the airway open (using the head-tilt, chin-lift maneuver), pinch the nostrils shut for mouth-to-mouth breathing and cover the person's mouth with yours, making a seal.
2. Prepare to give two rescue breaths. Give the first rescue breath — lasting one second — and watch to see if the chest rises. If it does rise, give the second breath. If the chest doesn't rise, repeat the head-tilt, chin-lift maneuver and then give the second breath. Thirty chest compressions followed by two rescue breaths is considered one cycle.
3. Resume chest compressions to restore circulation.
4. If the person has not begun moving after five cycles (about two minutes) and an automatic external defibrillator (AED) is available, apply it and follow the prompts. Administer one shock and then resume CPR — starting with chest compressions — for two more minutes before administering a second shock. If you're not trained to use an AED, a 911 or other emergency medical operator may be able to guide you in its use. Use pediatric pads, if available, for children ages 1 through 8. Do not use an AED for babies younger than age 1. If an AED isn't available, go to step 5 below.
5. Continue CPR until there are signs of movement or emergency medical personnel take over.

To perform CPR on a child, 1 to 8 years

The procedure for giving CPR to a child age 1 through 8 is essentially the same as that for an adult. The differences are as follows:

- If you're alone, perform five cycles of compressions and breaths on the child — this should take about two minutes — before calling 911 or your local emergency number or using an AED.
- Use only one hand to perform heart compressions.
- Breathe more gently.
- Use the same compression-breath rate as is used for adults: 30 compressions followed by two breaths. This is one cycle. Following the two breaths, immediately begin the next cycle of compressions and breaths.
- After five cycles (about two minutes) of CPR, if there is no response and an AED is available, apply it and follow the prompts. Use pediatric pads if available. If pediatric pads aren't available, use adult pads.

Continue until the child moves or help arrives.

To perform CPR on a baby

Most cardiac arrests in babies occur from lack of oxygen, such as from drowning or choking. If you know the baby has an airway obstruction, perform first aid for choking. If you don't know why the baby isn't breathing, perform CPR.

To begin, examine the situation. Stroke the baby and watch for a response, such as movement, but don't shake the baby.

If there's no response, follow the CAB procedures below and time the call for help as follows:

- If you're the only rescuer and CPR is needed, do CPR for two minutes — about five cycles — before calling 911 or your local emergency number.
- If another person is available, have that person call for help immediately while you attend to the baby.

Circulation: Restore blood circulation

1. Place the baby on his or her back on a firm, flat surface, such as a table. The floor or ground also will do.
2. Imagine a horizontal line drawn between the baby's nipples. Place two fingers of one hand just below this line, in the center of the chest.
3. Gently compress the chest about 1.5 inches (about 4 cm).
4. Count aloud as you pump in a fairly rapid rhythm. You should pump at a rate of 100 compressions a minute.

Airway: Clear the airway

1. After 30 compressions, gently tip the head back by lifting the chin with one hand and pushing down on the forehead with the other hand.

2. In no more than 10 seconds, put your ear near the baby's mouth and check for breathing: Look for chest motion, listen for breath sounds, and feel for breath on your cheek and ear.

Breathing: Breathe for the infant

1. Cover the baby's mouth and nose with your mouth.

2. Prepare to give two rescue breaths. Use the strength of your cheeks to deliver gentle puffs of air (instead of deep breaths from your lungs) to slowly breathe into the baby's mouth one time, taking one second for the breath. Watch to see if the baby's chest rises. If it does, give a second rescue breath. If the chest does not rise, repeat the head-tilt, chin-lift maneuver and then give the second breath.

3. If the baby's chest still doesn't rise, examine the mouth to make sure no foreign material is inside. If the object is seen, sweep it out with your finger. If the airway seems blocked, perform first aid for a choking baby.

4. Give two breaths after every 30 chest compressions.

5. Perform CPR for about two minutes before calling for help unless someone else can make the call while you attend to the baby.

6. Continue CPR until you see signs of life or until medical personnel arrive
   - Open the airway by tilting the head and lifting the chin. Do not tilt the head back too far.
   - If the baby is not breathing, give 2 small mouth-to-mouth breaths. Do so by covering the infant's mouth and nose with your mouth. Each breath should be1½ to 2 seconds long. The infant's chest should rise with each breath.
   - Next, start *gentle* chest compressions, *only* about ½" to 1" deep, by positioning your 3rd and 4th fingers in the center of the chest half an inch below the nipples. The compression rate should be approximately 100 per minute, or close to two compressions per second.
   - Continue CPR, administering one breath for each 5 compressions. After 1 minute of repeated cycles call 911. Continue the CPR efforts. Check for the return of breathing every 2 minutes.

See the extensive health care and diet information available on the Mayo Clinic web site. http://www.mayoclinic.org

Heat and Cold-Induced Illnesses
Heat Cramps

Heat cramps are painful, involuntary muscle spasms (cramps) that usually affect people who sweat a lot during strenuous activity. The sweating depletes the body's salt and moisture, and a low salt level in the muscles can cause painful cramps. These cramps are different from exercise-type muscle cramps in that only a small section of a muscle (and not the entire muscle) is involved. Heat cramps can also appear in people with the more serious condition of heat exhaustion (see below).

Symptoms:

- Muscle discomfort that wanders and usually occurs in the legs of people exercising in high temperature areas. Cramps can also occur in the abdomen, arms or any muscles involved in the exercise
- Patient usually has normal body temperature.

Causes:

- Salt depletion and drinking water without adequate salt or minerals.

Treatment:

- Stop the activity and try to provide a cool location.
- Drink clear juice, water, or a sports beverage containing minerals (an electrolyte solution, such as Gatorade)..
- Replace lost salt with salt tablets if available.

Heat Exhaustion

This is an intermediate form of heat-related illness that can develop after several days of exposure to high temperatures and inadequate or unbalanced replacement of fluids. This condition may evolve from the milder condition of heat cramps if the exercising person does not stop. Most prone to heat exhaustion are elderly people, people with high blood pressure and people working or exercising in a hot environment. The symptoms often begin suddenly. However, if regular meals are consumed, salt depletion is very unlikely.

Symptoms:

- Body temperature is usually normal, but may be slightly elevated. The victim is sweating heavily, or in some cases, not sweating. The skin may be cool and moist.

Pulse rate and respiration are increased. There may be paleness; muscle cramps; tiredness; weakness; nausea and vomiting; headache; fainting.

- An exercising individual in a hot environment can complain of any of the following: headache, dizziness, nausea, vomiting, irritability, and muscle cramps.

Causes:

- The loss of salt and water from the body.

Treatment:

- Remove individual from the sun and get them to a cooler or air-conditioned area.
- Use a fan and/or spray the person with cool water.
- Loosen any tight or restrictive clothing.
- If the person is conscious and not vomiting, give them a half-filled glass of cool water or an electrolyte-containing sport drink every 15 minutes.
- Apply cool towels or cloths to the body.
- If the symptoms are severe and/or the patient is vomiting and needs intravenous fluids, has high blood pressure or heart problems, seek medical attention promptly to avoid progression to heat stroke.

Heat Stroke (The most serious)

Heat stroke occurs when the internal mechanisms (internal temperature control, sweating) that respond to body over-heating are lost. As the body is unable to cool itself adequately, the temperature rises rapidly. Body temperature may rise to 106F or higher in as fast as 10 to 15 minutes. If emergency treatment is not provided, death or permanent disability could result.

Causes:

- Usually occurs in ill and or elderly individuals who have been exposed to several days of high temperature while living in poorly ventilated homes.
- Also can occur in athletes in a location with high temperature, sometimes combined with high humidity and limited access to or availability of water. Can occur in children exercising in the heat.
- Some people are born with an impaired ability to sweat normally
- Other risk factors include obesity, alcohol use, cardiovascular disease and dehydration.

Symptoms:
- Very high body temperatures, above 103°F orally
- Rapid strong pulse
- Rapid and shallow breathing
- Red, hot and dry skin (no sweating)
- Confusion,
- Unconsciousness.
- Throbbing headache
- Dizziness and nausea
- Delirium

Treatment:
- Call 911 for emergency assistance.
- Attempt immediate cooling by exposing as much of the body surface as possible, and applying cool to lukewarm water (65°F-75°F) with either a towel or sheet, or running water.
- Continuous large electric fanning can prove helpful.
- Monitor body temperature, and continue cooling efforts until the body temperature drops to 101-102°F.
- Help the cooling process by applying ice packs to the groin, armpits and chest.
- If emergency help is delayed, call the hospital emergency room for further instructions.
- Do not place objects in the mouth and do not give fluids. If there is vomiting, make sure the airway remains open by turning the victim on his or her side.
- <u>DO NOT place the victim of heat stroke in an *ice*-water bath</u>, as this could make things worse.

Heat Rash

This is a skin irritation that occurs when there is excessive sweating in hot, humid weather. Heat rash is most common in young children.

The rash is a red cluster of small pimples or blisters, and generally affects the neck and upper chest, groin, under the breasts and elbow creases.

Treatment
- A victim of heat rash should try to stay in a cool low humidity environment.
- Keep the affected area dry and avoid creams and ointments.
- The condition will eventually clear itself without additional treatment.

Sunburn and Sun Exposure

If sun exposure is prolonged or for sensitive people, red, painful and warm skin usually occurs within a few hours, after the exposure. Electromagnetic radiation from the sun in the form of ultra-violet light (UV) burns the skin and can lead to skin cancer. Discomfort from sunburn is usually minor and healing generally occurs within a week. More extensive and severe sunburn may require medical attention.

Treatment:
- If the person is less than one year old, or if there is fever, rash, blisters or severe pain seek medical help.
- Immerse the involved region in cool water or apply a cold compress. A cool bath or shower may be of help
- Place moisturizing lotion (Aloe Vera lotion) on the affected areas. Avoid salve, butter or ointments containing alcohol or benzocaine*.
  * The Food & Drug Administration (FDA) recently issued a communication regarding a rare adverse effect in professional and over-the-counter consumer products containing benzocaine. In particular, the FDA recommends that caregivers of children under the age of two years old should consult their physician or healthcare professional before use.
- Do not break any blisters, as they are nature's way to speed healing and help avoid infection. If a blister bursts, apply antibacterial ointment on the open area and cover with a sterile gauze bandage.
- Call the doctor for any of the following conditions:
  o Severely painful sunburn
  o Fever over 100.5° F
  o Sunburn on an infant less than one year or age
  o Multiple blisters or infected-appearing blisters
- Seek immediate care if an affected child has eye pain or cannot look at lights, is dizzy or faints when standing, or has signs of dehydration such as dry mouth, no tears when crying, no urine output for 8 to 16 hours, or dark-colored urine.

Prevention:
- Wear wide-brimmed hats in the sun; baseball caps don't cover enough of the face and neck to offer much protection.
- Wear a sunscreen with an SPF of at least 15 for even brief periods spent out of doors, and remember to reapply your sunscreen every few hours and after swimming.

- Wear sunglasses to protect your eyes.
- Try to schedule outdoor activities early in the morning (before 10 a.m.) or after 3 p.m. The sun's rays are weakest at these times.
- Wear long-sleeved shirts and pants to cover as much of your skin as possible when you're outside.
- Remember that an overcast sky does not mean that the sun's rays will not affect you. Continue with your regular sun-care regimen at each exposure.
- Anyone can develop skin cancer, but those with fair hair and skin are the most vulnerable to the sun's effects. The sun's rays age the skin prematurely and significantly increase the risk of skin cancer. To reduce their risk, everybody needs to limit their overall exposure to the sun as much as possible. The American Cancer Society estimates that 80 percent of all skin cancers can be prevented by sun protection.

Frostbite: Superficial

Frostbite occurs when the skin and underlying tissues have been exposed in a cold, moist, windy climate. With that in mind, the areas that are most prone to frostbite are the hands, feet, nose and ears.

Symptoms:
- Affected areas of the body are white and waxy, with diminished sensitivity.

Treatment:
- Re-warm the affected areas in a warm (105°F) water bath.
- Use mild analgesics (acetaminophen) if the re-warmed area becomes painful. This painful reaction is not uncommon.

Frostbite: Deep

Any part of the body exposed to temperatures less than 44°F for over 7-10 hours IS prone to develop severe injury to the tissues that go as deep as the muscles and tendons. Although this temperature is still above the freezing mark, the fact that part of the body is exposed to such a low temperature for such a long time can cause severe frostbite.

Symptoms:
- The affected body tissue appears hard and frozen.

Treatment:
- Hospitalization is required because of this condition's severity. Rapid re-warming should be attempted in the interim.
- In the event that immediate hospitalization is not possible:
- Remove any wet clothing and change into dry clothing.
- Put the affected area into warm water *(not hot, as it will burn the skin)* to thaw the frozen tissue.
- If warm water is not available, then try to warm the affected parts by using body heat such as putting affected hands under the armpit or using hands to warm your nose and ears.
- If you must move to get help, do not warm the affected area, as getting additional frostbite to the same area of the body after it has been warmed might increase damage to the tissue.
- Unless there is no alternative, do not walk on frostbitten toes or feet.

Hypothermia

Hypothermia occurs if the body temperature drops below 95°F. The body's temperature control mechanisms that would usually maintain normal body temperature fail. This is commonly encountered when there is immersion in cold water and exposure to cold environments. Wet or damp clothing increase the likelihood of hypothermia.

Persons at increased risk for hypothermia would be older adults; infants; young children; lean individuals or those with impaired mental function (Alzheimer's patients, those intoxicated or homeless). In addition, anyone trapped in a vehicle in cold weather; anyone suffering from malnutrition; cardiovascular disease; under-active thyroid; extensive psoriasis; or any illnesses that decrease physical mobility; or those who on certain medications that are used to treat anxiety, depression, nausea or insomnia are all at increased risk.

Symptoms:
- May develop slowly with gradual loss of mental and physical ability. The victim may be unaware of need for emergency medical care.
- There is usually a period of shivering, although this may stop when the body temperature is below 90°F. Shivering is the body's attempt to make heat.
- Mental functions are affected and will result in reduced attention, lightheadedness, slurred speech and possibly coma.
- Look for the "umbles" such as stumbles, mumbles, fumbles and grumbles (mental and physical impairment).

- Breathing may be impaired with abnormally slow breathing. Blood pressure may be low and the pulse weak.

Treatment:
- This serious condition requires hospitalization so that the proper medical care can be delivered. Call 911.
- Perform CPR if the victim is not breathing until assistance arrives.
- If the person's clothes are wet, remove and replace them with warm, dry clothes.
- Warm up the victim by using blankets and keep them in a warm environment.
- Don't apply direct heat, hot water, a heating pad or a heating lamp to the victim. Don't warm just the arms and legs, as the applied heat could cause cold blood to move back to the heart, lungs or brain, resulting in a further drop in core body temperature.
- Do offer warm, non-alcoholic drinks if patient is not vomiting.
- Handle the victim gently because they are at risk for cardiac arrest.

Moving an Injured Person

While it is always best not to move an injured person if at all possible until medical personnel arrive, in some situations it is necessary to remove an injured person to protect them from imminent or potential danger. If this is the case, here is information on how to move them safely.

Treatment:
- Take care. An injured person should not be moved or shaken unless absolutely necessary. Jarring their body may increase their injuries.
- Check for the presence of head, neck and back injuries.
- Whenever possible, render first aid before transporting the injured. Reduce their pain and make them as comfortable as possible
- When possible, use a regular stretcher, or fashion a substitute with sheets, blankets and a slab of wood.
- Take a stretcher to the injured person, rather than the person to the stretcher.
- If the injured *must* be moved, steady their head and injured body-parts and gently pull *lengthwise*, not sidewise.
- With great care, carry the injured person without bending him/her anywhere *(take special care that the head, neck and back do not bend).*
- If possible, have another person put the stretcher in position and carefully place the injured patient on the stretcher.

- If there is any chance that the person's head, neck or back is broken, put tightly folded clothing on each side of the head and tie the person's forehead and body on the stretcher to keep him or her from moving,
- Always move the patient feet first so the rear bearer can watch for any signs of difficulty breathing.

Poisoning

A poison is anything that someone eats *(ingestion)*, breathes *(inhalation)*, gets in the eyes *(ocular exposure)*, or on the skin *(dermal exposure)* that can cause sickness or death if it gets into or on the body. Poisons are found in a number of forms such as solid, liquid, spray or gas or drug overdose.

A poison *exposure* is the ingestion of or contact with a substance that can produce toxic effects. A *poisoning* is a poison exposure that results in bodily harm. Poison exposures can occur by accident without intent, and these exposures are defined as *unintentional poisonings*. In some situations, poison exposures are the result of a conscious willful decision; these cases are defined as *intentional poisonings*.

More than 90% of poison exposures occur in the home. Of these, over 50% occur among children younger than age 6. Children most commonly ingest household products such as cosmetics, personal care products, cleaning substances, pain relievers, foreign bodies and plants. Adults are most commonly poisoned by ingesting pain relievers, sedatives, cleaning substances and antidepressants.

Carbon monoxide results in more fatal unintentional poisonings in the United States than any other agent, with the highest number occurring during the winter months. **If you suspect poisoning of any type, call the local POISON CONTROL CENTER immediately at 1-800 222-1222.** Do not wait for anyone to either look or feel sick.

Symptoms and Signs:
- Burns or redness around the mouth and lips that can result from drinking certain poisons.
- A breath that smells like chemicals, such as gasoline or paint thinner.
- Large (dilated) or small (constricted) pupils.
- Burn stains and odors on the person, their clothing, furniture, floor or rugs.
- **Call 911 immediately if the victim has any of the following symptoms:**
  - Unconsciousness or seizures
  - Difficulty breathing
  - Difficulty swallowing

- o Drowsiness
- o Increased irritability
- o Nausea, vomiting and/or stomach pain
- o Blisters or burns on lips or mouth
- o Unusual drooling
- o Strange odors on a child's breath or in the stools

Treatment:
- First, get the poison away from the person. If there is any of the substance remaining in the mouth, make them spit it out or remove all of it with your fingers. Note: Do *not* discard the material removed.
- Call the Poison Control Center for advice. 1-800-222-1222
- Provide your name, address, zip code, and phone number to the Poison Control Center to ensure ongoing communication.
- When speaking to the Poison Control Center or emergency personnel, be prepared to provide the following information:
  - o What type and how much poison has been ingested? If there is a bottle or a container, keep it with you while speaking on the phone.
  - o If possible, give information as to existing medical conditions, such as a list of medications being taken by the victim and the name and phone number of the victim's physician.
- If skilled help is not immediately available, take the following steps:
- If the substance has caused injury to the lips or mouth, rinse the area with large quantities of cold water.
- If there is poison on the skin, remove any contaminated clothing and rinse the skin with water for 10 minutes.
- If the substance is in the eye, flush the eye for 15 minutes using a large cup filled with clean, lukewarm water. Then call the poison center.
- Do not induce vomiting unless instructed by knowledgeable persons. Ipecac syrup is no longer recommended as a treatment, as there is no scientific evidence that vomiting will actually help anyone who either ate or drank something poisonous.
- Administer CPR if necessary.

Poisonous Fumes, Gases, Smoke and Other Inhalants

These damaging agents may cause skin burns, burns of the mucus membranes (of the mouth), and irritation to the lungs or the passageways to the lungs (bronchus, trachea). They can be absorbed into the body with serious consequences and a potentially fatal outcome.

The symptom list is the same as the previous general symptom list for poisoning.

- Unconsciousness or seizures
- Difficulty breathing
- Difficulty swallowing
- Drowsiness
- Increased irritability
- Nausea, vomiting and/or stomach pain
- Blisters or burns on lips or mouth
- Unusual drooling
- Strange odors on a child's breath or in the stools

Causes:

- Such things as a car engine running in a closed garage, leaky gas vents or unlit pilot lights can result in carbon monoxide poisoning.
- Wood, coal or kerosene stoves that do not work properly.
- Strong fumes from such products as household or industrial cleaners, solvents, insecticides, fumigants, silver polish, artificial fingernail remover, or film developer.
- The accidental mixture of bleach *(sodium hypochlorite)* with toilet bowl cleaner *(sulfuric acid)* can produce poisonous chlorine gas. Also, bleach with ammonia can produce chloramine gas.

Treatment:

- Take the victim away from the offending agent and into fresh air right away.
- For poison on the skin and mucous membranes, wash with plenty of room temperature water for about 10 minutes.
- Because of the possibility of delayed effects, call the Poison Control Center for advice, even if the person is breathing without a problem.
- If the individual is not breathing or is having breathing difficulties, first perform CPR for 1 minute. If no one else is immediately available then you should call 911.

Food Poisoning

Food-borne illnesses affect millions of people each year. Many of those who think they have the flu or a virus are really victims of a mild case of food poisoning. Particularly vulnerable to food poisoning are young children, the elderly, pregnant women (because of the risk to the fetus) and persons with chronic or serious illnesses.

Causes:
- Eating foods that contain certain types of bacteria or viruses that result in an intestinal infection causes most food-borne illnesses.
- Foods can also cause illness if they contain a toxin or poison produced by bacteria growing in food.
- Do not eat improperly canned foods; they may be breeding grounds for bacteria.

Prevention:
- Thoroughly wash your hands before and after handling food.
- Always wash your hands after using the toilet, changing diapers, smoking, blowing your nose, coughing or sneezing.
- Wash your hands after touching raw meat, seafood, poultry, or eggs before handling any other foods.
- Do not use wooden cutting boards for cutting raw fish, poultry, or meat. Choose plastic boards, which are easier to sanitize. They should be sanitized with Clorox® or washed in the dishwasher.
- Thoroughly clean any food preparation surface or cooking utensil after each use.
- Cook poultry, beef and eggs thoroughly before eating.
- Do not eat or drink any beverages or foods made from raw or undercooked eggs, poultry, meat or non-pasteurized milk, or any dairy products made from non-pasteurized milk.
- Avoid leaving cooked foods for over two hours out of the refrigerator.
- Wash all fresh produce thoroughly before eating. You should wash all fruit and vegetables even if you are going to peel and discard the skin. This will avoid the inside becoming contaminated when cutting through the unwashed skin.
- Avoid cross-contamination of foods by keeping your fresh produce, cooked foods and ready- to-eat foods separate from uncooked meats and raw eggs.

Symptoms:

Many people with mild cases of food poisoning think they have the stomach flu. However, the onset of symptoms of food poisoning is usually very sudden and abrupt, often within hours of eating the contaminated food. While each person may experience symptoms differently, the most common symptoms include:

- Abdominal cramps, distension and gas
- Watery and or bloody diarrhea
- Nausea and vomiting
- Headache
- Fever

.Treatment:

- If you think you or someone else has food poisoning, do not give the victim anything to eat or drink.
- Call the Poison Control Center at 1-800-222-1222 for assistance.
- Remember that most food poisoning cases are mild and self-limited, meaning that the poisoning clears itself without any specific treatment.
- In mild cases, drinking sufficient liquid is usually effective.
- If the symptoms persist, call a doctor.
- Discuss with your doctor what, if any types of anti-diarrhea medications to keep on hand or in your medicine cabinet. However, do not take these types of medications without consulting medical personnel. Only use anti-diarrhea medications as directed by your doctor.

Lead Poisoning

Lead poisoning can be a serious problem particularly for children under 6 years of age, although this type of poisoning is less common today as a result of constant monitoring by environmental agencies. The Environmental Protection Agency *(EPA)* and the Center for Disease Control *(CDC)* have established guidelines for childhood lead testing. This should be done once a year for children under the age of six.

Children are naturally curious, so they tend to crawl and play in potentially hazardous places. They also lack an awareness of safety and sanitary habits, and of course their frequent hand-to-mouth activity increases the risk for contamination.

When there is a case of lead poisoning, it can be particularly serious for a child as the developing brain and nervous system can be adversely affected by the increase in lead concentration and can result in a variety of long-lasting and permanent disabilities.

Prevention
- Fix any peeling paint, especially paint in homes built prior to 1978.
- Remove any paint chips and old, painted toys and furniture.
- Do not store food or liquids in lead crystal or lead glazed pottery.
- Eating some foods such as leafy greens, citrus fruits and dairy items can reduce lead absorption.

Note: *Boiling water that has any lead content will not remove the lead.*

Animal Bites

Most animal bites are from home pets - dogs and cats. Bites from domestic animals that are not immunized, and especially wild animals, carry a risk of rabies. Rabies is more likely to result from bites of raccoons, skunks, bats or foxes than a bite from a dog or cat.

Treatment of minor bites:
- If there is minimal skin breakage, apply the same treatment as for a minor wound. Wash thoroughly with soap and water; apply antibiotic cream and cover with a clean bandage.

Treatment of deep bites:
- If there is a deep skin breakage, or the skin is badly torn and bleeding, apply pressure with a sterile gauze pad if possible, or a clean cloth to stop the bleeding. Get medical attention.
- High-risk bites are those involving the hands, feet, head and face, injuries over 6-12 hours old, deep puncture wounds, crush injuries, human bites, cat bites, and bites in elderly individuals and those with reduced immunity.
- If there is any infection or if rabies is a possibility, contact medical care.
- A Tetanus booster is recommended if not provided within the past 10 years.

Snake Bites: Non- Poisonous

The majority of snakebites are from non-poisonous snakes.

Symptoms:
- Pain and swelling at the bite site.
- Acute allergic reaction

Treatment:
- Same as treatment for animal bites, minor wounds and deep wounds. If there is an allergic reaction, (see the Allergic section)

Snake Bites: Poisonous

Snakebites are rarely fatal, although extensive local tissue damage and destruction can occur. Poisonous snakes in the United States are rattlesnakes, copperheads, water moccasin and coral snakes. Prompt expert medical therapy will help to manage this problem.

Treatment:

First aid and emergency room treatment of a venomous snake- bite is controversial at present. New recommendations are made every 2 to 3 years, but the current consensus of recommendations is as follows:
- If there is uncertainty as to whether the snake is poisonous, treat the bite as if it were poisonous.
- Arrange for transportation to a medical emergency or trauma center.
- Call your local poison control center AT 1-800- 222-1222.
- Keep the victim calm and reassured. Allow them to lie flat and avoid movement of the affected bite area.
- *Do not cut or incise into the bite*, and do not apply ice to the wound.
- For those who are hiking in snake-infested areas you probably have a suction device, venom suction kit. If so, place it over the wound (as is) to help draw venom out of the wound. If you don't have the kit, then try suctioning by mouth. This is recommended *only as a last resort (fortunately, swallowing the venom is not toxic as it is destroyed in the stomach).* Suction after 30 minutes is ineffective, as the body has absorbed the venom by this time.
- Tourniquets are currently not recommended, as they can isolate venom in a small area and concentrate the damage. A partially constricting band that does not cut off venous circulation might be OK.
- Don't waste time attempting to capture the snake. However, if the snake is dead, bring it in for identification.
- Cover the affected area with a clean, cool compress or a moist dressing to minimize pain and swelling.

Stings (Fire Ants, Bee, Wasp, Hornet, or Yellow Jacket)

These kinds of bites induce local swelling, redness, and pain. Fire ant stings can result in small pustules, or white pimples that are arranged in a semi-circular pattern. Some people have allergic reactions to insect stings that range from very mild to, in some cases, severe and even fatal reactions. People with known allergies to insect stings should always carry an insect sting allergy kit and wear a medical bracelet or necklace stating their allergy.

Treatment:

- Bees leave behind a stinger attached to a venom sac. *Do not* try to pull the stinger out, as this may release more venom. Instead, gently *scrape* it out using some gauze wiped over the area, or scrape a fingernail or blunt-edged object, such as a credit card or dull knife, over the area.
- Wash the stung area carefully with soap and water. Continue to do this several times a day until the skin is healed.
- Apply a cold or ice pack, wrapped inside a cloth, for a few minutes.
- Take acetaminophen for pain, if necessary. It may be helpful.
- Topical steroids and oral anti-histamines can help the local reaction
- Seek immediate medical attention if you are stung in the mouth or nose, as subsequent swelling may block your airway passages.
- Seek emergency care if *any* of the following symptoms are present, as these could indicate an allergic reaction:
  - Large areas of swelling
  - Hives
  - Abnormal breathing
  - Tightness in throat or chest
  - Fainting or dizziness
  - Nausea or vomiting
  - Persistent pain or swelling

Seizures and Convulsions

Seizures are caused by abnormal electrical discharges in the brain. In addition to known seizure behavior in a patient (due to some form of epilepsy), seizures can be associated with: alcohol use, drug overdose, intoxication, fever in young children, head injury, poisoning, venomous bites and stings, hypoglycemia (low blood sugar), very high blood sugar or head injury.

Seizures appear as sudden, involuntary contractions of the muscles. They may be obvious when they cause jerky movements and stiffening and are repetitive. At times they produce violent body muscle shaking. The eyes may roll back in the head. There may be loss of bowel or bladder control. Some seizures are more subtle with reduced muscle tone, peculiar hand or face movements, unintelligible noise making, altered thought processes, and/or periods of staring. Seizures may be minor and short-lived, or major, prolonged and/or recurrent. Some result in a loss of consciousness.

Prevention
- People who are known to have seizures (*epilepsy*) should wear medical alert tags and be sure to take their prescribed medication.
- With the first signs of increased temperature try to control any fevers, especially in the case of children, by using cool water, and treat like a mild case of heat exhaustion.

Treatment:
- Call for emergency medical assistance if the seizure lasts longer than 2 minutes or if there is a series of recurrent seizures.
- Time the seizure.
- Try and prevent the victim from injuring themselves by removing them from areas where thrashing might cause injuries.
- Lay the victim on the ground, clear of sharp objects and furniture, and loosen tight clothing, especially around the neck.
- Place something soft, like a folded jacket, under the head.
- If some restraint is required, lay the victim on their side, but do <u>not</u> actively restrain them and do not try to stop their movements.
- If there is vomiting, turn the head to the side in an attempt to keep the airway clear and the vomit from aspirating into the air passages (*trachea*).
- Do *not* put anything in the victim's mouth, or between the teeth, during a seizure.
- Do not try to force the mouth open with any hard implement or fingers, as persons having seizures do not swallow their tongues. Trying to hold the tongue down can injure the teeth or jaws.
- If a child is experiencing seizures for the first time, assume they have swallowed a poison and treat as a poisoning. If it likely that a high fever is the cause, slowly cool the child with cool cloths, tepid water and an age-appropriate dose of acetamino-phen (Tylenol®). *Do not immerse the child in ice water.*

- Following a seizure, the victim may fall into a deep, sleep-like state ("post ictal"). Upon awakening, they may be disoriented for a period of time.
- When the victim is able to talk, determine if the victim has a history of seizures, and what medication they are taking.
- If the victim is a diabetic, when fully awake and not experiencing nausea or vomiting have him eat or drink something with high sugar content.
- Do not perform CPR, rescue breathing or give the victim anything by mouth until the seizure has stopped and the patient is not breathing.

Splinter Removal
Treatment:
- Sterilize a needle or tweezers using a flame from a fire, gas range or a candle, and then let the needle cool before use.
- If the splinter is sticking out from the skin, grasp the protruding end and pull it out at the same angle that it entered. If it is just under the skin, gently loosen the skin around the splinter with a sterile needle and remove it with tweezers.
- Consult a doctor if the splinter went deeply into the skin, or if signs of an infection develop, such as redness, swelling, streaking, discharge or fever.
- When removed, wash the area with soap and water.

Sprains, Fractures and Dislocations
A *sprain* is an injury to the soft tissue (ligaments) around a joint. A *fracture* is a broken bone. An *open fracture* is a broken bone that pokes through the skin. A d*islocation* is when the bone comes out of the socket. Because it is difficult to know right away if someone, especially a child, has suffered a sprain or a fracture, the same first aid treatment (detailed below) should be used for each condition. Then the advice of a doctor should be sought.

Symptoms:
Each of these injuries can result in pain, swelling and inability to move or bear weight.

Treatment:
- Call 911 in the event of any of the following: the absence of a pulse below the injury *[if you are trained in pulse detection)*, severe pain, signs of shock, or injuries to the femur *(thigh bone)*, hips, back or neck.
- Do not move the person until emergency medical personnel arrive.

- Stabilize the injured area. Splint the injured area with a magazine, newspaper, Popsicle˙ stick or board, securing with some tape, shoelaces or a scarf.
- Do not try to straighten or change the position of the injured bone. Move the area as little as possible
- Ice the injury to help minimize swelling
- Raise the injured limb above the level of the heart with a sling or pillows.
- If the fracture is open, cover with a clean cloth or bandage and call 911.
- If the injury is to the foot or ankle, remove the shoe. If necessary, cut the shoe so as not to disturb the injury.
- Acetaminophen or ibuprofen should be given for pain as directed by the doctor.
- Avoid moving the injured area, and allow appropriate time for healing before returning to normal activity.
- An elastic bandage may help ease the pain. Ask a doctor first, though, before use, and check frequently for decreased circulation (numbness or tingling). Loosen the bandage if this occurs.

TICKS

Awareness of diseases transmitted by tick bites in the United States has been heightened in recent years by the recognition of Lyme disease. Other tick-borne diseases include typhus, babeosis, and Rocky Mountain Spotted fever. Usually, the only early finding of a tick bite is the discovery of a tick attached to some part of the body, most frequently at the hairline or in the scalp. Lyme disease generally starts as a flu-like condition, but is characterized by an enlarging red rash and later may be accompanied by joint pains and swelling, heart rhythm disturbances and meningitis. A physician should direct diagnosis and treatment (antibiotics).

The tick barb is usually deeply embedded under the skin and may be difficult to remove. Attempt to remove with tweezers close to the skin and apply steady, slow traction while trying to avoid detaching and leaving the head in the wound. (The tick carries and can transmit the agent *Borrelia burgdorferi* that causes Lyme disease.

Prevention
- Persons should be aware of ticks in their communities or areas they intend to visit and wear protective clothing.
- After leaving potential tick areas, carefully inspect the body for any ticks.
- Protect exposed skin areas with insect repellants that contain DEET.
- Sprays *(containing permethrin)* of clothing may be helpful.

WOUND
See Animal Bites in Poisoning Section

I hope you have found the information in this chapter interesting and helpful. It is strongly advised that you attend demonstrations to learn and practice the procedures for CPR and Heimlich as well as on line or in-person first aid courses.

You and all your loved ones should be well.

CHAPTER **Eight**

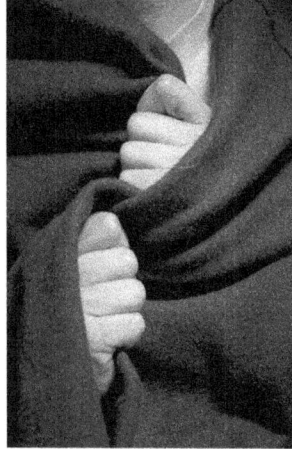

Natural Disasters Happen, So… Be Prepared!

Fortunately, the warning often given with most natural disasters usually provides enough time for you to carry out pre-made plans and minimize any damage that could affect your property. However, unless you make contingency plans that take into account the types of disasters that can occur in your area, you are unlikely to be able to fully prepare yourself and your family in the time that exists between a warning and the onset of an actual disaster.

The first step and the best way you can handle a disaster is to learn what can be done for the particular types that are likely to occur in your neighborhood. Once you know the type of disaster that can be expected, you can make the appropriate preparations, and in doing so you will be better able to help protect yourself and family.

When you have lived most of your life in one place, you get to know your local climate and the types of preparations that are needed to prevent excessive damage to homes from severe weather. However, if you move to a new area, you must make sure you learn about the types of weather that can occur, and the preparations you should make for potential local disasters. All the information you are going to need to make this evaluation is available from the State Emergency Management Agency, civil defense office or the local chapter of the American Red Cross. They can tell you the types of natural disasters that can happen in your area. Go to www.GettingSafer.com for companies and State and Federal Agencies that can provide useful services in the event of natural disasters.

In this chapter you'll learn ways to create your own disaster plan and ways to protect yourself in a variety of natural disaster conditions, from hurricanes to severe snowstorms. Since you are only likely to need to prepare for some of these conditions, just focus on those that occur where you live.

PREPARING FOR POTENTIAL DISASTERS

Many of the things that need to be done to prepare for natural and other potential disasters are the same as those listed previously in the Home Preparedness chapter of this book. Since there are so many similarities the preparations are included in the following list of things to do.

- Inquire about any disaster plans that already exist at your work place, children's school, day care and any other places where you or your family spend a lot of time.
- Learn about your community's warning signals. All radio and TV stations emit an emergency warning sound. This is then followed by instructions about what you should do when you hear the warning. In some cases, emergency services personnel will drive around your area and call out verbal directions using loud speakers.
- Other methods of communication include warnings delivered via phone, email or text.
- If there is sufficient time to warn people, newspapers will print information about the emergency.
- Take First Aid and CPR classes as part of your prevention and preparation tactics. For more about First Aid and CPR in the Basic First Aid chapter.
- Learn about the best ways to help elderly or disabled persons in an emergency.

BEWARE

- Make arrangements in advance for pets and animal care in case of any disaster. Emergency shelters generally do not take animals unless they are special service animals for a person with disabilities. You need to make arrangements to have some pre-determined alternative place which deals exclusively with pets.
- You should have a pre-arranged out-of-town family contact in the event of a disaster. Put this person's contact information on your emergency list, and memorize the telephone number.
- Consult professionals on the best ways to safety-proof your home against the hazards of such things as moving furniture or how to prevent objects from falling.
- Conduct a home hazard hunt, looking for anything that can fall, break or move.
- Eliminate hazards by bolting or strapping down such things as water heaters and major appliances, and attaching bookcases, cabinets and tall furniture to wall studs.

- Install strong latches on cupboards, and fasten shelves securely to the walls, placing heavier items on the lower shelves.
- Always hang pictures and mirrors away from any beds, and bolt larger items to the wall.
- Store flammable products away from heat sources.
- Repair defective wiring, and cracks in ceilings and foundations.
- Have professionals clean and repair chimneys, and clean flue pipes, vent connectors and gas vents.
- Make sure you have a smoke detector on each level of your home, especially outside each sleeping area. If you sleep with doors closed, put a detector inside each bedroom.

BEWARE
- Install *at least one* carbon monoxide detector in your home *(there should be one on each level.)* The high pitched warning from this kind of an alarm could save your life.
- Check alarm batteries each month; replace them at least once a year.
- Smoke and carbon monoxide alarms deteriorate over time, so replace them every ten years or sooner if recommended by the manufacturer.

- With your eyes closed, practice leaving your bedroom, and walk to get out of your home according to your home evacuation plan

BEWARE
- You should have at least one fire extinguisher in your home and know how to operate it properly. It is vital to know how to operate a fire extinguisher if you have one, otherwise you can actually make a fire *worse* by not using it properly! Get instructions on its use from your local fire department.

There are many different types of fire extinguishers, for fire, electrical or grease fires. An ABC extinguisher will work on most types of fires. Ideally, you should keep an extinguisher specifically designed for grease fires in the kitchen.

For more information about fire extinguishers contact the National Fire Protection Association, on the web at www.NFPA.org, or your local fire station.

Developing Your Family Disaster Safety Plan

It is really important to develop a workable family disaster safety plan with the members of your family in advance. Make your own list of things to do from the following:
- Talk about the various types of disasters that are most likely to happen in your area, and discuss with your family members what can be done to minimize damage in each case.

- Involve everyone, including children, in the planning process of a home escape plan. It is possible for schools to get involved, and your children's school system should make it an assignment for children to develop and practice a home escape plan.

- Prepare an evacuation plan, and make sure that *everyone* in your household knows what to do. Then practice what you have planned.

- Inform caregivers or baby sitters of your plan. They are in charge when you are out or away from home … and accidents and emergencies can happen at any time.

- Create an emergencies information sheet (example follows) as part of all the pertinent and important things that you have planned to do in any emergency, depending upon where you live and the type of property you occupy.

EMERGENCIES INFORMATION SHEET *sample*   COMPLETE

Our Cell Phone Number: _ _ _ _ _ _ _ _ _ _ _ _ _ _ Name: _ _ _ _ _ _ _ _ _
Neighbor's Phone Number _ _ _ _ _ _ _ _ _ _ _ _ Name: _ _ _ _ _ _ _ _ _
Local Hospital Emergency Number _
24-Hour Pharmacy Phone Number
Meeting Location 1: _ _ _ _ _ _ _ _ _ _ _ _ _ Location 2: _ _ _ _ _ _ _ _ _
Do Not Forget: Take Emergency Kit *(located under stairs by front door)* and if time permits, turn off all utilities *(see utility location map located in Emergency Kit.)*

- Find safe places in your home for each type of disaster. Show them in the plan of your home. Designate an interior room, if possible, as your 'safe room.' It should be on the ground floor and not in a basement. Ideally there should be no windows in the 'safe room', and you should store a battery-powered radio and a telephone there.

- Keep a copy of emergency phone numbers in your wallet.

Download a sample of the following form at www.gettingsafer.com so you can insert your appropriate phone numbers.

EMERGENCY PHONE NUMBER CARD SAMPLE   COMPLETE

BEWARE

Local Police - 000-111-2222
Local Hospitals - 000-111-3333
Kids Schools - 000-111-4444
Neighbors - 000-111-5555

- Place a copy of your emergency numbers list next to each phone, and explain the purpose of each number to all your family members.
- Teach children how and when to call 911. Make sure they realize 911 should be used only if property or a life is in serious danger.
- Each family member, if they're old enough, should know how and when to use your fire extinguisher, as well as any other emergency equipment. They also need to know where the equipment is kept. Make sure the equipment is easily accessible.
- Everyone in your home should learn what to do in case of a power outage.
- Know when, where and how to turn off utility valves and switches *(water, gas and electricity)*. Mark the turn-off locations on the plan of your home.
- Prepare and stock emergency supplies and kits. *See the lists of likely contents for your EMERGENCY KITS at www.GettingSafer.com*
- Make arrangements with your neighbors that you check on each other in an emergency.
- For emergencies, have at least two pre-designated meeting places for your family: one outside your home, and the other away from your neighborhood. Ideally you should make these meeting place arrangements for every place at which you spend a great deal of time, such as home, work, or school.
- Ask an out-of-state friend to be your "family contact." After a disaster, it's often easier to call long distance. Other family members should call this person and tell them where they are. Everyone must know your contact's phone number.
- Discuss and practice what to do in the event of an evacuation.
- Plan how to take care of your pets.

Escape Routes
- Plan two escape routes from each room in your house.

Consider getting some escape ladders for rooms on a second floor. There are a lot of different types of ladders, including roll-up types designed for emergency situations. These ladders fold up and take up very little space when not in use. It is important to practice, become familiar with and know how to use all your escape equipment and routes.

Practice your escape plan twice a year. The more familiar you are with the procedures, the less you and your family will panic in a real emergency.

Arrange a place to meet outside your home, after a fire or any other emergency.

Evacuation

- Listen to the radio and follow the local emergency official's instructions
- Wear some kind of clothing that will provide protection, and especially wear shoes (keep a pair under your bed) to protect your feet against broken glass.
- As you leave with the rest of your family, take your disaster supply kit. It should be located near your exit. Do not expect to have time to look for anything else in your home. You may not have sufficient time, and every second wasted looking for possessions puts you in greater danger.
- Keep the local streets clear for emergency vehicles, and do not use your own vehicle unless you have an emergency and must travel somewhere.
- Use travel routes and roads specified by the authorities. Avoid any short cuts as they may be impassable or dangerous.
- Try and meet your family at your agreed-upon designated points.
- If time permits, leave a note prominently placed telling others where you are going, and shut off the water, gas and electricity.
- Take care of your pets in accordance with your pre-arranged plan.

Explosion

- If there is a gas or other type of explosion, remain as calm as possible. Follow the emergency plans that you have prepared and practiced.
- If you are trapped in debris, use a flashlight or whistle, if possible, to help rescuers find your location. Otherwise, tap on a pipe or wall from time to time so rescuers can locate you by the noise.
- Shout only as a last resort. Shouting can cause you to inhale large amounts of dust and will sap your energy.
- Stay in one area so you don't kick up dust, which could also make your breathing difficult.
- Cover your mouth with clothing to prevent dust from going into your lungs.
- Once you get outside, stay out, until the authorities tell you that it is safe to return.

After Rescue:

- Check yourself and others for possible injuries. Protect yourself in a damaged building from further injury by putting on clothing with long sleeves, as well as pants, shoes and gloves.
- Look for small fires and extinguish them.

- Check for gas leaks. Don't use candles, lanterns or open flames unless you're absolutely sure the gas has been turned off and the area aired out. Even fumes can ignite. Don't take chances.
- Report gas leaks to the utility company. They are also the only ones who should relight the main pilot.
- Listen to the radio for instructions.
- Inspect your home for cracks and damage, including the roof, chimneys and foundation.
- Clean everything that got wet.
- Don't eat any spoiled food. If you are not sure that it is safe to eat, throw it away.
- Only drink water that you know is safe.
- Limit your use of the phone, using it only to report serious injuries.

NATURAL DISASTERS

There are different of types of disasters. Many disasters are caused by a variety of natural and weather-related conditions. According to the National Oceanic and Atmospheric Administration, the U.S. has more severe storms and flooding than any other nation in the world. Typically, every year that translates into about 10,000 thunderstorms, 5000 floods, 100+ tornadoes and many hurricanes.

However, another type of potential disaster is of the man-made variety: terrorism. As terrorism is in a category of its own this book has a chapter that deals specifically with this problem.

Natural and weather-related disasters are discussed alphabetically in this chapter, for convenience's sake. Please remember that the amount of damage each disaster causes will depend on the type and severity of the disaster and the length of time it lasts. The amount of damage you sustain, if any, will also be related to the amount of preparation that you have made to cope with the disaster.

Drought

Drought is a normal and recurrent feature of climate, and occurs to varying degrees in virtually all parts of the world. It originates from a shortfall of precipitation over a period of time. This could be a shortfall of rain or less snow than normal. Other factors such as high wind, high temperatures or low relative humidity can also have a bearing on the degree and extent of any drought.

Generally in more populated areas of the country, the effect of a drought is that, as a result of an extended period of insufficient rainfall, there is extensive damage to crops. On the personal level for those with individual homes, it can also cause damage to gardens and lawns when watering is restricted.

Drought can have a serious impact on the economic life of a region or the country as a whole. A shortage of water can mean a reduction of hydroelectric power that can affect manufacturing. Drought can and invariably does lead to a shortage of food grains, vegetables and even fish. In addition, drought can result in extensive forest and wildfires.

The costliest weather disasters in the US haves been due to a hurricane two separate droughts and another hurricane. For example, Hurricane Katrina in 2005 cost 1833 lives and over $133 billion. The US drought in 1988 cost 7500 deaths and $71 billion. A drought in 1980 cost 10,000 lives and $55 billion and Hurricane Andrew in 1992 cost $40 billion and 61 lives were lost.

As this book deals with these topics alphabetically, Hurricane Preparations are addressed later in this chapter.

Signs:

The signs of a drought include little or no rainfall or snow, compared to its year in, year out averages in a specific region.

- Extremely heavy rainfall on very dry soil can cause runoff, and in that situation the soil cannot absorb the rain. This leads to a shortage of moisture in the soil … and drought.
- Inadequate rain or melting snow will mean that the levels of reservoirs start and continue to fall. Riverbeds will dry up. The farming community is the first to feel the impact of drought, and it is only later, when water in reservoirs starts to dry up, that those living in cities and towns become affected.

Action:

As a homeowner there are a number of things that one can do to help reduce the burden of drought:

- Reduce or eliminate car washes.
- Reduce the number of baths, or when showering, turn off the water until you need to rinse.
- In the garden, grass needs water, but it can be watered early in the morning or late in the day when there is less evaporation. It is better to water a lawn deeply once a week than a little watering 3 or 4 times a week.

- Reduce nitrogen fertilization so you are not accelerating growth.

The above may seem insignificant measures, but when they are undertaken by thousands or millions of people in an area, they can have a significant beneficial impact.

Earthquakes

Earthquakes occur when the earth suddenly moves, and that movement is usually followed by a series of shakes that travel quickly. The earth's movement can result in landslides and building collapses, and if gas lines are severed, can result in fires or explosions and additional damage. Some parts of the country are more likely to have significant and noticeable earthquakes, although these movements can and do occur almost everywhere.

Signs:

You may hear a noise like an approaching train before you feel any movement. This noise may give you--literally--just a few moments to get prepared for the actual quake.

Mini-earthquakes, called "aftershocks," usually follow earthquakes. These smaller shocks can occur from time to time over a period of several days, and sometimes for weeks after the initial earthquake.

Preparation:

Unfortunately earthquakes cannot be prevented, but you can prepare to lessen the destruction that they may cause.

IDEA

- Practice getting to safe, sturdy structures in each room at home, work or school, such as a doorway, table or desk under which you can seek cover. As you do so, practice the "Drop, Cover and Hold On" technique. This is an exercise when you drop to the floor, take cover and protect your head and neck with your arms. Hold on if you are under a sturdy piece of furniture.
- Try to make the interior of your home as earthquake-proof as possible. Bolt down large items like water heaters and gas appliances. Place and secure heavy objects and fragile items on lower shelves. Fasten shelves and cabinets to the wall, and brace or anchor high or top-heavy objects.

Action:

- If an earthquake hits, immediately get under a protective cover. Move about as little as possible, taking only a few steps to get to a safe place. The greatest danger is from falling objects or even a ceiling.

- Once under a sturdy object, hold on and protect your eyes by pressing your face against your arm.
- If there is nothing sturdy and close enough under which you can hide, sit next to an interior wall where there is nothing heavy that can fall on you.
- If you are in bed, stay there and hold on. Protect your head with a pillow.
- After an earthquake, get outside if your home or building is unsafe. If you need to exit a high rise building, only use the stairs, never an elevator.
- If you are outdoors and an earthquake occurs, quickly move away from buildings, street lights, power lines, trees and anything else that could fall on you. Wait until the shaking stops and until you are sure there are no immediate aftershocks. Do not enter a building to hide.
- In a stadium or theatre, stay in your seat but get below the level of the back of the seat for protection and cover your head. Do not try to rush for the exit.
- Make sure that you and others are not hurt as a quake starts to subside.
- Be careful when you start to move about, and be very careful near things that have fallen or are unsteady and may still fall.
- Look out for small fires, unsteady ground or loose electrical wires.

Earthquake Information for Motorists:
- You may not feel the earthquake while driving and only become aware of it because you hear a report on the radio.
- If you are driving when an earthquake hits, gradually decrease your speed and pull to the side of the road when it is safe to do so.
- Once you stop the car, keep your seatbelt fastened and remain in the car until the shaking and aftershocks stop.
- Do not stop on or under overpasses or bridges. Avoid parking near trees or downed power lines, and stay away from buildings.
- Keep your car radio tuned to a local channel and listen for advisories.

Fire

One of the most common disasters is fire, although most of them are preventable. If a fire occurs you will be better able to deal with it if you know what to do and have made some advance preparations. Accidents will happen, but taking preventive measures will minimize your risks.

Knowing how to light a fire is one thing. Learning and knowing how to put out a fire is another. Being responsible and practicing prevention is important so that in an emergency you are ready and able to act. The Red Cross and your local fire station personnel will be happy to help you when you are ready to receive more information.

Prevention:

- Teach your children that matches, lighters and candles are not toys and can cause serious accidents.
- Let youngsters know that if they see children playing with matches or a lighter, they must tell an adult immediately, so that a possible accident can be prevented.
- Make sure that your home heating sources are clean and in working order. Many fires start from faulty furnaces or stoves, cracked or rusty furnace parts and chimneys with soot buildup.
- Make sure that all vents and filters are kept clean and replaced as needed.
- Candles are the cause of too many fires even when residents are at home. Make sure that when lit they are placed well away from anything flammable. They also need to well-protected so they cannot fall when lit.
- Cigarettes are the cause of thousands of major fires every year. To reduce accidents, extinguish a cigarette promptly when finished.
  - Nobody should ever smoke in bed or when inebriated.
  - Smoke detectors can provide a warning, giving you a few extra minutes or seconds that can make the difference between life and death. *Make sure your detectors are installed in the correct locations and working properly.*
  - Test smoke detectors once a month and change the batteries once a year.
- Purchase emergency ladders for each room on the second floor of your home and for any higher floors as well.
- As part of your safety plan, have your entire family practice using the ladders twice a year.

Action:

- If you hear a fire alarm or smell smoke, shout "Fire! Fire" several times to warn others, and immediately exit the building.
- Get out, and then call 911 from a neighbor's house or a cell phone.
- Grab your emergency kit as you exit but do not stop to take or pick up any other personal property.
- Since so much furnishing is made from synthetic materials that are petroleum-based, the fumes they produce as they burn are frequently toxic.

- If your clothing catches fire, *Stop, Drop and Roll* until all the flames are extinguished. Use a heavy non-flammable blanket to beat out the flames.
- Do not try and hide from a fire, and never try and hide in a closet. Firefighters will have a difficult time finding you.
- Because heavy smoke and poisonous gases collect near the ceiling, crawl, stay low and cover your nose and mouth with a wet cloth.
- If smoke, heat or flames block all your exits, stay in whatever room you are in with all door and ventilation cracks blocked with rags.
- Stuff rags, preferably wet ones, under door and ventilation openings to prevent smoke from coming into a room.
- If you cannot get out, try to signal for help from a window by waving your arms, using a flashlight or hanging brightly-colored clothing from the window.
- When you reach a door, feel the door with the back of your hand for heat or blistering before opening. If it is not hot, open the door slowly, but if it is hot do not open it. Look for another way out.
- If there is a phone in the room call the fire department.
- If you are in a multi-story building do not use the elevators. Always use the fire escape stairs.
- Once outside, do not re-enter the building until it is fully checked and you are given the okay.

Fires: Wildfires and Canyon

Wildfires and canyon fires frequently start unnoticed and spread quickly, igniting bushes, trees and homes. Sometimes these fires occur by accident, but unfortunately, there are times when they are deliberately set. At other times lightning can cause them. No matter how they start, the end result can be the same if you are in the path of the smoke and flames.

Prevention:

- Make sure fire vehicles can find your home by clearly displaying its address.
- Make sure all driveway entrances are clearly marked and free of any obstacles.
- Immediately report to authorities any hazardous conditions that might cause a fire, or any sign of an actual fire.
- Teach all family members about fire safety and the importance of never playing with fire. (*In some states, parents can now be held responsible if their children set a fire.*)

- If the damage you incur has been caused by a criminal act, your home insurance may not cover any costs for damages. If you want this coverage, check your policy or ask your insurance company or agent for clarification.
- Keep matches and other combustible items locked up and out of reach.
- Plan different escape routes away from your home, including ways by foot or by car.
- Plan with neighbors to create a network that will work together during and after a fire.
- Check your roof material and, if necessary, change it for fire-retardant roofing material if possible.
- Regularly clean the roof, chimneys and stovepipes of your home, and inspect them at least once a year. Maintain dampers in good working order, and make sure that they are fitted with spark arresters that meet National Fire Protection Association Code 211. You can find information on this and other fire prevention and protection topics and products at www.nfpa.org.
- Install a smoke detector on every floor of your home, especially near bedrooms; test the detectors monthly and replace the batteries at least once a year.
- Smoke, rather than causing you to wake, can actually make you fall into a deeper sleep if you are not awakened by an alarm.
- Install and make sure everyone in the household knows how to use the fire extinguisher (*ABC type*) and its location.
- Have a ladder that reaches the roof.
- Consider installing protective shutters or heavy fire-resistant drapes.
- Create and maintain an emergency fire tool kit. It should contain a rake, axe, handsaw or chainsaw, as well as a bucket and shovel.
- Arrange a meeting with your local fire station personnel to discuss any concerns you might have.

Fire Prevention-Safety Zone:

BEWARE

- Contact your local fire department to obtain information on creating a defensible space (*a firebreak*).
- To help reduce the exposure of your home and property to flames, ideally create a 30 to 100 foot safety zone.
- Plant ornamental landscaping plants that are fire-resistant and non-invasive near your home, such as ice plants.
- If you live adjacent to government land or near canyon property, you need to check the regulations regarding the type of clearing activities that you are either

allowed or required to perform. Check with your city's Development Services for the Development and Permit Information for legal considerations and guidelines.

- Remove anything combustible that touches your home or extends over the roofline. Trees near your home should not form one continuous planting mass.
- Clear all flammable vegetation and rubbish that is near or under your property.
- Remove all dry leaves, dead limbs and twigs. Clean any dead leaves from the roof and gutters.
- Remove any tree branches that grow in the 15-foot space between the tree crowns and the ground. Prune any trees or branches within 15 feet of a chimney or stovepipe.
- Remove vines and vegetation from the walls of your home.
- Mow grass regularly.
- Keep flammable outdoor chairs and furniture at a safe distance from home structures.
- Request that the power company clear any branches from power lines.
- For safety, clear a 10-foot area around barbecues and propane tanks. Place a non-flammable mesh screen no coarser than a quarter inch over the grill to prevent flying burning ash.
- Soak any fireplace or grill ashes for two days, in a metal bucket filled with water, and then bury the cold ashes in soil.
- Regularly dispose of newspapers and cleared vegetation at an approved site.
- Store flammable material, including gasoline and oily rags, in approved safety cans away from other combustible materials (i.e. paper, wood).
- Stack firewood 30 to 100 feet away from the home and uphill. Any other combustible material should be stored at least 20 feet away.
- Identify and maintain an adequate outside source of water, such as a swimming pool, a well, a cistern or hydrant.
- Have a garden hose that is long enough to reach all areas of the home and any structures on the property.
- Install freeze-proof exterior water outlets on at least two sides of your home and near any other structures. If needed, install additional outdoor water outlets about 50 feet from the home.
- As an added precaution, a portable, gasoline-powered pump could be of use to help supply water if the electrical power is cut.

Action:

BEWARE

- If you are warned that a wildfire or canyon fire is threatening your area, listen carefully to the radio for instructions and evacuation information.
- Follow the instructions of the local officials and firefighters.
- Put your emergency supply kit and other valuable property in the car.
- Back your car into the garage and close the garage door, or park your car in an open space that faces the direction of your exit route. The car doors and windows should be closed, but not locked, to keep the car smoke-free. Make sure you leave the car keys in a very accessible place, but not in the unlocked car, so you can get away quickly.
- Disconnect any automatic garage door opener in case the electric power is cut off.
- Confine pets in one room and make plans for them in case you need to evacuate.
- Arrange temporary housing outside of the threatened area.

Things to do *inside* your home, if time permits:

IDEA

- Close all the windows, vents, doors, Venetian blinds and heavy drapes.
- Remove any lightweight window coverings that can ignite quickly.
- Turn off all pilot lights and shut off gas at the main valve.
- Open fireplace dampers and close fireplace screens.
- Move flammable furniture into the center of the room away from windows and sliding glass doors.
- Turn on a light in each room for better visibility in heavy smoke.

Things to do *outside* your home, if time permits:

IDEA

- Seal any attic and ground-level vents with pre-cut plywood or commercial sealant to help prevent smoke or flames entering the house.
- Turn off propane tanks.
- Move any combustible outdoor furniture and items into the house.
- Connect garden hoses to outside taps.
- Set up gasoline-powered pumps, and place sprinklers on the roof and near above-the-ground fuel tanks.
- Wet the roof and decking thoroughly, and wet or remove shrubs within 15 feet of the home.

Evacuation Procedure:
- Once you are told to evacuate by fire or police personnel, do so immediately.
- Lock your home if time permits.
- Choose a route away from the fire hazard, and carefully watch for changes in the speed and direction of the fire and smoke.
- Let someone know when you are leaving your home and where you are going, so you can be contacted easily.

Flooding

Every small stream, gully, creek, dry riverbed or low-lying ground has the potential to flood at some point in time. In many parts of the country where flash floods frequently occur, there are signs indicating the potential for flash floods. Be very careful, as these areas can be extremely dangerous even though they appear quite harmless in dry weather.

It is important to know the meaning and the differences in the terminology used to identify the different types of flood warnings.

Terminology:

Flood/Flash Flood Watch: This means that flooding or flash flooding may occur within the designated "watch area." Be prepared to take action.

Flood/Flash Flood Warning: This means that flooding or flash flooding has been reported or is imminent. Take any necessary actions immediately.

Prevention:

Find out if you live in a flood plain. If you do, contact your local emergency management office or the Red Cross and learn what actions you can take and the types of supplies you will need to protect your home.
- Know the elevation of your property in relation to streams and dams so you will know if forecasted flood levels could reach your home.
- If you live in a flood-prone area, consider adding storm shutters, and keep a supply of plywood or plastic sheeting, if appropriate, for future use to reduce damage or loss of property.
- Obtain sandbags when necessary to help shore up your property, especially around doors. *Do not pre-fill sandbags*, as moisture in the sand will rot the bags. Sandbags should only be half-filled when needed, or they can burst.

Action:

- Floodwaters can rise very quickly, so *every minute counts*. You should be prepared to evacuate before the water level reaches your property.
- Stay away from power lines and electrical wires, and remember that electrical current can run through water. Report any downed wires to the appropriate authorities.
- If you come upon floodwaters, stop, turn around, and go the other way.
- Look for and go to the highest ground possible. *(This should be pre-planned)*.
- Stay away from already flooded areas; the waters may rise higher quickly and without warning, and you could find yourself trapped.
- Do not walk in, dive into or try to cross water. Floodwaters can move very quickly and knock you off your feet.
- If you are in your car, get out and move to higher ground.
- Watch out for snakes around flooded areas.
- Throw away all food that has come into contact with floodwater; eating contaminated food could make you very sick.
- Never allow children or anyone to play near high water, storm drains or ravines.
- If a flood warning has been issued and you are at home, you should have time to:
  - Turn off all utilities.
  - Collect water in bathtubs, sinks and jugs so you have a supply of clean, uncontaminated water.
  - Move valuable items to upper floors if possible.
  - Bring in movable outdoor possessions.
- After any floodwater has subsided, walk carefully, as floors that have been covered with mud can become very slippery.

Hazardous Materials

Since chemicals and solid types of hazardous materials are now being transported frequently by roads, railways and waterways, a hazardous materials accident could occur almost anywhere. Most manufacturers dispose of waste material in correct ways that may involve transporting the waste to an approved site some distance from their plant.

In some areas, communities that are located near chemical manufacturing plants can be at greater risk for an accident simply because of the greater amount of activity involving hazardous materials. If an accident occurs in your neighbor- hood the authorities will notify you and tell you about the most appropriate actions to take.

There are many hazardous materials and some do not have a taste or odor, therefore becoming difficult to detect. On the other hand, some chemical materials can be detected easily because they cause physical reactions, such as watering eyes or nausea. An oil or foam-like appearance just above the surface of the ground usually indicates the likely presence of hazardous materials beneath the surface of the ground.

Action:

• If you see or think there has been a hazardous material accident, call 911 or the local fire department immediately to report the nature and location of the accident. Give your name, the phone number you are calling from, and your distance from the incident and location.

• Avoid coming into contact with any spilled substance. Do not walk into, touch or try to inhale any of the material, gases, fumes or smoke. Cover your mouth and nose when in the area, even if there is no odor.

• Move away from the accident scene as quickly as possible, and help to keep others away.

• Stay upwind, upstream or uphill, and away from the hazard. Cover all exposed skin if possible, and protect your respiratory system using a handkerchief or some cloth to cover your mouth and nose.

• Stay away from any accident victims until the hazardous material has been identified, and the authorities indicate it is safe to go near them.

If you are advised to remain indoors:
• Bring pets inside.
• To prevent contaminants from entering your home, turn off air conditioning units. Seal all vents using plastic sheeting, wax paper or aluminum foil and duct tape. Do the same with any bathroom and kitchen exhaust fans, as well as stove and dryer vents using duct tape and plastic sheeting, wax paper or aluminum wrap.
• Close and lock all windows and doors.
• Seal all gaps under doorways and around windows with wet towels and/or duct tape.
• Close fireplace dampers and turn off the ventilation system.
• Seal off nonessential rooms such as storage areas, laundry rooms and extra bedrooms.
• Fill up bathtubs or large containers so you will have a water supply, and turn off the water intake valve to the house.
• If any gas or vapors could have entered the building, cover your mouth and nose with a cloth and take shallow breaths.

- Do not eat any food or drink any water that may be contaminated.
- Listen for the Emergency Broadcast System on radio or TV stations for all updates, and remain indoors until authorities indicate it is safe to go outside.
- Don't try to approach or care for victims of a hazardous materials accident until the substance has been identified and authorities indicate it is safe to go near them.
- As soon as you are advised that it is safe, move any victims into fresh air, and then call for emergency medical help.
- Remove contaminated clothing and shoes and place them in a plastic bag. Unless instructed otherwise, wash anyone that has come into contact with chemicals by immediately pouring cold water over the skin or eyes for at least 15 minutes.

If you are advised to evacuate:
- Leave immediately, and avoid the contaminated area on the way out. Follow the routes recommended by the authorities. *Do not take shortcuts because they may not be safe.*
- If you have time, reduce the chances of contamination getting into your house by closing all windows, shutting all vents, and turning off attic fans.

Upon returning home from an evacuation:
- Come back to your home only when authorities say it is safe to do so.
- Follow the authorities' advice concerning food and water safety.
- Closely follow instructions from emergency officials concerning clean-up methods, and dispose of residue carefully.

Heat Waves

Heat waves are prolonged periods of excessive heat and humidity. The National Weather Service makes a special effort to alert the public during periods of excessive heat and humidity.

A good web site for more information about the effects of extreme heat and how to act during it is: http://www.redcross.org/services/disaster/keepsafe/treat

Prevention:

- If a heat wave is predicted, prepare to slow down and avoid strenuous work or activity.
- If you must do strenuous work, do it during the coolest part of the day, which is usually in the morning between 4:00 and 7:00 am.

- Stay indoors as much as possible. If air conditioning is not available, stay on the lowest floor away from sunshine, and try to spend some time each day at a public building, such as an indoor mall, that has air conditioning.
- Use electric fans; even if they do not cool the air, they do help sweat to evaporate, which cools the body.
- Wear lightweight and preferably light-colored clothing that will help to reflect some of the sun's energy.

Office of Emergency Management Heat Index Chart

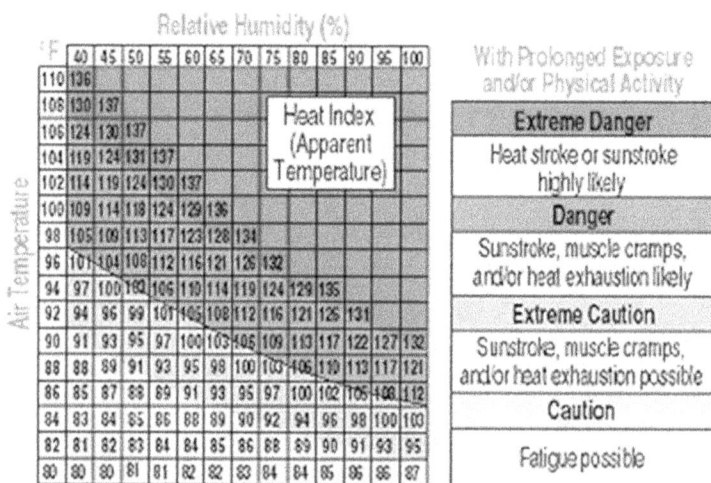

Relative Humidity (%)

°F	40	45	50	55	60	65	70	75	80	85	90	95	100
110	136												
108	130	137											
106	124	130	137										
104	119	124	131	137									
102	114	119	124	130	137								
100	109	114	118	124	129	136							
98	105	109	113	117	123	128	134						
96	101	104	108	112	116	121	126	132					
94	97	100	102	106	110	114	119	124	129	135			
92	94	96	99	101	105	108	112	116	121	126	131		
90	91	93	95	97	100	103	105	109	113	117	122	127	132
88	88	89	91	93	95	98	100	103	106	110	113	117	121
86	85	87	88	89	91	93	95	97	100	102	105	108	112
84	83	84	85	86	88	89	90	92	94	96	98	100	103
82	81	82	83	84	84	85	86	88	89	90	91	93	95
80	80	80	81	81	82	82	83	84	84	85	86	86	87

Air Temperature

Heat Index (Apparent Temperature)

With Prolonged Exposure and/or Physical Activity

Extreme Danger
Heat stroke or sunstroke highly likely

Danger
Sunstroke, muscle cramps, and/or heat exhaustion likely

Extreme Caution
Sunstroke, muscle cramps, and/or heat exhaustion possible

Caution
Fatigue possible

- Drink plenty of water every 10 to 15 minutes throughout the day. This means that you will drink about a gallon of water (128 oz) a day during a heat wave.
- Avoid drinks that contain alcohol or caffeine. Those drinks may make you feel better temporarily, but they are dehydrating and will make the heat's effect worse.
- Eat small meals and eat more often than usual. Foods that are high in protein will increase metabolic heat (i.e. meat, eggs and beans), so avoid them.
- Avoid using salt unless directed by a physician.
- If you are taking any medications or if you have a medical condition that may cause poor blood circulation or which reduces your ability to tolerate heat, discuss your concerns with your physician.
- If you feel dizzy or weak call for medical help *immediately*. If possible, go to a cool place, drink some water and wash your face with cool water.

Heat Cramps

Heat cramps are painful, involuntary muscle spasms (cramps) that usually affect people who sweat a lot during strenuous activity. The sweating depletes the body's salt and moisture, and a low salt level in the muscles can cause painful cramps. These cramps are different from exercise-type muscle cramps in that only a small section of muscle (and not the entire muscle) is involved. Heat cramps can also appear in people with the more serious condition of heat exhaustion, (discussion follows).

Symptoms:

- Muscle discomfort that wanders and usually occurs in the legs of people exercising in high temperature areas. Cramps can also occur in the abdomen, arms or any muscles involved in the exercise.
- Patient usually has normal body temperature.

Causes:

- Salt depletion and drinking water without adequate salt or minerals.

Treatment:

- Stop the activity and try to provide a cool location.
- Drink clear juice, water or a sports beverage containing minerals (an electrolyte solution, such as Gatorade").
- Replace lost salt with salt tablets if available.

Heat Exhaustion

This is an intermediate form of heat-related illness that can develop after several days of exposure to high temperatures and inadequate or unbalanced replacement of fluids. This condition may evolve from the milder condition of heat cramps if the exercising person does not stop. Most prone to heat exhaustion are elderly people, people with high blood pressure and people working or exercising in a hot environment. The symptoms often begin suddenly. However, if regular meals are consumed, salt depletion is very unlikely.

Symptoms:

- Body temperature is usually normal, but may be slightly elevated. The victim is sweating heavily or in some cases, not sweating. The skin may be cool and moist. Pulse rate and respiration are increased. There may be paleness; muscle cramps; tiredness, weakness; nausea and vomiting; headache; fainting.

- An exercising individual in a hot environment can complain of headache, dizziness, nausea, vomiting, irritability and muscle cramps.

Causes
- The loss of salt and water from the body.

Treatment
- Remove the individual from the sun and get them to a cooler or air-conditioned area.
- Use a fan or spray the person with cool water.
- Loosen any tight or restrictive clothing.
- If the person is conscious and not vomiting, give them a half-filled glass of cool water or an electrolyte-containing sport drink every 15 minutes.
- Apply cool towels or cloths to the body.
- If symptoms are severe and/or the patient is vomiting and needs intravenous fluids, has high blood pressure or heart problems, seek medical attention promptly to avoid progression to heat stroke.

Heat Stroke (The most serious)

Heat stroke occurs when the internal mechanisms (internal temperature control, sweating) that respond to body overheating are lost. As the body is unable to cool itself adequately, the temperature rises rapidly. Body temperature may rise to 106F or higher in as fast as 10 to 15 minutes. If emergency treatment is not provided, death or permanent disability could result.

Causes:
- Usually occurs in ill and or elderly individuals who have been exposed to several days of high temperature while living in poorly ventilated homes.
- May occur in athletes in a location with high temperatures, and combined with high humidity and limited access to water. Can occur in children exercising in the heat.
- Some people are born with an impaired ability to sweat normally
- Other risk factors include obesity, alcohol use, cardiovascular disease and dehydration.

Symptoms:
- Very high body temperatures, above 103°F orally
- Rapid strong pulse
- Rapid and shallow breathing
- Red, hot and dry skin (no sweating)

- Confusion,
- Unconsciousness.
- Throbbing headache
- Dizziness and nausea
- Delirium

Treatment:
- Call 911 for emergency assistance.
- Attempt immediate cooling by exposing as much of the body surface as possible, and applying cool to lukewarm water (65°F-75°F) with either a towel or sheet, or running water.
- Continuous large electric fanning can prove helpful.
- Monitor body temperature, and continue cooling efforts until the body temperature drops to 101-102°F.
- Help the cooling process by applying ice packs to the groin, armpits and chest.
- If emergency help is delayed, call the hospital emergency room for further instructions.
- Do not place objects in the mouth and do not give fluids. If there is vomiting, make sure the airway remains open by turning the victim on his or her side.

BEWARE

- ***Do not place the victim of heat stroke in an ice-water bath***, as this could make things worse.
- If the person refuses to drink the cool water or is vomiting or there are changes in their level of consciousness, do *not* give them anything to drink.

Hurricanes:

A hurricane is a form of tropical cyclone and is accompanied by thunderstorms with winds that reach more than 74 miles per hour. The wind in this region of the World - the Northern Hemisphere including the USA - blows in a large counter-clockwise spiral around a relatively calm center.

You need to be prepared for this type of weather system if you live in an area that receives hurricanes. *This natural disaster results in a number of people being killed each year.*

Terminology:
- Hurricane Watch: A hurricane may strike within 24 hours.
- Hurricane Warning: A hurricane or hurricane conditions are expected in your area within 24 hours. Coastal areas may require evacuation.

Signs:

The sky will begin to darken and winds will increase as the hurricane approaches.

A hurricane usually builds up over water and as it nears land, may bring heavy rains, strong winds and extremely high tides.

Prepare:

- Plan and discuss with your family what each one will do if a hurricane strikes, and the steps to take if you need to evacuate. You need to figure out where will you go and what things will you take with you.
- Cut plywood to cover your windows if you live in a hurricane zone.
- Appoint a contact person in another state so everyone in your family, as well as friends, can call and check in.

Action:

- Listen regularly to the radio and television for instructions.
- If asked to evacuate, go to a designated or pre-selected shelter, taking your emergency supply kit with you.

Radiation Exposure

Everyone receives some kind of natural or background radiation exposure every day from the sun. There are also small radioactive elements in the soil and rocks, as well as in household appliances such as television sets and microwave ovens. Medical and dental x-rays, and even the human body, also emit radiation. These levels of natural and background radiation are normal and not harmful.

Although the construction and operation of nuclear power plants are closely monitored and regulated, an accident, although very unlikely, is possible. If there is any release of radiation, authorities from the utility, as well as federal and state governments will be monitoring the levels of radioactivity, to determine the potential danger to the public and put emergency plans into action.

Radioactive materials that are handled improperly or are accidentally released into the environment can be dangerous because of the harmful effects of certain types and amounts of radiation on the body. The longer a person is exposed to radiation and the closer the person is to the radiation source, the greater the risk.

Signs:

Radiation cannot be detected by the senses (sight, smell, etc.) but is easily found by scientists with sophisticated instruments that can detect even the smallest levels of radiation.

Prevention:

- Contact local emergency management officials for information about radioactivity and the safety precautions set out in local, industry, state and federal plans.
- Ask where the nearest nuclear power plants are located.
- Learn the warning systems and signals in your community.
- Learn about the established emergency plans for schools, at work, day care centers, nursing homes and any other places where any of your family members might be.
- Read and become familiar with emergency information material that is regularly delivered to your home (via brochures, the phone book, calendars, utility bills, etc.).
- Residents living within a 10-mile radius of a nuclear facility are in a special emergency-planning zone, and should regularly receive emergency materials containing information and instructions about what to do if there is a radiation leak.

Action:

If You Are Alerted

BEWARE

- If there is a radiological emergency, the Alert and Notification System will be activated quickly to inform the public of any potential threat from natural or man-made events. This system uses: sirens, radio and TV tone alerts, public announcement systems or a combination of these to notify the public to tune their radios or televisions to an Emergency Alert System (EAS) station (TV and radio). In addition, the tone alert is also used to inform the public about a variety of emergency situations, including a practice test, a nuclear power-plant emergency, tornadoes, fire or flood situation, etc. The tone alert is then followed by a broadcast detailing the emergency.
- When you hear a siren or tone alert, it does not mean you should evacuate. It *does* mean you should promptly turn to an EAS station to determine the nature of the emergency, and follow the directions about what to do.
- Do not call 911 for information, as this will only tend to block the emergency line. In case of a nuclear accident, special emergency numbers and information will be provided to the public either during the EAS message, in the utilities' public information brochure, or both.
- Check on your neighbors, particularly if they are elderly. Make sure they are okay and know what to do.
- In a nuclear power plant emergency, you might be advised to go indoors instead of evacuating. If this is the case, close all windows, doors, chimney dampers and other sources of outside air, and turn off any forced air heating and cooling equipment, etc.

If Advised to Remain at Home:
- Bring pets inside.
- Listen to emergency information.
- Close and lock all windows and doors.
- Turn off air conditioning, fans and furnace, and close any vents.
- Close fireplace dampers.
- Go to the basement or other underground area.
- Stay inside until authorities say it is safe.

If Advised to Evacuate the Area:
- Stay calm, and do not rush anywhere.
- Listen carefully to emergency information.
- Close and lock windows and doors.
- Turn off air conditioning, vents, fans, and furnace.
- Close fireplace dampers.
- Only take necessary items and your emergency kit with you.
- Use your own transportation if possible. For those who do not have other means, public transportation should be made available.
- Keep car windows and air vents closed, and listen to an EAS radio station as you drive.
- Follow the evacuation routes provided.
- If you need a place to stay, special information and emergency accommodations will be made available.

When Coming In From Outdoors:
- Shower and change clothing and shoes.
- Put items worn outdoors in a plastic bag and seal it. The clothing may have become contaminated or it may need to be tested for exposure.

Medical Treatment:

- If a radiological release occurs at a nuclear power plant, the state and your local authority will provide the public with stable iodine, or a potassium iodide, pill. This will saturate the thyroid and protect it from absorption of radioactive iodine. For such tablets to be effective, they must be taken within 3-4 hours of exposure. If you live in a high-risk area, or for your own peace of mind, you may want to obtain your own supply in advance. Potassium iodide tablets are inexpensive, do not require a prescription and they have a long shelf life. Although these tablets used to be readily available in pharmacies, they may now require a special order. Your pharmacists will be able to tell you more.

- Many states are developing plans to distribute potassium iodide tablets to the public and create centers (such as schools) from which they will be distributed in times of need. Residents will be advised by radio and TV, as well as notified by loudspeaker or door-to-door if necessary.

Three Ways to Minimize Radiation Exposure

Time: Most types of radioactivity will lose their strength fairly quickly. Limiting the time spent near the source of radiation reduces the amount of radiation exposure you could receive.

Distance: The greater the distance between you and the source, the less radiation you will receive. In case of a serious nuclear power plant accident, local officials will most likely call for an immediate evacuation, thereby allowing you to increase the distance between you and the radiation source as quickly as possible.

Shielding: The greater the amount of heavy and dense materials between you and the source of radiation, the better. This is why local officials could advise you to remain indoors if an accident occurs. In some cases, the walls in your home or workplace would be sufficient shielding to protect you for a short period of time.

Thunderstorms/Lightning

Signs:

Dark towering clouds or distant flashes of lightning and loud thunder usually signal the arrival of a thunderstorm. Severe thunderstorms also may result in heavy rains that can include flash flooding, strong winds, hail and tornadoes.

A thunderstorm is always accompanied by lightning.

Action:

- If you see or hear a thunderstorm, seek shelter in a sturdy building or car.

  - If you feel your hair stand on end, it signifies lightning is about to strike.
  - Because lightning will strike the highest point in an area, move away from trees, towers, fences, telephone lines or power lines, as these will attract lightning.
  - *Never* stand beneath a single large tree that is out in the open.
- To avoid being hit by lightning, make sure you are not the tallest object around, and don't stand beside the tallest object.

- When outdoors, stay away from mountaintops.
- On a golf course you are safer in a cart than standing in the open.
- At home stay out of the bath or shower. Lightning can be conducted through water pipes, telephone lines, electrical wires, TV cables or computers or steel rods in concrete.
- If outdoors and unable to shelter nearby, find a low area and crouch down with your feet together, protecting your ears and head with your hands. Do not lie flat as this makes you a larger target.
- Stay away from metal objects that may attract lightning and act like a lightning rod, such as umbrellas, baseball bats, fishing rods, camping equipment and bicycles.
- If you are in or near water when swimming or boating, get to dry land as quickly as possible.
- Unplug all appliances, including computers, televisions, telephones and air conditioners. The use of electrical appliances during a storm can become dangerous.
- Lightning can occur up to 6 miles ahead or behind a storm, so even if you are under a blue sky, lightning could strike literally out of the blue. If a bolt hits someone it generally flashes over the body but does not enter it. But burns can occur if the person struck by lightning is wearing rings or a belt, as those objects are heated rapidly.
- Since the electrical charge from lightning does not enter the body, it is safe to touch someone to help them. You will not get shocked.
- Lightning *can* strike twice in the same place, so move a victim carefully if possible, and commence CPR if necessary within a few seconds. (*See also Electric Shock, in the chapter dealing with Health, for more information on treating a victim of electric shock*).
- Injuries *can* range from minor, such as temporary blindness and deafness, amnesia, or a ruptured eardrum, to moderate, such as disorientation, some paralysis, and coma, to the most severe, including cardiac arrest, brain damage, and/or trauma to internal organs.

Tornadoes

A tornado is nature's most violent storm, and can wreak devastation in seconds. Tornadoes can occur at almost any time of the year in most parts of the United States, but they especially do so east of the Rocky Mountains.

Terminology:

Tornado Watch: Weather conditions are right for a tornado to occur. Be alert and on the lookout for approaching storms. Note: This does not mean that a tornado will definitely develop.

Tornado Warning: A tornado has been sighted and the situation is very dangerous. Go to a safe place and listen to instructions on a battery-operated radio.

Signs:

A rotating, funnel-shaped cloud that spins like a top and may sound like an airplane or train. It strikes the ground with speeds of up to 250 miles per hour, and can damage an area up to 50 miles long and a mile or more wide.

Prepare:

- Everyone should know the safest places to shelter in your home, at work and school. Choose places away from windows or heavy items that could tip or fall on you.
- If you do not have a basement or storm shelter, find out how to reinforce an interior room on the lowest level of your home to use as a shelter.
- Identify a safe place to hide in case you are outside and unable to reach your shelter.
- Store an emergency kit including a battery-operated radio in your pre-determined shelter location, along with some food and water.

Action:

- If you see or hear a tornado approaching, take cover immediately.
- *Do not open windows.* This would allow the strong wind to enter the structure and cause even more damage.
- If you are in a house or a building, go to the basement or storm cellar. If there is no basement, go to the middle of the lowest level, and if possible, stay in a bathroom or closet for protection. If those options are not available, hide under a sturdy object like a heavy table and protect your head from falling objects by covering it with your arms and hands.
- If you are in a car or mobile home at the time of a tornado warning, quickly go to the basement of a nearby sturdy structure.

Winter Storms/Snowstorms
Signs:

Winter storms can deliver anywhere from several inches of snow falling in a few hours to blizzard conditions that may last for several days and deliver several feet of snow.

Extreme cold, heavy snowfall, freezing rain and high winds usually accompany these storms. Real dangers can result from these extreme storm conditions. People can become trapped in their home, stranded in their car or at work and/or left without utilities or other services.

Preventive measures:

IDEA

If you live in an area that is likely to have winter storms:

- Have the type of emergency heating equipment that can be used if the utilities do not work properly. Plan to have at least one room that you can keep warm where everyone can gather.

- Make sure your home is properly insulated. To prevent excessive heat loss, insulate walls and attic, and caulk and weather-strip doors and windows.

- Install storm windows, or at least cover all windows with plastic on the inside to create a double-glazed effect. This will greatly reduce the loss of heat, and the cost of utilities.

- Before the winter season starts, clear rain-gutters and repair any roof leaks.

- Check the structural ability of the roof to carry unusually heavy weight from the accumulation of snow or water if the drains on a flat roof do not work.

- Prevent water pipes from freezing by wrapping them in insulation or layers of old newspapers and covering with plastic to keep out moisture.

- Allow faucets to drip a little to avoid freezing.

- If the pipes freeze, remove any insulation or layers of newspapers and wrap the pipes in rags. Completely open all faucets and pour hot water over the pipes, starting where they were most exposed to the cold (or where the cold was most likely to penetrate).

- Know how to shut off water valves.

- Stockpile food and water, as well as heating fuel, so that you have emergency supplies available during peak storm periods.

- For extreme conditions, when you may need to evacuate, keep emergency kits in your car(s) as well as at home. Put special, winter-appropriate items in the kit, such as extra blankets, sleeping bags, extra-warm clothing and hand and toe warmers, as well as window scrapers, a shovel and salt or kitty liter that can be used for traction along with the other recommended items such as food and water.

Action:

BEWARE

- Stay indoors during a snowstorm.

- After a snowstorm, if you need or want to go outside, make sure to dress warmly with many layers of clothing. Wear a hat, gloves and warm socks. Many thin layers of clothing will trap warm air, and as a result provide more warmth than a single thick layer.

- If clothing becomes wet, change it as soon as possible for something dry.

- When you are outside, cover your mouth with a scarf to protect your lungs from extremely cold air.
- Take lots of breaks and go indoors periodically to warm up.
- If you become tired, start to shiver, turn pale or any of your extremities such as nose, fingers, ears or toes become numb, immediately return inside and tell anyone that can help you to get warm.
- Avoid overexertion in cold weather because it may strain the heart.

Automobile Concerns in Winter
Preventive Maintenance:
- Make sure that your car is in the best condition possible, and that you are prepared for auto related emergencies. So, before winter sets in, have a mechanic check the following items:

• Antifreeze	• Ignition system
• Battery	• Lights
• Brakes	• Thermostat
• Defroster	• Wipers & windshield washer fluid
• Exhaust System	• Heater
• Flashing hazard lights	• Oil Level

- As recommended, replace existing oil with winter-grade oil or the appropriate grade of oil depending upon the season and your vehicle.
- Install good winter tires. Make sure that the tires have adequate tread. All-weather radials are usually adequate for most winter conditions, although some areas of the country require that vehicles be equipped with chains or snow tires with studs.

IDEA

- Keep a windshield scraper and small broom in the car for ice and snow removal.
- Always maintain at least a half tank of gas during the winter season.
- Keep an In Vehicle Emergency Kit in the car

In addition, if you are going to travel any real distance and in case you become stranded, you should have some cold weather-specific items on hand such as:
- Extra newspapers for insulation
- Several blankets
- Sleeping bags
- Plastic bags (for sanitation)
- Extra gloves, mittens, socks and hat

- Rain gear and extra clothes
- Cards, games and puzzles
- Brightly-colored cloth to use as a flag
- Small sack of sand *(for generating traction under wheel)*
- Set of tire chains or traction mats
- Flashlight

Action to take when Winter Driving:
- If trapped in a car during a snowstorm, remain there and try to keep yourself warm.
- To stay warm, turn on the car's engine for ten minutes every hour. This will conserve fuel and also prevent the engine from freezing.
- While the engine is running, turn on the heater and dome light to help you stay warm. For additional warmth, huddle with another occupant if you are not alone in the vehicle.
- Use newspapers, maps and even the removable car mats for added insulation on windows.
- Do some minor exercises to keep up your circulation. Clap hands and move arms and legs occasionally. Try not to stay in one position for too long. If more than one person is in the car, take turns sleeping. Wake up the sleeping person at regular intervals.
- Try to attract attention by hanging a brightly-colored cloth from the antenna or window, and raise the car's hood. However, if any snow is still falling do not raise the hood.
- To avoid carbon monoxide poisoning when the engine is running, open a downwind window slightly for ventilation and keep the exhaust pipe clear of snow.
- Only leave the car if help is visible *within* 100 yards. You do not want to become disoriented or lost in blowing or drifting snow.

Frostbite: Superficial

Frostbite occurs when the skin and underlying tissues have been exposed in a cold, moist, windy climate. With that in mind, the areas that are most prone to frostbite are the hands, feet, nose and ears.

Symptoms:
- Affected areas of the body are white and waxy, with diminished sensitivity.

Treatment:
- Re-warm the affected areas in a warm (105°F) water bath.
- Use mild analgesics *(acetaminophen)* if the re-warmed area becomes painful. This painful reaction is not uncommon.

Frostbite: Deep

Any part of the body exposed to temperatures less than 44°F for over 7-10 hours is prone to develop severe injury to the tissues that go as deep as the muscles and tendons. Although this temperature is still above the freezing mark, the fact that part of the body is exposed to such a low temperature for such a long time can cause severe frostbite.

Symptoms:
- The affected body tissue appears hard and frozen.

Treatment:
- Hospitalization is required because of this condition's severity. Rapid re-warming should be attempted in the interim.

In the event that immediate hospitalization is not possible:
- Remove any wet clothing and change into dry clothing.
- Put the affected area into *warm* water *(not hot, as it will burn the skin)* to thaw the frozen tissue.
- If warm water is not available, then try to warm the affected parts by using body heat such as putting affected hands under the armpit or using the hands to warm your nose and ears.
- If you must move to get help, do not warm the affected area, as getting additional frostbite to the same area of the body after it has been warmed might increase damage to the tissue.
- Unless there is no alternative, do not walk on frostbitten toes or feet.

BEWARE

Hypothermia

Hypothermia occurs if the body temperature drops below 95°F. The body's temperature control mechanisms that would usually maintain normal body temperature fail. This is commonly encountered when there is immersion in cold water and exposure to cold environments. Wet or damp clothing increase the likelihood of hypothermia.

Persons at increased risk for hypothermia would be older adults; infants; young children; lean individuals; or those with impaired mental function (Alzheimer's patients, those intoxicated or homeless). In addition, anyone trapped in a vehicle in cold weather; anyone suffering from malnutrition, cardiovascular disease, under-active thyroid, extensive psoriasis or any illnesses that decrease physical mobility; or those on certain medications (those used to treat anxiety, depression, nausea or insomnia) all are at increased risk.

Symptoms:
- May develop slowly with gradual loss of mental and physical ability. The victim may be unaware of need for emergency medical care.
- There is usually a period of shivering, although this may stop when the body temperature is below 90°F. Shivering is the body's attempt to make heat.
- Mental functions are affected and will result in reduced attention, lightheadedness, slurred speech and possibly coma.
- Look for the "umbles" - stumbles, mumbles, fumbles and grumbles (mental and physical impairment).
- Breathing may be impaired with abnormally slow breathing. Blood pressure may be low and the pulse weak.

Treatment:
- This serious condition requires hospitalization so that the proper medical care can be delivered. Call 911.
- Perform CPR if the victim is not breathing until assistance arrives.
- If the person's clothes are wet, remove and replace them with warm, dry clothes.
- Warm up the victim by using blankets and keep them in a warm environment.
- Don't apply direct heat, hot water, a heating pad or a heating lamp to the victim. Don't warm just the arms and legs, as the applied heat could cause cold blood to move back to the heart, lungs or brain, resulting in a further drop in core body temperature.
- Do offer warm, non-alcoholic drinks if patient is not vomiting.
- Handle the victim gently because they are at risk for cardiac arrest.

CHAPTER **Nine**

Terrorism

Terrorism is best described as the purposeful intent or action to carry out any act with the purpose of terrorizing or causing panic and disrupting normal ways of life.

There are many parts of the world where there are high instances of terrorism. This is particularly true of volatile political regions. People who live in such places have, by necessity, become more sensitive to anything out of the ordinary, and are constantly on guard for signs of terrorism.

Unfortunately, unlike natural weather-related disasters that can usually be predicted, terrorist attacks will most likely occur with little or no visible sign or warning. Therefore, the best we can do as individuals to help prevent, or at least minimize, the likelihood of terrorist acts is to work in our neighborhood with law enforcement and report anything unusual. We should also work on our personal safety plans. With these activities we will be able to help protect one another. By becoming active, rather than passive, we will be important participants in the national effort to defeat terrorism.

At the very least, working together in our neighborhood will help eliminate local crime and minimize the likelihood of effective terrorist acts.

There is little doubt that at present most individuals in the United States are under-prepared for almost any type of disaster. The fact that you have read this book this far indicates your interest in developing more safety measures and security for yourself and your family. Overall, if more and more people would make the effort to learn how to deal with a variety of emergency situations, the chances of widespread panic in the event of a terrorist attack would be greatly reduced or virtually eliminated.

This chapter, in addition to the added safety you will achieve by learning and practicing what to do in different emergency situations, will also help you gain more confidence. As that confidence grows you can get on with life and not become paralyzed by the fear of possible disasters, or an attack that may never come anywhere near your home town.

PRECAUTIONS

There are lots of precautions you can take and things you can do that will help you reach a comfort level so that you can get on with your life:

- Be alert at all times, and look out for any conspicuous or unusual behavior.
- Trust your intuition when something looks out of place, or someone looks suspicious or is acting in an unusual manner.
- If you see, hear or even suspect a potential problem, report it to the police. They have the training and the tools to determine the seriousness of your report. The more help you can give the police and other agencies, the more they can do to make everyone safer.
- No matter where you live, or how safe you believe your area to be, always be cautious and willing to report anything unusual. Terrorists are trained to hide out and blend into the most unlikely places; this is the reason you need to be vigilant in your neighborhood and at work too.
- Recognize that your neighbors and colleagues depend on you, and that you need to be able to depend on them.
- Be extremely careful if you are in or near places such as city centers, airports, subways, resorts, historic landmarks, sports stadiums and entertainment events where large numbers of people gather. Those areas are regarded as the most likely targets for a terrorist attack. Always make sure you know where the nearest exits are placed and how to get to them if you need to exit quickly.
- When traveling, never leave your luggage or hand baggage unattended, or accept anything from strangers *(see Travel,* Chapter Five.)

- Do not tell strangers where you live or give out *any* personal information.
- If you are in a building that is on fire, try to stay close to the floor and below the smoke. Cover your mouth and nose, preferably with a piece of wet cloth, and leave as quickly and cautiously as possible. Never open any doors without checking the surface with the back of your hand for heat first. If exit routes are blocked, look for an alternate route. Never use an elevator.
- If you are near an explosion, try to leave the area as quickly and calmly as possible. If you are in an affected building and items start to fall, protect yourself under a sturdy table or similar object, and leave when it is safe to do so.
- If you become trapped in debris, cover your mouth, and tap on a wall or pipe so that rescue workers can identify where you are. Shout only when necessary.

BEWARE

- Untrained persons should not try to rescue people from a collapsed building; instead, wait for emergency personnel to arrive and let them know if you suspect that a person is trapped in a particular area.
- If there is a possibility that any hazardous chemical agent is present, authorities will give you instructions and then tell you to either, seek shelter, seal your premises or immediately evacuate. Wait for their instructions.

PERSONAL AND FAMILY PREPARATIONS

- Create your own family disaster plan and make sure to include escape routes, as well as a designated meeting point at each of your most frequented locations (i.e. one for school, home and work. *See* EMERGENCY CONTACT AND MEETING PLACES *Chapter 6 for more specifics).*
- Develop plans and discuss the details covering any potential hazards and threats that are of special concern to your family.
- Practice, practice and practice again. When you frequently practice what you have planned to do in the event of an emergency, your reactions will become second nature. Then, at times of emergency all the planning and practice will help prevent panic.
- Remember there are three main things to consider with all types of disasters:
  - How will you communicate with family?
  - Where will you go?
  - What disaster supplies will you need if you must to go to a shelter for a short time?
- Take First Aid, CPR and disaster-preparedness classes.

- Always keep vital emergency telephone numbers printed and accessible *(in your wallet and in or next to telephones).*

Create the appropriate Emergency Kits to meet your own planning needs.

SUPPLY KIT FOR DISASTERS

IDEA

You need to create a supply kit that will enable you to be self-sufficient for several days in the event of an emergency, as stores may have to close without notice and social services could be disrupted.

To hold your emergency supplies, some of which are heavy, consider using a covered trashcan, preferably one on wheels if it is practical. Alternatively, use some smaller containers that can be carried easily.

In your selected container(s) you should store a variety of long shelf life canned food items such as: tuna, meat, fruit, vegetable juices, milk and soups. These canned goods do not need refrigeration and will not be damaged by heat. Other items to include would be: high energy snacks, peanut butter, jelly, crackers, trail mix, non-chocolate candy, cookies, instant coffee, teabags, and any special baby or elderly foods.

Avoid salty items, as they make you drink more. Note the expiry or "best if used by" dates, and change the items as needed, but at least every 6 months. Other items that should be packed are a simple hand-operated can opener, a cell phone (and charger), goggles (swimmers' type) and respirators-filtered fiber masks with N95 certification. Depending upon your specific needs, you can add other items from the other lists in this book.

PROTECTIVE MASKS

Since there are many types of protective masks on the market it is important to decide what you want to protect against. If it is for protection from smoke or dust in the event of, say, a fire, then there are some adequate protective masks readily available. If on the other hand, you are thinking about protection from chemical or biological elements, then that is very different. For those types of cases you would first of all need to have the mask with you so you can put it on immediately or prior to being in an environment when such an attack occurred. Putting a mask on after the event will not do much good.

There are some very important things to know about masks in general.
1. To be effective any mask must fit correctly. That means when buying one, have it made to fit perfectly.

2. Putting a mask on after exposure is too late.
3. There are three categories of protective masks:

*   Full face (*entire head*), such as a P100 mask that is the best type to protect against biological agents.
*   A ½ face, for mouth and nose. This is a rubbery ½ mask with replaceable filters. It should be approved and reliably tested for you to have any confidence that it will work when needed. The filters have a finite life and they will need to be replaced after a period of time depending upon the make and model.
*   Disposable mask (the mask itself is disposable). This type is a simple filter mask that covers the nose and mouth. It will block tiny particles, and is one of the least expensive masks to purchase.

One of the mask types available, the N95, will eliminate 95% of particles, but not eliminate all. Again, these N95 masks must be fit-tested to be effective and even facial hair will interfere with their efficiency.

None of the above-cited masks will prove effective against chemical agents. It is expected that quite soon NIOSH (National Institute for Occupational Safety and Health) and the Department of Defense will publish specific approval standards for protection against chemical and biological weapons.

See www.cdc.gov/niosh/docs/2009-132

You should get credible advice before you invest in any masks, either for yourself or anyone in your household.

BIO-TERRORISM

Bio-terrorism *(biological or germ warfare)* is a form of terrorism that specifically refers to the intentional release of potentially deadly bacteria, viruses or toxins *(diseases)* into the air, food or water supply, in an attempt to spread infectious diseases

The first indication that a bio-terrorism attack has occurred will probably be noticed with the development of symptoms by those exposed in the days or weeks after the attack. By the time the attack is discovered, the perpetrator is likely to be far away, and almost impossible to discover.

The types of diseases that could be used for bio-terrorism have been known in their natural form for hundreds of years. The difference now is that there are countries that have developed these diseases into weapons with advanced levels of sophistication and delivery methods.

As a result of the experiences gained from the 2001 anthrax contamination in Washington, D.C., the EPA (Environmental Protection Agency) has been developing better methods for decontaminating buildings where bio-terrorism agents have been released.

We also are starting to understand more about how to prepare for, and respond to, biological weapons. Since 2001, many medical professionals across the U.S. have been concentrating on learning about all the implications of infectious diseases, and how they can best help in an emergency. What this means is that doctors and nurses will primarily be the ones in the front line when it comes to bio-chemical attacks, not police or fire personnel. The knowledge they develop will go a long way towards helping to reduce personal anxiety and stress, and minimizing the chances of paralysis in our lives.

Remember that there is a big difference between *living in fear* and *being prepared.*

Although there are a number of potential biological weapons that could be developed and used against the United States, the main threats in the biological arena are anthrax and smallpox. To hopefully help put your mind at ease, I have also listed other possibilities and some information about each. Some of the more outrageous media print startling misinformation from time to time; the real facts about the other biological diseases should not get you overly upset, as most are very unlikely to be used.

THE MOST LIKELY BIO-WEAPON CANDIDATES

Anthrax

Anthrax is an infectious disease that can affect animals and humans. There are three ways the disease can be contracted, depending upon how it enters the body. Via the skin (through broken skin or wounds); by the inhalation of its spores, that can prove the most deadly, especially for the elderly or anyone with a weakened immune system; or by eating contaminated foods.

Anthrax is *not* contagious and cannot be passed from one person to another. There *must* be direct contact with the agent, such as through the handling of infected animals or contaminated products like wool or hide; the inhaling of spores; or eating contaminated food, such as under-cooked meat from infected animals. So while anthrax could potentially be used as a weapon of mass destruction, it would be extremely difficult to convert it to be of use for this purpose. If used at all, it is most likely to be in individual locations and designed to cause disruption.

If there is a known exposure, there are preventive antibiotics that can be given to persons who might have been exposed. These antibiotics are most successful if they are administered before the spores release toxins.

If you develop flu like-symptoms you might think that you have been exposed to anthrax. However, you should assume you have the flu unless there are reported cases of anthrax exposure in your area, or people around you are coming down with the 'flu' and also have suspicious skin sores. A true case of anthrax will probably cause some additional non-flu-like symptoms, such as vomiting, X-ray abnormalities and fluid around the lungs.

A blood culture test can determine if the disease is present, and gives accurate results in 2 to 3 hours. Other tests are available that could indicate the presence of anthrax within 45 minutes. In the case of suspected anthrax, the earliest diagnosis is critical.

Do not take antibiotics "just in case." The drug Cipro is effective, but it should not be taken unless needed. Every emergency room has sufficient antibiotics, and as of this writing, additional supplies can be made available within 12 hours to anywhere in the country.

Also, there is a vaccine for those more likely to come in contact with anthrax, such as members of the military and mission-essential Dept. of Defense employees assigned to a threat area. Since 1970 the vaccine has routinely been administered to veterinarians, laboratory personnel and livestock handlers. Currently supplies of this vaccine are limited. For that reason, and with a need for a more advanced vaccine, the government currently considers it a priority that new vaccines be developed.

Precautions against Mail Tampering

Whenever you are handling mail, the CDC *(Center for Disease Control)* together with the US Postal Service recommend a number of precautions. They advise:

- Never sniff or hold letters close to your nose.
- Never shake or jostle the contents of a package.
- Always wash your hands after opening the mail.

Assume that any mail you receive could be dangerous, especially if it is marked "Confidential," "Personal," "Do Not X-ray" or if it is postmarked from a city that is different from the return address. Other suspicious indications are such things as: excessive postage, misspelled words, a strange or no return address, an incorrect title or just a title and no name. See 'Mail Tampering' in this book.

Check the outside of every envelope or package for any powdery substance that can be seen or felt through the surface. Be cautious if there is any appearance of oily stains, discoloration, odor, an uneven envelope or excessive packaging material.

If you receive any suspicious-looking mail, don't open, shake, or sniff it. Leave the mail where it is, close off the area, make sure nobody else is there and shut off ventilation to that particular room.

Anyone who has touched suspicious mail should immediately wash their hands with soap and water. Then call 911 about your suspicions, and make a list of the names of anyone who was in the area. If possible, put all the clothing anyone was wearing at the time they may have touched the suspicious mail into plastic bags for law enforcement agents. Then shower off with soap and water.

Smallpox

Smallpox is a highly contagious virus that, until recently, used to claim millions of lives every year. However, as a result of the most successful World Health Organization public health effort ever, smallpox was eradicated. As of this writing there is no smallpox disease anywhere in the world.

Although the disease was eradicated worldwide, the virus was kept for scientific purposes in two places: the CDC in Atlanta, and The Institute of Virus Preparations in Moscow. Unfortunately, in violation of an international agreement, Russia produced a quantity of the virus for use in bombs during the Cold War era. It is believed that some of this Russian-produced virus may have fallen into the hands of other nations such as Iraq and North Korea.

In the unlikely event of an outbreak the CDC recommends isolating anyone infected and to vaccinate anyone in contact, such as family and friends, since smallpox does not always prove fatal. There is a vaccine, which, if administered in 1 to 3 days, will offer protection. So, early detection is vital.

Remember that since smallpox is highly contagious, anyone within 6 feet of an infectious person will likely develop the disease. The CDC is currently training local and state health personnel to prepare them for a response to a potential outbreak. However, although it could be used as a biological weapon, smallpox would be extremely difficult to engineer for this purpose as its contagious nature makes it extremely difficult to control.

As routine smallpox vaccinations ended in 1972, everyone in the United States would need to be vaccinated now if there was a widespread outbreak. At this time, sufficient vaccine is available to protect everyone in the United States if it is deemed necessary. As mentioned earlier, if there is an outbreak, vaccination within 3 days will protect against severe symptoms. The administration of vaccinations would most likely be given in homes or, in a major outbreak, at a central location like a school.

A cure for the disease is quite likely to be discovered soon, as there are already many known drugs that will kill the virus in a test tube. Work is currently moving at a rapid pace to determine if these drugs will work with humans and what, if any, the side effects could be.

Other Bio-Weapon Possibilities

The following are not really going to be practical to use as biological weapons, but you should know about them in case you read or hear about them as a threat.

Botulism

This sometimes-fatal disease of the nervous system is acquired from eating spoiled foods in which botulism is present. The disease always begins with muscles in the head, face and neck, and if untreated will work its way down, paralyzing the entire body as it goes.

The nerve toxin that causes botulism is the most poisonous substance known. However, the disease is not contagious, and is usually contracted from uncooked or improperly cooked food. Note: Cooking at or above 185°F for 5 minutes destroys the toxin.

As it is extremely difficult, for the purpose of bio-terrorism, to create an aerosol version of botulism, using the toxin to contaminate food or beverages would be easier.

Usually products that are served cold are more at risk for contamination, such as salad bar items, condiments, unheated beverages, beer, soda and bottled water. Any of these types of products could become dangerous.

Although there is no vaccine for botulism readily available at this time, there is an anti-toxin kept by the CDC that can be shipped immediately throughout the nation twenty-four hours a day. Once it is administered the vaccine will prevent the toxin from circulating; however, it will not reverse any paralysis that has already occurred.

The good news is that American military and civilian scientists announced in August 2002 that they have produced the first drug that can be mass-produced to prevent or treat botulism. A shot of the newly developed drug will protect against the toxin within one to two hours, and the protection will last for three to six months. As a treatment, it is effective when given up to two days after exposure.

Drinking Water

With concern about the safety of drinking water and the threat of contamination by terrorist activities, the EPA as the lead agency for water supplies, together with state and local governments, is working to protect the nation's drinking water from terrorist attack from chemical, biological or radiological agents. The FBI is also working with the local water utilities to provide extra security. So, with this increased security and vigilance, it would be difficult now to introduce large quantities of any contaminant into a reservoir without being detected.

In the unlikely event of an attack on a local water system, the utility would shut down, notify the public of any emergency steps to take (like boiling water before drinking it), and provide an alternative source of water if needed. In any event, the treatment of drinking water before it comes out of the tap will, in many cases, remove the pollution or any threat to public health. Therefore the general water supply is considered to be safe because toxins *(unless present in huge quantities)* cannot survive the treatment of chlorinating and aeration.

In some cases, boiling water can remove some contaminants and kill organisms that can cause disease. However, boiling water that contains lead and nitrate will only increase the concentration and create potential risk. Thus you should check with your local water utility or health department to ask if boiling water is necessary.

Bottled water is not necessarily safer from a terrorist attack than your tap water. Most bottled water is originally from tap water, so it depends on the source of the bottled water and the safety plans and procedures in place at the bottling plant. Bottled water does have its uses, and it is very valuable for all types of emergency situations when tap water is not accessible.

Since September 11th, greater security and safeguards have been instituted at most ports to examine different foods and beverages that are being imported. To provide enhanced security at all entry points, especially for food imports, the U.S Customs has set up a new joint government and business relationship to better control products entering America. The Customs-Trade Partnership against Terrorism (C-TPAT) initiative increases co-operation between importers, carriers, brokers or warehouse operators and manufacturers. This program provides enhanced vigilance and security throughout the supply chain, and also develops a strong anti-terrorist partnership with the trade community. Additional information is available at www.cbp.gov/ctpat

You can learn more about botulism from the CDC, Centers for Disease Control and Prevention Internet web site, www.cdc.gov/botulism

Plague

Plague is an infectious, epidemic disease that is caused by a bacterium. It causes high mortality if not treated promptly.

The disease can be given to humans by infected fleas that have fed on infected rodents such as squirrels, prairie dogs and sometimes even rabbits or cats. (As a precaution, be careful when you are around or near any of these rodents and pets.)

There are a number of different kinds of plague:

- <u>Bubonic plague</u>, which can affect different organs, is like other forms of the plague but is only spread from infected fleas. People with this form of plague are not contagious.
- <u>Pneumonic plague</u>, however, is a form that moves to and develops in the lungs and is then easily passed from one person to another through coughing and sending the bacteria into the air.

If there were an outbreak of this type, wearing a properly fitted N95 respirator mask would provide protection if you were at risk for exposure.

Although all the information about plague seems terrible, it is highly unlikely that this will become a weapon of mass destruction as it is so difficult to control. Currently, although there is no vaccine available to protect against plague, there is an antibiotic treatment that must begin within 24 hours after symptoms first appear in order to be effective.

Tularemia

This is primarily an animal disease that is carried by small mammals such as rabbits, hares, squirrels, voles, mice and water rats. Humans can become infected if bitten by infected ticks or, less often, by flies. Tularemia can also be contracted if any bacteria enter the skin via a wound when handling infected animals or carcasses. Eating undercooked rabbit meat or drinking contaminated water can also cause this disease.

This disease does not spread from person to person.

Tularemia could be developed for use as a bio-weapon. There is a vaccine, but it does not protect against an inhaled form of the disease. The vaccine also takes 14 days to provide protection.

In the event of an outbreak the most effective treatment would be to use an effective antibiotic that the government will immediately make available from the national pharmaceutical stockpile.

Ebola

Ebola is a disease that can be spread from person to person by direct body contact with infected blood, or any body fluids.

Even though there has never been an outbreak of Ebola in the USA, it does exist in some African countries and the virus could be used as a bio-terrorism weapon. However, because it needs to be spread from one individual to another, it would not work very well as a weapon of mass destruction.

There is no vaccine to treat the disease. Any treatment would involve isolation of the affected patient and taking every possible precaution, such as wearing protective clothing and masks, hand washing and other barriers in order to help to contain the disease.

Specifically in the case of this disease, it is critical to avoid any body contact with the fluids or clothing and bedding of those infected, as any of these items can spread the disease among family and friends.

Chemical Weapons

Chemical weapons are less likely to be used by terrorists because they cannot cause the mass casualties that can be inflicted with biological weapons. Their most likely use would be in small areas, to try to cause panic. However, with that said, the most likely chemical weapons would be nerve or blister agents.

Nerve agents are the most toxic of the known chemical agents. They are hazardous in their liquid as well as their vapor states, and can cause death within minutes after exposure.

Blister agents are chemicals that cause burn or blister type wounds and, if inhaled, could damage the respiratory tract.

Both these types of chemical agents can be dispersed in the air, by water or onto surfaces we touch. In the case of a biological attack, it may not be detected for days or weeks. On the other hand, a chemical weapons attack could be detected almost immediately by signs of the chemicals' presence: smell, large numbers of dead insects, fish or animals, numerous surfaces with oily droplets or film, or water surfaces with an oily film.

If you see a number of people on the ground choking, it is probably a sign of a chemical attack. In this instance be extra careful and if possible try to leave the area immediately as the area could still contain hazardous gas. Call 911 as soon as you are able. Try to remain as calm as possible, and get yourself checked as soon as possible by paramedics or a physician. *(Note: If you see a single person on the ground choking or in convulsions, it is probably a heart attack or seizure, and not a chemical attack.)*

Because some chemical agents linger and do not evaporate within 24 hours, exposure to contaminated clothing is quite likely unless precautions are taken immediately. If you believe you have been exposed, remove your clothing as well as contact lenses. All must be placed in plastic bags for disposal. However, if you wear glasses they can be washed carefully and worn again.

Since most chemical agents will penetrate your clothing quickly, remove everything. Do not pull clothing over your head; cut it away instead if at all possible. It is important to wash and bathe, preferably within the first couple of minutes after exposure, with soap and water so as to prevent the chemical from being absorbed or spread over the body.

Disposal of contaminated clothing must be done very carefully using rubber gloves, tongs, sticks or anything else that can be used so that you can avoid touching the items. Put everything into a plastic bag and seal it. Then put that bag into another plastic bag and seal that too. Do not try to dispose of or handle the bags again, but tell the health department or local emergency personnel exactly what you have done with your clothes.

Once you have sealed the contaminated articles, you should then dress in clothes that have not been contaminated. Clothes that have been in a closed closet or in drawers are un-likely to have been contaminated, so you could wear those.

Defending Against Biological Terrorism

With the passage in Congress of the USA Bio-terrorism Act of 2002, funding has been made available to enhance the abilities of the nation's health system to respond rapidly to bio-terrorism.

For national security reasons, as well as general health safety, there is an urgent need to find cures to deal with biological diseases. Aggressive research and development programs focused on developing specific new vaccines, medicines, and diagnostic tests will result in our ability to respond not only in the event of a biological attack, but also to quickly curtail outbreaks of naturally-occurring diseases.

As has been stated, "Disease has long been the deadliest enemy of mankind. Infectious diseases make no distinctions among people and recognize no borders. We have fought the causes and consequences of disease throughout history and must continue to do so with every available means. All civilized nations reject as intolerable the use of disease and biological weapons as instruments of war and terror."

At the time of the September 11th attacks only 1 in 5 hospitals in America had any bio-terrorism preparedness plans in place. Since that time, the other 80% have been changing rapidly for the better.

Among the changes being made is ongoing development of systems and procedures that are aimed at eliminating overlapping work, and establishing better-coordinated methods between public health agencies and laboratories, hospitals and health-care facilities and all levels of emergency personnel.

It is realized that the detection and management of a bio-terrorist attack needs to be a shared responsibility of federal, state, local and private entities. To meet that responsi-bility, the nation is now developing an effective "early warning" system against a possible bio-terrorist attack, and the ability to mount an effective operational response to manage its medical consequences.

State and local medical personnel are a principal line of defense against bio-terrorism. These people are likely to be the first to recognize that we are under a biological attack. Ensuring that these healthcare providers have the appropriate tools and training is critical.

Programs are underway to enhance both state and local health systems, including the improvement of medical communications and disease surveillance capabilities. These improvements are designed to maximize their contribution to the overall bio-defense as well as the general health of the nation.

The healthcare system is being improved, especially in the ability to manage both contagious and non-contagious biological attacks. Hospitals and other healthcare facilities are being modified to be able to better handle a big increase in the demand for their services, should the need arise. There are also changes being made to increase the public health laboratory capabilities.

The Department of Defense is accelerating its efforts to develop better detection, identification, collection and monitoring technology in relation to biological terrorism. Additionally, scientists under Defense auspices are now working to support law enforcement, national security and medical communities by improving the understanding of how potential bio-terrorism pathogens may be made into weapons, transported and disseminated.

The government is providing considerable new funding for contracts and grants to aid the elimination of, and safe transportation and storage for, biological, chemical, nuclear and other weapons, and to establish programs to prevent the proliferation of weapons, components and related technology.

The success of our response to an act of bio-terrorism depends in large measure on the quality and effectiveness of our diagnostic tests, vaccines and therapeutic drugs. Some of the diagnostics, vaccines, and therapeutics available to us today were developed during the Cold War and do not harness the full power of modern biomedical science. Now modern biomedical science is taking a new look at testing, vaccination and drug treatment so as to effectively short-circuit bio-terrorism activity.

Improvements to the communications network that links the acute care providers of our communities with their public health counterparts is also being improved, so that vital information on the detection and treatment of disease can flow swiftly.

At the CDC in Atlanta, the Epidemiological Intelligence Service (EIS) teams of epidemiological scientists are working with their counterparts in foreign countries to provide information, research, awareness, and early warning of potential health threats from abroad on all types of epidemics.

Homeland National Security

As a result of the September 11th 2001 attacks and subsequent intelligence, the Director of Homeland Security position was created; this has evolved into The Department of Homeland Security. This new department has a critical mission to:

- Prevent terrorist attacks within the United States
- Reduce America's vulnerability to terrorism
- Minimize the damage and speed recovery from any attacks that do occur on our soil

In America many federal alert systems are already in operation. Each is tailored and unique to different sectors such as: transportation, defense, agriculture and weather. All of these systems fill vital and specific requirements for a variety of situations in both the commercial and government sectors, and they can also be used for the communication of the nature and degree of terrorist threats.

Notwithstanding all the systems that were already in place none were completely sufficient when the country was being threatened by terrorists. So, in March 2002 the Homeland Security Advisory System was set up to build a comprehensive and effective communications structure for the dissemination of information regarding the risk of terrorist attacks to all levels of government and private industry and the public.

As of March 2004 the National Cyber Alert System was up and running. It is designed to provide timely information about current and emerging threats and vulnerabilities, as well as advice about protecting your computer and network. You can sign up to receive this information via email at http//www.us-cert.gov

Using this advisory system, and based on any threat level, federal agencies will implement appropriate 'Protective Measures.' Before issuing a Threat Advisory Condition, federal agencies assess the threat based on a variety of factors, such as:

- Is the threat credible?
- Is the threat corroborated?
- Is the threat specific and/or imminent?
- How grave is the threat?

Based on the information ascertained, a 'Heightened Threat Advisory Condition' can be declared for the entire nation or for a specific geographic area. These public announcements of threat advisories and alerts can help deter terrorist activity. Once the advisory is announced, the public's extra vigilance may help in detecting and preventing some terrorist activity. The announcement will also notify law enforcement and state and local government officials of the type of threats, inform the public about local or government preparations and provide the public with the appropriate information necessary to respond to the threat.

Until April 2011 a color coded *Five Threat Conditions* warning signals system was in place.

Now, The National Terrorism Advisory System, or NTAS, has replaced the color-coded Homeland Security Advisory System (HSAS). This new system will more effectively communicate information about terrorist threats by providing timely, detailed information to the public, government agencies, first responders, airports and other transportation hubs, and the private sector.

It recognizes that Americans all share responsibility for the nation's security, and should always be aware of the heightened risk of terrorist attack in the United States and what they should do.

Security Information Systems

To help prevent future terrorist attacks, the Department of Homeland Security is developing a system that will ensure more effective use of intelligence and ensure a closer coordination of information and activities across all levels of government. The new system will be capable of combining everything from incoming visitors and those leaving the country, to threat information, and then transmitting any appropriate warning as needed to all relevant law enforcement and public safety officials.

This Homeland Security information project has two key objectives:
- To design and help implement an interagency information architecture that will eliminate duplicate and unwarranted information within the federal government
- To support efforts of the United States to find, track, and respond to terrorist threats within the United States and around the world

Information technology is an important key to keeping track of short-term foreign visitors. It will allow the Immigration and Naturalization Service (INS) to implement an entry-exit system to track the arrival and departure of non-U.S. citizens. This process will dramatically improve the ability to deny access to those individuals who should not enter the United States, as well as speed the entry of routine, legitimate traffic.

In addition to intelligence-gathering capabilities, the FBI and other agencies are working with enhanced technology capabilities so that any planned attack can be disrupted before it can happen.

The struggle against terrorism is a national struggle, and all government agencies, as well as the private sector, must work seamlessly together. Having the right system of communication - content, process, and infrastructure -is critical at all levels to protect and defend against future terrorist attacks, and to effectively manage incidents whenever they should occur.

21st Century Technology and Cyberspace-Security

America's information infrastructure is a source of both great strength and considerable vulnerability. Modern information technology is essential to not only make our nation more prosperous but to make our homeland more secure.

Security on the Internet is being strengthened to protect the critical infrastructure. This is being achieved through a voluntary public and private partnership, including corporate and non-governmental organizations.

The Critical Infrastructure Protection Board has, since October 2001, organized national committees to streamline initiatives and address emergency planning. The board has initiated research into potential methods to isolate and protect critical government information that carries vital communications. It has fostered an unprecedented national government-industry partnership to provide alerts and warnings for cyberspace threats.

Other components of this national strategy include:
- National Infrastructure Protection Plan This provides a unifying framework to integrate efforts to enhance the safety of the US infrastructure.
- Priority Wireless Access. This is a wireless priority access program that will give authorized users priority on the cellular network, so that first responders have priority for cellular phone coverage during emergencies.
- National Infrastructure Simulation and Analysis Center at the Department of Energy. This Center promotes collaboration between federal research efforts and the private sector to better understand the dependencies between the Internet, our critical infrastructure and our economy.
- Advanced Encryption Standard. This is designed to protect sensitive but unclassified information. In limited circumstances, it may also be used for classified national security information. This new standard of encryption is expected to be used widely in the private sector and benefit millions of consumers and businesses.
- Cybercorps Scholarships. To provide scholarship funding into universities across America, the Cybercorps Scholarship for Service program encourages college students to become high-tech computer security professionals within the

government. Managed by the National Science Foundation and the Office of Personnel Management, this program also helps to build academic programs at universities in the area of computer security.

Government and industry are currently undertaking a tremendous amount of work that is geared to better assure our safety. The bottom line, however, is that the nation depends on each of us to do our part in the overall protection of the values we cherish.

Should you have any questions or need additional information about Homeland Security, the following address may prove useful:

Federal Bureau of Investigation
935 Pennsylvania Avenue NW
Washington, D.C. 20535
Or call Tel: 202.324.3000

CHAPTER **Ten**

Neighborhood Security

Since the September 11th, 2001 and subsequent terrorist attacks, most Americans have come to the realization that we are no longer secure and safe in our own country and isolated from overseas terrorism. Although this realization is disconcerting, we have to realize that the kinds of terrorism we see on the nightly news broadcasts from around the world could happen here.

Unfortunately we must also acknowledge that even in our own neighborhood there could be dangers other than from accidental fires and the usual types of crimes that have been perpetrated in the past. We know too well, from recent events and activities, that there is a possibility that terrorists, who are trained and determined to cause death and destruction in America, and to disrupt our way of life, could be living or working very close to us.

Especially now, in addition to all the usual reasons to become involved in neighborhood security, there is an urgency to work on both our personal and neighborhood safety plans. By working with others that we trust, we can learn, plan, organize and practice what would need to be done in various types of disasters. By working with our families and neighbors, and practicing what we learn, we will be far better able to cope in the event of an actual emergency.

As safety and security is also a matter of national importance, it is important, if at all possible to volunteer some of our time and join community organizations or neighborhood groups. There is no doubt that by working together we will become stronger within our own neighborhoods. It follows that as more and more neighborhood groups arrange to work together we will become even stronger as a country.

The clear advantage of having a local neighborhood group is that it provides additional security and safety. There is no doubt that when we work as a team with neighbors, anyone or anything in our area that is out of the ordinary can more easily be identified and reported immediately to the authorities.

Neighborhood groups are usually formed to improve safety, discuss the concerns of their members and work to resolve local problems. The concerns addressed are sometimes confined to a particular neighbor's problem and at other times it might involve something that can affect the entire area. There are probably quite a few things that you can think of in your own neighborhood that could do with some attention. It could even be a problem with which you could use some help near your home. Well, there is no time like the present to take the next step, make up your mind and get involved.

One obvious advantage to becoming a member of your neighborhood group is that you will most likely meet people with whom you have a lot in common. As a start, you and your neighbors have a mutual interest in making your homes and families safer by making arrangements for everyone to look out for one another.

Becoming involved in your neighborhood group is the *right* thing to do. And since you are going to benefit in many ways, you should seriously consider making the effort as soon as possible to join and devote some of your own time to help achieve common goals.

It is a proven fact that wherever neighborhood groups have been formed and run properly, the residents have successfully launched programs to achieve the goals they have set for their area.

There is probably a neighborhood group already in your area. The local library, police or fire department will help you to find out where and when they meet. The meetings are usually not very frequent, but worthwhile.

Each neighborhood group of residents usually makes their own arrangements for programs. They arrange schedules so that most or all will be able to attend, and receive information, training and educational programs from law enforcement, fire, first aid and other agencies. In a short time, whether as individuals or a group, you will have gained sufficient knowledge and training that, in the event of an emergency, you will be able to be of help to emergency personnel.

It has been shown that belonging to and participating in neighborhood activities is also beneficial to personal health. A study by the Centers for Disease Control and Prevention has shown that when people feel good about their neighborhood they are more likely to exercise. It appears that belonging to and participating in activities with the group increases the level of comfort and safety making outdoor exercise more appealing.

From time to time, the group in your area will probably organize social gatherings so that everyone gets to know one another. At other times they will arrange to have speakers come to a meeting and give a talk on a specific subject. When there are talks about safety you'll learn firsthand from the experts about the correct things to do, how to react and how to be better organized to handle a number of different potential emergencies.

A useful topic from an invited law enforcement officer could be a course about the right ways to report unusual activities, so that the police can act decisively with the least loss of time. You might even have a speaker come to your group to talk about the best ways to talk to children about disaster planning without frightening them, and how to get their active participation in such planning.

Since safety in all its facets is of paramount importance to everyone, speakers from law enforcement, fire, paramedics, Red Cross and other agencies are likely to come to your meetings, if invited, to provide advice and training.

You, your family, friends, neighbors and fellow workers can all play active roles to improve security. There is no doubt that the combined safety and security activities of tens of thousands of citizens in neighborhood groups across the country would have a major impact in helping to reduce crime in general. There would also be less likelihood of further terrorist acts if the terrorists had much more difficulty in hiding their identity and intentions. What a great way to ensure that life goes on in an orderly way throughout the country!

Although you can learn a lot on your own from reading or searching on the Internet, the support you can gain from within a neighborhood group can be invaluable.

There are many things you can learn about that would be potentially lifesaving in an emergency. These could be things you should or should not do, and places you should or should not go to. You should know the best ways to get help in an emergency situation. You can learn how to let the authorities know correctly that someone either is, or is not, in a burning building, so that others do not needlessly put their lives at risk. There are correct ways to report unusual activities in your area that will allow the police to act decisively with the least loss of time. It has been proven that with the correct information and some hands-on training and practice, you and your neighbors can make a significant difference. In effect you will be able to relieve some of the pressure that falls on police, fire and medical personnel in the event of natural disasters, emergencies or even a terrorist attack.

Since everyone in your neighborhood is learning the same skills, you will develop confidence in each other. This confidence will enable you to cope better, on a daily basis, with everyday neighborhood security and safety issues. You will certainly feel more secure in calling on neighbors in the event of an emergency.

There is no time like the present to talk with your family and friends about making the important plans for security that you have delayed for too long. Your neighbors could prove to be a great help in getting you started, keeping you on the right track, and helping you to put your plans into practice. Remember that everyone around you has a vested interest in your safety, as you have in theirs.

A NEIGHBORHOOD NETWORK

Neighborhood groups are formed for a variety of reasons. Usually the basic purpose is to develop a local network so that people nearby can share skills, information and supplies towards a common goal. To achieve these goals, the groups usually discuss their priorities and then arrange to provide education and prepare for potential emergencies or catastrophes. On the lighter side many of these groups also create activities for "getting-to-know-you" type of events and for holiday celebrations.

You should understand that if you become a founder or part of an existing neighborhood group, it does not mean that you'll have to be heroic, or put your life at risk. Nor should the network take much of your time, as meetings are usually quite short unless there is a special presentation.

It is through working with our families, friends, business associates, neighbors and the community at large that we will be helping to develop a safer and more secure environment for our families. Ultimately, of course, everyone will benefit as we create a more secure region and country.

Neighborhood Watch Program

A popular type of neighborhood group that is prevalent around the country is called 'Neighborhood Watch.' These groups are formed primarily to allow neighbors to look out for each other and to increase their community's safety. Their programs are organized not to be, or to act, as vigilante groups, but to reveal the willingness of all the neighbors to look out for anything suspicious in their area, and report the activity to law enforcement as well as to each other in the group.

In many communities there are families in which both parents are working and the neighborhood is relatively deserted during the daytime. In these areas it is particularly important for the group to meet with the local police and let them know the situation so that, along with the residents who are usually at home, they can help to provide some additional protection for particular properties.

One of the prime activities of the Neighborhood Watch program is crime prevention, which focuses on ways to help eliminate the opportunity and the places where crimes can be committed. This is done through learning and activities programs in cooperation with law enforcement. It allows everyone in the group to give something back to their neighborhood by working together to make the area safer and improve the quality of life.

If any type of disaster occurs and help is needed quickly, the best people to assist you are those who are living near you and whom you know you can trust. By creating or belonging to the group in your area, you make an agreement with others to look out for and help each other when there is a pre-determined need. With the right organization in your neighborhood, you can help to prevent crimes and other problems in the most effective way: before they start!

If there is no existing group in your area, here are some suggestions and ideas that will help you to create and maintain a neighborhood group in preparation for emergencies.

IDEA

- Call a meeting of neighbors to create an in-depth preparedness plan.
- Develop a network for sharing skills and supplies.
- Ask for people to volunteer as coordinators who will make lists of the neighbors who have skills, equipment and tools that may be useful during or after a disaster.
- Create specific committees and make assignments for each participant's responsibility. These responsibilities could include such jobs as looking after new members, secretarial work, home watch management, first aid supplies control or communication, transportation and search and rescue.
- The police, fire departments and the Red Cross offer training in many areas of safety and emergency preparedness. Just contact your local representatives to discover the services they can offer your group.
- Arrange for education, and encourage neighbors to train in first aid, CPR, fire suppression, search and rescue, and damage assessment.
- Establish a meeting place, in the event of a disaster, for reuniting and for checking in.

- Set up a place to store vital medical and survival supplies in the neighborhood.
- Set up areas for triage, first aid and treatment.
- Make plans to care for those with special needs such as the elderly, the disabled, and those with special medical conditions or limited English skills.
- Authorize people to turn off utilities, if necessary, for safety reasons.
- Meet at least twice a year. One time should be to review and update plans and to include any new members. The other time is for practice drills where everyone becomes familiar with his or her role.

From experiences throughout the country it has been found that there are generally five steps that are necessary to create and maintain a neighborhood group in preparation for disasters or emergencies:

1. Plan strategies that address problems in your area.
2. Build a good relationship between law enforcement officers and the residents.
3. Assess and discuss the neighborhood needs, and reach agreement between law enforcement and residents as to what is important to the neighborhood.
4. Select and train volunteers and maintain motivation.
5. Develop meaningful objectives to keep enthusiasm going. This can mean developing on-going projects such as building a playground or painting over graffiti or any other project that everyone agrees upon as important to the neighborhood.

To learn more about Neighborhood Watch programs, contact your local police department, sheriff or satellite office, and ask for help from the Community Relations Officer, Community Service Officer or Community Coordinators.

Benefits of Neighborhood Watch:
- Neighbors get to know each other and work together towards a mutual objective.
- Neighbors look out for each other and solve problems in their communities with the problem-solving techniques learned through the Neighborhood Watch program.
- Citizens are trained to recognize and report suspicious activities in their neighborhoods.
- Crime prevention strategies, such as creating better security for your home, are taught.
- The size of the law enforcement task force in any given area is limited; therefore, citizen involvement is essential to help fight crime. With training from law enforcement, fire and medical personnel, you and your neighbors can become better informed and make a big difference in an emergency.

- Your neighbors will most likely be the first ones to spot a burglar breaking into your home when you are out or away. If they see someone attacking or threatening you, they will be the ones who will call for help.
- Neighbors can befriend local children and keep them from joining gangs.
- As a group, neighbors can file suit in small claims court to shut down undesirable places like crack houses.
- Neighbors can also arrange the trimming of overgrown shrubs, and pressure the city to improve lighting to remove hiding places for criminals.
- Training programs are developed within the group to meet local changing needs.

Neighborhood Anti-Terrorism Programs

Neighborhoods just like yours, as well as the places where people shop, work or play, are all areas that need crime control. Almost every area today can be prone to criminal activities and even a potential site for acts of terrorism.

In addition to the general neighborhood programs, government as well as law enforcement agencies such as The National Sheriff's Association, have developed anti-terrorist plans. These will help neighborhoods and groups of citizens better understand what needs to be done to prevent future disruptive attacks. These new programs have been created to educate citizens on the detection of potential terrorist activity. By learning about and becoming active participants we can each become critical aids in the detection, disruption and elimination of terrorism.

As a result of this special planning effort, law enforcement agencies will be working more closely than ever with neighborhood groups to enable residents to recognize signs of potential terrorist activity. Any information you and your group can provide to law enforcement about unusual activities or unknown persons in your neighborhood will make your contribution to the detection, prevention and disruption of terrorism very important.

No matter how trivial it seems, *let the police know if anything appears unusual.* They will decide what to do. They would rather have too much information than too little. Even anonymous tips are helpful.

CRIME PREVENTION

Ten Things Adults Can Do To Stop Violence:
1. Set up a Neighborhood Watch or a community patrol that works with police.
2. Make sure your streets and homes are well lit.

3. Make sure that all the youth in the neighborhood have positive ways to spend their spare time, in activities such as: organized recreation opportunities, tutoring programs, part-time work and volunteer opportunities.

4. Build a partnership with police that is focused on solving problems *in advance* rather than reacting to crises. Make it possible for neighbors to report suspicious activity or crimes without fear of retaliation.

5. Take advantage of "safety in numbers" to hold rallies, marches and other group activities to show you're determined to drive crime and drugs out of your neighborhood.

6. Clean up the neighborhood! Involve everyone - teens, children, senior citizens. Graffiti, litter, abandoned cars and run-down buildings send a signal to criminals that you don't care about where you live or each other. Call the local public works department and ask for help in cleaning up.

7. Ask local officials to use some new or alternative ways to get criminals out of your building or neighborhood. These include enforcing anti-noise laws, housing codes, health and fire codes, anti-nuisance laws and drug-free clauses in rental leases.

8. Work with schools to establish drug-free zones.

9. Work with recreation officials to do the same for parks.

10. Develop and share a phone list of local organizations that can provide counseling, job training, guidance and other services that can help neighbors.

Reporting a Crime

Eyewitness information is frequently the key to solving many crimes. To be most effective it is important to call the police immediately: every second counts! Tell the police everything that you remember. Details are important, and no detail is too small or trivial. And never disturb a possible crime scene so that every type of evidence is preserved. It's this kind of cooperation that will definitely help the police make your neighborhood a safer place.

The following is a list of the types of questions you might be asked when reporting a crime. Don't try to memorize the questions. Just read through the list to familiarize yourself with the types of questions that you are likely to be asked by the police.

You will probably be asked to relate:
*   What occurred?
*   When did it occur?
*   Where did it occur?
*   Who was involved?
*   What was said?

- How many people were involved?
- What did they look like?
- What did their vehicle look like?
- What are the names, numbers and addresses, if you have knowledge of them?
- What was done or taken?
- Were weapons used? What kind?
- Which way did they go?
- Were there witnesses? If so, who?
- Was anyone injured and in what way?
- What other information do you think is important?

The fact that you have read this list, and may remember some of it around the time of a crime, could help you provide the police with the answers they need to track down the likely perpetrators.

Graffiti is a Crime

There are usually a number of things that could need attention in a neighborhood. Perhaps there are unsafe sidewalks, poor street lighting or one of a dozen of other things. Whatever the problem, the easiest way to get it solved is with the help of a well-organized neighborhood group.

Graffiti is one of those things that can be a real problem. Perhaps it's not on the walls on your street, but it could be on your way to work or near a school. Everyone should understand that it's not only a nuisance and an eyesore, it is illegal. Furthermore, the presence of graffiti can have a specific meaning or purpose, as most of it is the result of gang activity.

Gangs use graffiti to mark their territory, identify conflicts between gang members or promote the sale of illegal drug use. It can also be the result of juveniles "tagging" or marking walls or any locations with graffiti simply for peer recognition. With a good neighborhood watch program and co-operation from law enforcement, you can greatly reduce, or in most cases eliminate, graffiti in your area.

Here are some things you need to know about graffiti:
- Graffiti decreases the value of your property and neighborhood, and will probably lead to more crime and unsavory elements near where you live.
- Leaving graffiti on your property is a temptation, and an open invitation, for more vandalism and crime. If you discover graffiti on your property, remove it immediately.

At the least, have it removed within 24 hours. By doing so, you are discouraging further vandalism.

- Use matching paint to cover graffiti whenever possible so that you do not create a "canvas" for more graffiti. To remove the paint, try using 'Graffiti Remover' on glass, unpainted metal surfaces, brick and walls, or M.E.K. *(Methyl Ethyl Keytone)* on glass or previously painted metal surfaces.
- Report all instances of graffiti to the police and prosecute all apprehended vandals as a sign that you "mean business".
- Do not try and apprehend, on your own, any vandals you see who are drawing graffiti. Instead, get a good description of the person and their vehicle, if any, and make a report to the authorities.

Crime-Proofing Your Home

As discussed earlier in Chapter Six, one of the most common crime problems for homeowners is burglary. One in every ten homes is burglarized every year, and almost everyone will have something of value stolen from them one way or another during their lifetime. For information on creating a secure environment both in and around your home, and for the best ways to prevent a burglary, please review, the Crime-Proof Your Home material earlier in this book. Within that section there is also some material that covers how to act if you are a victim, or present, during a robbery.

Keeping Children Safe in Your Neighborhood

As part of your neighborhood program, there should be discussions as well as some invited specialty speakers on the subject of keeping children safe in various situations. There are a lot of things that most parents need to learn about this topic so they can help their children be safe.

One of the great things about children is their natural trust in people, especially in adults. As a result, it's sometimes difficult for parents to teach their children how to balance this trust with caution. But kids today need to know common-sense rules that can help keep them safe, and at the same time build the self-confidence they need to handle emergencies. Since common sense is not always common, a lot of things need to be taught carefully to children.

Would children in your neighborhood know what to do if...
- They got lost at a shopping mall?
- A nice-looking, friendly stranger offered them a ride home after school?

- A friend dared them to drink some beer or smoke a joint?
- The babysitter or a neighbor wanted to play a secret game with them?

The following are a number of basic safety measures that the children in your neighborhood need to know. These are relatively easy measures for parents to teach, so devote some time to letting your children know how to stay safe.

The Basics

IDEA

- As soon as they are old enough, make sure children know their full name and address with city and state, as well as their phone number with the area code.
- Be sure that kids know to call 911 or "O" in emergencies, and that they know how to use a cell-phone, landline or a public phone. Get them to practice making emergency calls with a make-believe phone.
- Tell them never to accept rides or gifts from someone that both they and you don't know well.
- If in doubt about someone, they should know to ask for a code word. (See www.GettingSafer.com for more information about the use of code words.)
- Teach children to go to a store clerk, security guard or police officer, or a mother with kids, for help if they are lost.
- Set a good example with your own actions. Lock doors and windows, and see who's there before opening the door.
- Take the time to listen carefully to children's fears and feelings about people or places that scare them or make them feel uneasy. Tell them to trust their instincts.

At School and At Play:

- Encourage children to walk and play with friends, not alone. Tell them to avoid places that could be dangerous - vacant buildings, alleys, playgrounds or parks with broken equipment and litter.

BEWARE

- Teach children to settle arguments with words, not fists, and to walk away when others are arguing. Remind them that taunting and teasing can hurt friends and make enemies.
- Make sure your children, and those of your neighbors, take the safest routes to and from school, stores, and friends' houses. Walk the routes together with your children, and point out places they could go for help, if needed.

- If you see a neighbor's child walking somewhere unsafe, be sure to let their parents know. Both the parent and the child may be unaware of the danger.
- Encourage kids to be alert in the neighborhood, and to tell an adult - you, a teacher, a neighbor, a police officer - about anything they see that doesn't seem quite right.
- Check out the school's policies on absent children: are parents called when a child is absent?
- Check out daycare and after-school programs. Review certifications, staff qualifications and rules on parent permission for field trips. Also check teachers' reputations in the community, any programs involving parent participation, and policies on parent visits.

All precautions and any practicing that involves your children can and must be done in ways that should not frighten them. But above all, they still need to realize that they always need to be observant and careful to be safe.

Protecting Children from Sexual Abuse

This difficult subject should not be ignored. If a child is not informed about what to do or how to react, sexual abuse can result too easily. Discussing the topic after the fact is much too late. As a parent:

- Let your child know that he or she can tell you anything, and that you'll be supportive.
- Teach your child that no one - not even a teacher or a close relative - has the right to touch him or her in a way that feels uncomfortable, and that it's okay to say no, get away, and tell a trusted adult.
- Don't force kids to kiss or hug or sit on a grown-up's lap if they don't want to. This freedom gives them control and teaches them that they have the right to refuse.
- Always know where your child is and whom they are with.
- Tell your child to stay away from strangers who hang around playgrounds, public restrooms and schools.
- Be alert for changes in your child's behavior that could signal sexual abuse. Psychological warning signs include: sudden secretiveness, withdrawal from activities, refusal to go to school, unexplained hostility toward a favorite babysitter or relative or increased anxiety. Some physical signs of abuse include bedwetting, loss of appetite, venereal disease, nightmares and complaints of pain or irritation around the genitals.
- If your child has been sexually abused, report it to the police or a child protection agency immediately.

- If your child is a victim of any crime, from stolen lunch money to sexual abuse, don't blame him or her. Listen and offer sympathy. They need to understand that they can talk to you.

Helping Children Learn to Handle Conflict

Children learn how to manage conflict in the same way they learn to do many other things, by watching what goes on around them. They learn from you, from teachers and other adults, from other children, and from television, movies, and other media. So how can you help them learn the best strategies? Here are some tips you may find helpful in your role as parent.

- Give your child some special time each day. This may be really tough in today's busy world, but experts tell us that 20 minutes of positive adult attention per day dramatically reduces a child's aggressive behavior.
- Teach your child to ask for attention *constructively*. Sometimes the purpose of a fight with a brother or sister is simply to get attention.
- Encourage your child to ask for attention by expressing his or her needs.
- Catch your child doing something right. Praise your child for doing well, rather than reprimanding them when mistakes are made.
- Teach your child to recognize the feelings of others. You can point out when someone is happy, sad, scared or worried and so on. When children learn to recognize what someone else is feeling, they are better able to respond appropriately.
- Listen first, and then help your child negotiate a solution. Acknowledge your child's feelings about a conflict before helping to work out a solution.
- Use positive methods to discipline your child. Avoid using physical punishment and yelling. Through your example, your child will see that force is not the best or only choice.

The following are some additional topics on the web site of the National Crime Prevention Council at http://www.ncpc.org. This web site is well worth a visit. It has information on a wide range of topics such as: At Home Alone; Back-to-School Safety; Raising Streetwise Kids; Bullying; Cell Phone Safety; Conflict Resolution; Halloween Safety; Media Literacy; Guns and Other Weapons; Bicycle Safety and Drugs & Alcohol. The site also contains a section devoted especially to children using the McGruff® characters.

In 1980, the McGruff® character arrived with his motto "Take A Bite Out Of Crime®." People began to change their minds and take charge of crime prevention themselves. Today, more than three out of four Americans believe they personally can take actions to reduce crime, and that their neighborhoods and communities can act to prevent crime.

McGruff® is a registered mark of the National Crime Prevention Council.

Protecting Yourself

To reduce your risk of being attacked there are a number of things you can do, depending upon the circumstances. Some may seem very obvious, but they still should be stated.

If you are walking outdoors at night, avoid dark and unfamiliar places. Instead of walking alone, try and go out in a group, walk with purpose and avoid contact with strangers. Don't show off, and never flash money or jewelry. Most assailants usually look for an "easy" target and a secluded place in which to commit their crime. Don't make it easy for them by making yourself a target.

Unfortunately, even if you are careful, it may not be possible to prevent an attack of some sort. For that reason, you should spend a few minutes now thinking about what you could do in case someone tries to attack you.

By formulating different scenarios and responses, you will be better able to react quickly and automatically. However, no matter how you try to prepare, how many self-defense classes you have taken or how carefully you have thought through what you would do if you were attacked, the reality of being attacked will be very different than expected.

Each attacker is motivated for a different reason and may react to the same situation differently. What might frighten off one attacker may cause another to become more aggravated. Therefore:

- You should use your own judgment and commonsense if you believe that someone is approaching you with ulterior motives.
- Remain calm and act as rationally as possible.
- If possible, distract or divert the assailant and run towards an open business or group of people while screaming, "Help, Police!"
- Use whatever resources you have available to your advantage. Throw whatever you are carrying or wearing at the person to distract them. If you have an umbrella, use it to stab the person; use a purse or package to push the assailant away.
- Scream loudly and constantly to attract the attention of people nearby.
- If you are not able to get away, try talking with your assailant. Look them directly in the eye and be verbally and physically assertive. Try and convince the attacker that you are not an easy target.
- Stall for time.
- Try not to let the assailant move you to a different place or into a car.
- *If the attacker has a weapon*, think carefully about what you should do. Consider your own strength and physical abilities, what you think the physical abilities of your assailant are, and your location and how successful you think you will be. If

you believe that you will not succeed escaping or fighting off the attacker then just wait and look for another opportunity.

- Call the police immediately after you are free. If there are any witnesses, ask them to speak with the police as well. Any clue that you provide may be helpful in capturing the attacker and preventing them from assailing someone else.

- Carefully reconsider before you "arm yourself" with guns, knives or chemical sprays for your personal protection. Many of these items are illegal or could be taken from you and used against you by an attacker. Also, the legal system in this country can be tricky, and you might be held accountable if some "innocent" person gets hurt. There have been many cases where an intruder or attacker has ended up winning a lawsuit even though they were the one carrying out an attack or burglary.

EMERGENCY KITS

As a part of any overall safety strategy you will need to prepare some emergency kits for various eventualities. To make the selection of items in each category as simple as possible, a list of items for each type of kit follows. For your own purposes, select some or all of the items for each kit, depending upon your individual needs.

Just like everything else, the kits will not create themselves. You need to assemble them, so get started as soon as possible. Remember you will need to keep your emergency kits up-to-date, so track the expiry dates on such items as food, batteries etc. You can use a reminder application on your smart phone to make sure you don't forget. Supplies should be replaced when necessary, and everything checked at least twice a year.

You may find it helpful to make up your own list of the types of kits you need and the items that go in each kit. Check off the items as you assemble each kit; in this way, you can track your progress.

There are four basic kits listed here. Each kit is important in its own way, depending upon your specific need and circumstance.

The Four Basic Kits:
1. <u>Grab and Go Kit.</u> This should be a light and easily portable Emergency Supply Kit.
2. <u>Vehicle Emergency Kit.</u> This is a kit that is kept in your vehicle.
3. <u>Expanded Emergency Supply Kit.</u> This is a kit that would be used in a major emergency together with your Grab and Go kit. The two would be taken together, so the items in each should not be duplicated.

4.   <u>First Aid Kit.</u> With the advice of your medical practitioner you can select the items to assemble in this First Aid Kit that you would take with you in the event of an emergency. It should contain several days supply of prescription medication.

1. Grab and Go Kit

Items for this Grab and Go kit should be put into an easy-to-carry duffel bag, a small box or a container. This kit should be kept in an accessible place along your escape route, near the exit from your home.

For all medical-related items it is recommended that you speak with your doctor, who is familiar with your family's medical profile, for suggestions on what to pack.

- A copy of this book so you'll have useful information with you.(must be kept secure so there is no possibility of ID theft)
- Flashlight with plenty of batteries
- Battery- powered radio with extra batteries
- First Aid Kit with a first aid manual. (See #4 later in this section for First Aid Kit contents)
- Anti-diarrhea medicine
- List of doctor and pharmacy telephone numbers and addresses (keep up-to-date)
- Prescription medication(s) in the original bottle(s), along with a copy of the prescription (keep updated)
- Water – at least 2 liter bottles per person (change every 6 months)
- Food, packaged and non-perishable items (energy bars, nuts, dried fruit - note any expiry dates)
- Food and extra water for pets (check dates of products)
- Pocketknife
- Electrical/duct tape
- Sanitary items, i.e. diapers or feminine hygiene products (sanitary napkins also can be used as emergency bandages for wounds).
- Toilet paper, two rolls
- Cash, including a roll of quarters
- Map of the area
- Extra set of car keys
- Whistle
- Lightweight jacket/windbreaker.
- Large plastic bags and self-seal plastic bags for waste disposal or water protection
- Work gloves

- Fiber masks (like healthcare workers wear)
- Goggles
- Matches/lighter and candles (do not use unless certain that there are no gas leaks)
- Pre-moistened towels
- Soap
- Emergency blanket or thermal/aluminum foil space blankets
- Writing materials (paper and pencils)
- Adjustable pipe wrench for turning off gas and water (although it is really preferable to have these items already placed beside each utility)
- Rope
- Copies only, <u>not originals</u> of important papers. You should store some or all of the following documents in the kit in a sealed waterproof bag or container:
  - Driver's license or personal identification
  - Social security card
  - Medical and glasses prescriptions (keep updated with each change)
  - Small selection of your most important photographs
  - Important telephone numbers and addresses
- Reminder: Make sure you have originals of the following documents in your safe-deposit box and copies in a safe place but not in your home or in your kit:
- Proof of residence (copy of deed or lease)
- Insurance policies
- Copy of birth and marriage certificates
- Stocks, bond and other negotiable certificates
- Copy of wills, deeds and recent tax returns

2. Vehicle Emergency Supplies Kit

Depending upon the circumstances, your vehicle emergency kit should also contain some of the items listed above in the Grab and Go Kit. Look at the list and determine what you need. The kit should definitely contain the following, and should be stored in the trunk of your automobile:

- Small bag of abrasive material (sand, salt, kitty litter, gravel or traction mats) for hazardous or icy road conditions
- Ice scraper
- Small first aid kit
- Flashlight and batteries.
- List of personal emergency telephone numbers.

- Shovel
- Cloth/roll of paper towels
- Booster cables (jumper leads; know how to use them)
- Road map
- Window-washing solvent
- Warning devices (flares or triangles)
- Brightly-colored cloth, to attach to the antenna to signal that you need assistance
- Pen and paper
- Disposable camera

3. Expanded Emergency Supply Kit

Assemble this kit in addition to all the items in the lighter and more portable Grab and Go Kit.

Because of the greater number of items this expanded version of your emergency supply kit is not easily portable. However, ideally each family should have the items they have selected from the list below stored in a waterproof container that can be taken out of the house in the event of a major disaster when time is too short, and there would be little or no time to gather all these things.

- A copy of this book which contains handy emergency information (Make sure it is secure so there is no opportunity for ID theft)
- Flashlight with plenty of batteries
- Battery- powered radio with extra batteries
- First aid kit with first aid manual
- Anti-diarrhea medicine
- Prescription medication(s) in the original bottle(s), along with a copy of the prescription
- List of doctor and pharmacy telephone numbers and addresses
- Water, a three-day supply. Estimate one gallon per person per day.
- Food that does not require cooking, is not perishable and has high energy (for example, canned goods, energy bars, peanut butter, trail mix, dried fruits, nuts)
- Manual can opener
- Eating utensils (plates and flatware)
- Food and extra water for pets
- Disinfectants- iodine tablets or chlorine bleach (add eight drops per gallon to water to purify if necessary)
- Fire extinguisher (ABC type)

- Pocketknife
- Utility knife
- Plastic sheeting
- Electrical/duct tape
- Lightweight jacket/windbreaker
- Change of clothing and sturdy footwear for each household member
- Rain gear
- Sleeping bag or blanket and pillow for each family member
- Thermal/aluminum foil space blanket
- Sanitary items such as diapers or feminine hygiene products (sanitary napkins also can be used as emergency bandages for wounds)
- Toilet paper (a couple of rolls)
- Items that infants or elderly household members might require (Infants- formula, diapers, bottles, powdered milk and medications; Elderly- heart and high blood pressure medication, insulin, prescription drugs and denture needs)
- Entertainment for children (books, magazines, toys)
- Cash, checkbook, travelers' checks, ATM and credit cards. Include a roll of quarters
- Map of area
- Extra set of car keys
- Whistle
- Large plastic and zip-type plastic bags for waste disposal or water protection
- Work gloves
- Goggles
- Fiber masks (like healthcare workers wear)
- Matches/lighter and candles *(do not use until certain that there are no gas leaks)*
- Pre-moistened towels
- Soap
- Writing materials
- Charcoal grill or camping stove for outdoor cooking
- Tools- Adjustable pipe wrench for turning off gas and water, axe, crowbar, screwdriver, pliers, hammer, shovel, mop, broom, knife, scissors and rope

Most people have a variety of important documents that should be copied. When you have made copies of the documents you need, keep a set in a safe, secure place other than your home, because that copy could be destroyed by fire. In case you need to evacuate your home, keep a copy of your selected documents in your waterproof container.

The following is a list of the types of documents you should consider. (As a reminder, some of the items may need to be copied on both sides.)

- Driver's license or personal identification
- Social security card
- Medical and eyeglass prescriptions (keep updated with each change)
- Proof of residence (copy of deed or lease)
- Insurance policies
- Birth and marriage certificates
- Stocks, bond and other negotiable certificates
- Wills, deeds and copies of recent tax returns
- Family photographs, or copies, that you would not like to lose
- Important telephone numbers and addresses

4. First-Aid Kit

To be prepared for an emergency, make sure your medical first-aid kit contains the following items. Remember that some items will probably need to be replaced from time to time, depending upon shelf life.

- First aid manual
- Hydrocortisone cream or ointment
- Disposable medical exam gloves (latex or vinyl) Calamine lotion
- Mouth-to-barrier devices for rescue breathing
- Aloe Vera gel
- Adhesive bandage strips
- Acetaminophen *(non-aspirin pain reliever for adults and children, i.e. Tylenol)*
- Roller gauze and sterile gauze pads
- Elastic/Roller bandage *(ACE® bandage)*
- Aspirin
- Antibiotic ointment
- Ibuprofen
- Antiseptic ointment
- Eye drops
- Antihistamine
- Activated charcoal
- Antacid
- Medical/paper tape
- Anti-diarrhea medicine

- Thermometer
- Decongestant
- Tweezers
- Antiseptic wipes or hydrogen peroxide
- Scissors
- Antibacterial hand wash
- Syrup of ipecac
- Saline solution

CHAPTER **Eleven**

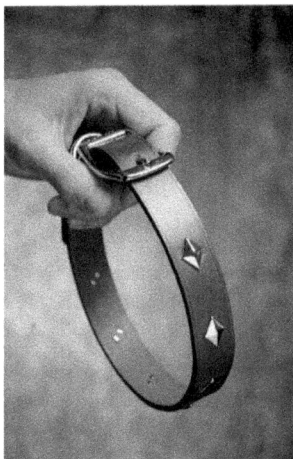

Pet Information and Protection

Your pet no doubt is an important part of your family and he or she depends on you to provide for their care every day. In a variety of emergency situations your pet might well require very special attention. However, when there is an emergency it's already too late to learn how best to take care of your pet's needs. Realistically, the best time to learn about what you can do to help your pet is long before an emergency occurs. Therefore their welfare needs to be part of your overall safety plan.

This chapter will help you list and keep track of all types of information about your pet, and provide advice and suggestions for keeping your pet safe in adverse situations.

If you have more than one pet, be sure you complete the pet information data for each one. When completed at www.GettingSafer.com your pet information then becomes part of your Lifeline Personal Data System.

Don't put it off; start now.

PET INFORMATION FORM

COMPLETE

Name of pet: ____
Type of animal: ____
Breed: ____
Color(s): ____
Sex: Male   Female
Birth Date: ____
Exterior Identification Tag: Yes   No
Microchip: Yes   No   Microchip Company: ____
Telephone Number: ____   Chip Number: ____
Pedigree: ____   Temperament: ____
Veterinarian: ____   Phone Number: ____
Address: ____   City: ____
State: ____   Zip: ____
Driving Directions to veterinarian's office from your home: ____

Business Hours: ____

Emergency Veterinarian:
Veterinarian: ____   Phone Number: ____
Address: ____   City: ____
State: ____   Zip: ____
Driving Directions to emergency veterinarian's office from your home: ____

Business Hours: ____

Pet's Medical History:
Weight: ____   Rabies tag: ____
Illnesses: ____

Operations: ____

Vaccinations: ____
Allergies: ____

Medications: ____
Copy of veterinarian record (a requirement if a pet needs to go to a shelter): ____
Location of record: ____
Pet insurance ____
Company: ____
Telephone Number: ____
Address: ____

Policy Number: ____   Renewal Date: ____
Pet License Number: ____

Foods: ____
Type and Amount: ____
Feeding Schedule: ____
Treats: ____
Toy Preference: ____
Exercise Schedule: ____

Is the Animal an   Indoor   or   Outdoor Pet?
Sleeping Preferences (i.e., cage, bed, blanket; alone or with others): ____

Grooming Contact Name: ____   Phone Number: ____
Alternate Caregivers:
Name: ____   Phone Number: ____
Special Abilities: ____

Location of a Photograph of Your Pet (can be used on notices if pet is lost): ____

Other Helpful Information: ____

STORAGE RECOMMENDATION: **Pet Information**

ENVELOPE	MAIN LOCATION	LOCATION 2	LOCATION 3
Open	Locked File Cabinet	Expanded Emergency Kit	
Actual Location(s):			

GENERAL PET INFORMATION

Licensing

If required, pet licenses and renewals can be obtained from veterinarian offices, animal shelters and/or county departments of animal control offices.

Micro-chipping

IDEA

Microchips are a reliable way to ensure that your animal, whether lost or stolen, can be identified

A microchip is a permanent form of identification that can be implanted by your vet, animal shelter or SPCA in the skin between your animal's shoulder blades. A unique number, which is never used again, is stored on the chip. If your pet becomes lost and loses its exterior identification tag, the pet can be identified by having the information on the chip read by a radio signal at a shelter, veterinarian office or animal control center. The identification information within the chip can be read in all U.S. states, as well as worldwide; therefore, if your animal is found far from home, it can still be identified.

Registering Your Pet's Microchip Information

When a microchip has been implanted in an animal you as the owner needs to register your pet. At this time there are many database companies that register microchips: AKC/Home Again and Avid are two that operate 24/7 worldwide. Vets and other animal care agencies have been trained to scan any microchips and call the appropriate registration company as indicated by the number, and report the status of the animal. The company then calls the owner and/or contact person of record and informs them where the pet is located. They also place a follow-up call to the owner to make sure that the animal is okay.

Some useful web site links are:
www.akcreunite.org
www.avidplc.com
www.petkey.org
www.rfid-usa.org

Pet Safety

Most children love their pets but they can hurt them accidentally. A very real danger to kittens and puppies is the way young children play with them. They can be quite rough unintentionally, and can even accidentally sit on a new pet, causing real harm. Make sure they are supervised or that they understand that their new pet needs to be treated carefully.

BEWARE

Remember that small toys can be a hazard to pets. Since young pets will chew almost anything, you need to make sure they have their own chewable toys, and that your child's small toys are kept out of their way to prevent possible choking.

To keep your pet safe outdoors there are a number of excellent products such as an invisible fence that can help keep a pet safe in an open area around your home. Your veterinarian or local pet store can provide more specific information, or you can find out about such products easily by entering 'invisible fence' in the search engine on the Internet.

While on the subject of safety outdoors, make sure that there are no fertilizers or insect killers in your garden that your pet can consume. Snail bait, for example, can be a problem, so get advice from your supplier for a pet-safe variety.

Your garage or storage area can be of concern as there are probably lots of potentially sickening or fatal products that your pet could ingest.

No matter where, make sure that any potential problem liquids such as anti-freeze, or powders, sprays, etc., are all out of reach of your pet and in sealed containers. If you have any doubts about a product ask your supplier or your vet about its safety.

Never wait to see what might happen if you think that your pet may have been poisoned. It could be too late. Just make a call to your veterinarian or your emergency vet or call the poison center immediately. Your quick action could be vital to your pets' safety.

Accidental poisoning can occur quite easily with most pets. Pets in general, and especially dogs, are prone to being poisoned, as they will eat almost anything. To avoid this type of danger you should make sure your pets are fed only appropriate pet food. Do not give scraps from the table, as the fat content can make them sick. Never give your pet chocolate, as it has an ingredient similar to caffeine and can cause numerous unpleasant problems for you and serious illness to your pet. Of course alcohol or drugs are also complete no-nos.

You should always check before you accept or bring any plants or flowers into your home. House plants, although beautiful, can become a major problem. Eating even a small amount of a plant can result in a variety of reactions or illnesses. Many ornamental plants have a sap that can cause an animal to vomit, salivate or have diarrhea. Plants such as hibiscus and Easter lilies can be very harmful to pets, and cats that consume these types of plants can go into renal failure. After ingesting hibiscus a dog can vomit and have bloody diarrhea to the point that they can lose so much body fluid that it can cause death.

Mistletoe and holly berries can be toxic to pets. Therefore holiday times can be especially dangerous to pets as everyone is busy and may not notice a pet eating the plants. The best policy to adopt is to make sure that indoor plants are always safely out of reach of your pet.

Because there are many plants that are potentially poisonous to pets, if you are in doubt call your veterinarian. Another source of information if you have questions on poisonous plants or other poison issues is the American Society for the Prevention of Cruelty to Animals (ASPCA) in Illinois They offer a 24-hour animal-based poison service and can be reached at 1-888.426.4435. As of this writing they will charge $65 to your credit card for this service.

Remember your pet depends on you for their safety, so it is vital to include your pet in any security and disaster planning. If you have to evacuate your home make sure you take your pet(s) with you. It is not sufficient to create a safe place for them in your home and leave them there. If it is a real emergency and your home is in danger of being destroyed, your pet may not be able to get out or someone could get killed trying to make a rescue.

So in case you ever vacate your home, make sure you have pre-arranged plans for your pet. Take into consideration that most disaster shelters cannot by law take pets, unless it is an animal that assists a person with disabilities. The best you can do for your pet is to contact hotels and motels in your area in advance and ask if they take pets. Even if they do not do so normally, ask if they make an exception in the case of emergencies. Keep trying until you have some places that will accept pets and then put those facilities along with their contact information on your emergency contact list.

Handling an Injured Animal

Any animal that is injured or in pain can bite or scratch and must be handled with care. Both dog and cat bites can become infected quickly so get medical attention immediately. If a pet is injured they will most likely require veterinary care. Call the veterinary office to get their advice about the best way to transport your particular pet. Their answer will depend on the type of pet and the extent of the injury.

Pet Emergency Kit:

To be prepared for an emergency make sure to have on hand:
- Supply of water and pet food, for at least one week
- Medications
- Containers or trash bags for waste
- Leash, carrier, cage (as appropriate)
- ID collar
- Current photos of your pet in case they get lost.
- Copy of current veterinarian records
- Pet toys
- Doggie coat (if necessary)

Insurance

Insurance can be purchased for dogs, cats, birds, reptiles and other pets. A policy can be obtained that will cover animals older than six weeks, as well as those with pre-existing conditions (if they have already been cured). However, there are only a few companies that offer pet insurance, so check with your veterinarian about your options. Pet insurance covers a very broad range of conditions, including more than 6,400 medical problems and conditions related to accidental injuries, poisoning or illnesses. Insurance for vaccinations and routine care coverage is also available.

Ensuring Your Pet Is Cared For If You Are Unable To

Pets usually have a short life span, so most people do not expect that they will be outlived by their pet. But occasionally, when someone dies or suddenly becomes incapacitated, a beloved pet can be left without someone to care for them. Just as you would want to ensure that someone cares for your children, it is very important that you make plans to care for your animals in case any such event occurs. The following discussions and advice will help you with some critical decision-making.

Emergency Caregivers

If something unexpected were to happen to you, your pet may be forgotten in any possible resulting confusion. Someone needs to take care of their immediate daily needs until a more permanent solution can be found, or until your legal documents can go into effect. Have you considered this possibility?

To prevent your pet from being forgotten or neglected, discuss with at least two potential emergency caregivers the possibility of needing their help. These people could be responsible family members, friends, neighbors or relatives. You should be willing to give them a house key (or let them know where or how to get one), as well as your pets' feeding and care instructions. They should also have the telephone number for your vet, as well as information concerning any permanent care decisions you may have made. It may not be easy, but keep going until you have found at least two people willing to help with your animal's care in an emergency situation.

Consider giving your friends, neighbors and relatives a list with the name of your pet and the emergency caregivers' contact information.

Create the list that can be given to friends and family by selecting the appropriate information from the Pet Information Form that you have already completed.

Carry a card in your wallet that will alert emergency personnel that you have a pet or pets, and that they will need to be looked after. Include the names of your animals and the contact information for the emergency caregivers.

PET CARE CARD *sample*

COMPLETE

My Name:

My Pet's Name:

In an emergency please contact Mary Smith at 222.555.7777 and ask her to take care of my dog and cat.

Place a sign (removable when your pet is not at home) inside a window or any prominent place to inform firemen or police, in case of an emergency, how many and what kind of animals are inside. Use a removable, non-permanent sticker or sign and keep the information updated. Remember to remove all outdated notices, as permanent and outdated stickers may result in rescue teams putting their lives at risk looking for animals that do not exist. Do not leave this type of sign visible whenever you take your pet out of your home. Accidents can happen at any time, and you do not want anyone risking their life to rescue a pet that is not there.

Keep the telephone numbers of your pet's emergency caregivers in a prominent place in your home along with other emergency telephone numbers.

Long-term Pet Care

You should consider make formal arrangements that clearly describe your wishes concerning the long-term care for your pets if you were to pass on.

Just getting an old friend to promise to look after your pet or leaving money in your will for them to use towards the animals' care is not enough. Circumstances change, and your friend may no longer be willing or able to take care of your animals as originally intended, or to provide the same type or amount of daily or medical care that you desire.

It is relatively simple to work with an attorney to draw up a legally binding document that will provide for the care and ownership of your pets.

Try to choose trustworthy short-term as well as permanent caregivers that are familiar with your pets and with whom your pets feel comfortable. It is a good idea to specify some alternate choices.

Discuss with your attorney (as well as the caregivers) your animal's condition and the level and extent of daily and medical care you expect. Both you and the agreed-upon caregivers should feel comfortable with each other knowing that they could have full discretion over your pet.

Remain in touch with the chosen caregivers over time to make sure that circumstances remain the same for both of you.

In the event that you decide that another choice of caregiver would be more appropriate, inform your executor or attorney. Have changes made to your documents indicating that you want your pets to be cared for by someone else.

If your executor is appointed the task of choosing a long-term caregiver, provide him or her with useful, realistic and non-confining instructions. The executor should be given broad discretion in making decisions concerning the animal and in appropriating estate funds.

Funds from your estate should be designated for the costs involved in obtaining both temporary and long-term pet care.

Enacting a Will

Remember that your Will only takes effect upon your death, and that there could be a long delay before it is enacted because of probate and any disputes.

Because of this potential delay, it is recommended that in addition to placing your pet instructions in your Will, you create additional documents that compensate for the Will's limits, such as a trust or a power of attorney.

Creating a Trust

Unlike your Will, a trust can be put into effect at the time you state. The instructions in the trust can apply whether you become ill, incapacitated or you die. Within the trust document, provisions can be made for money to be set aside to care for your pet, and you can choose a trustee who will control the funds.

Trust funds are excluded from the probate process, and can therefore be obtained with ease when needed.

Not all states enforce trusts on behalf of animals, so check with your attorney concerning the laws in your state. You should also look into this special aspect if you are moving at any time to another state.

Before you go ahead and make all the necessary arrangements and put provisions for your pet(s) into your trust, you need to be aware that there are costs of administering and maintaining trusts. It depends upon your circumstances if these costs are acceptable or prohibitive to you.

Granting Power of Attorney:

Power of Attorney is given to someone to conduct affairs on your behalf if you are unable to do so. See additional information about Power of Attorney in the chapter dealing with legal matters.

Giving a Power of Attorney to someone is simpler than creating a trust. It does not create a legal entity that needs to be maintained, so costs are not a concern.

Directions can be included in the Power of Attorney document to take care of your pets, allocate money to do so, and to place them with permanent caregivers. A lawyer can help you put this relatively simple document together.

Additional Long-term Care Options

Most humane organizations do not have the means to provide long-term care, nor is there any guarantee that your pet will be adopted from such an organization.

There are a few organizations in the USA that specialize in long-term pet care for deceased owners for a fee or donation; they may even try and place your pet with a family. You will find links to some of these organizations on www.GettingSafer.com

When choosing any "pet retirement home" or "sanctuary," carefully consider what type of care they can provide, as well as how the animals are fed, socialized, groomed and boarded. In addition, think about what will happen to the animals if the home loses funding or staff. With all these considerations in mind, choose well-established organizations that have good records of finding responsible homes quickly for the animals.

Remember that your pets are probably companion animals. They may never adjust to being institutionalized in a pet shelter, and may suffer terribly if left in such an environment.

Some people think their pets should be euthanized if they are no longer able to care for them, and they include orders to do so in their Wills. However, many states will rule this provision is illegal if the animal is young or in good health, and especially when other humane alternatives are available. Check with your veterinarian or lawyer for guidelines in your state.

It is important that whatever your decision, you need to carefully document the care you want for your pet, and ensure that copies be provided to the executor of your estate, as well as the pet's designated caregiver along with your attorney.

Pet Burial

Once your pet has passed away, you need to decide what you want to do with your pet's remains. Unless alternate plans are made, the veterinarian will dispose of the body for you. Other options are to have your pet buried or cremated. In many parts of the country there are sources for both of these options, including local pet cemeteries. You can obtain information about these options from your veterinarian or in the yellow pages.

Surprisingly, in most parts of the country it is illegal to bury your pet on private property. Check with the local authorities or your veterinarian for information concerning the local laws.

When Grief Counseling is Needed

Whenever a beloved pet has passed away many are grief-stricken. The death of a pet can be likened to that of a parent or a child, and the loss should be treated in many ways with a similar amount of respect and concern. The effects of the loss may have lasting effects. Most veterinarians can supply the names of special grief counselors whose services can offer support and comfort to the grieving owner or family.

For more information on providing future care for your pets, reach out to: The Humane Society of the United States: The Planned Giving Office: plannedgiving@hsus.org

APPENDIX **A**

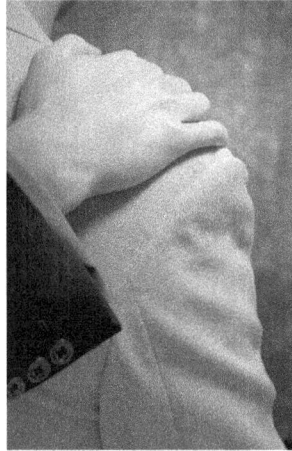

Coping with Accidents, Tragedies and Death

So far all the previous chapters have given you ideas that will help you to avoid or prevent health, monetary or legal problems and more. You have also been able to read, and hopefully plan and practice, a number of ways to deal with potential tragedies that could cause physical harm of one type or another.

This appendix about emotions and coping with grief is included to help you understand that in any adverse situation there is likely to be not only a physical aspect but also a psychological one with which you need to cope. Be assured, however, that you are not alone. In virtually any situation, others will have had the same or similar reactions, and there are ways in which you can either help yourself, or find places to help you get through a very stressful time.

As we go through life everyone experiences a range of emotions caused by the things we do, see or hear. Some events and experiences can be pleasant and cause us to be happy and feel joy. Others may not be pleasant and can cause sadness or grief. We really don't need much help when it comes to dealing with happiness, but grief, stress and upsetting experiences are much different matters.

The following information gives a preliminary, and yet helpful, overview of ways that can help you get through some difficult times that you might face. It also should help you to understand the emotions you are likely to experience.

REACTING TO DEATH

Even though we know that death is inevitable, when someone close to us dies it can be one of the most difficult things and times we face. Death can happen at any age, naturally, or by a tragic accident, a criminal act, a natural disaster, or even or terrorist attack. No matter how or when it occurs, it is always important that all family members are told as soon as possible.

It is almost impossible to predict how a particular person will take the news. In many cases it can depend upon the person telling the news or the way in which it is told. Reactions to hearing about the death of someone close can range from shock to denial to acceptance.

Most people feel uncomfortable talking about death, and find it especially difficult talking to young children who often cannot understand the finality of death. Regardless of the age of the person you are telling, be honest and tell the truth. Your honesty is necessary to help build a sense of trust. If you are unsure of the facts, it is definitely better to say that you don't know why someone has died rather than make up an answer. Adults frequently say very little or nothing at all about death because they are afraid of saying the wrong thing. When that happens, children especially can become more confused by the lack of information or silence.

Whenever the subject of death is being discussed, it is important to use the actual words "death" and "dying." Using these actual words allows adults, as well as children, to be open and honest about the event, and avoids disguising the truth. Whether speaking to children or adults you should realize that your voice as well as your body language is important. At the same time, be careful not to send mixed messages, such as telling children things like "the person went to sleep forever." That idea may frighten them to the point that they are afraid to go to sleep.

Children often need special care and handling when there has been a death of someone close, such as a grandparent or a very close friend. At such a time, it's a good idea to help them find something to do where they can have some control over the activity, such as their hobbies or sports. Let them decide what they want to do and what works for them. Sometimes it is helpful for them to express their emotions in some constructive way, such as making a scrapbook, photo album or memory box, or even to tell or write a story about the person who has died. It can often be quite helpful to encourage children especially, but adults too, to ask questions.

Adults frequently begin to feel somewhat better by talking openly or writing about the deceased person and the effect that he or she had on their life. However, it is very important to realize that each person is unique: they will react in their own way to death, and express their emotions in their own particular style.

Some may find it better to talk with a close friend, others to a pastor or other religious person, or others might choose a doctor or a counselor. If you are the one that has suffered the loss, it does not matter to whom you speak, but it is definitely best to express your feelings and not keep them bottled up.

Age-related Reactions to Death

A child's reaction to death will be different to that of an adult and will mainly depend upon the child's age and maturity.

Very young children who are exposed to TV-type cartoons do not understand that death is final. They will probably expect the deceased person to return to life at some point.

Between the ages of 5 to 10, however, children come to realize that death is final, although they are likely to think that it can only happen to older people.

When children who are just a little older, say between the ages of 10 and 13, they generally can understand death a little bit better. They are at an age when they are able to understand and appreciate the difference the deceased person had made in their life.

Adolescents between 13 and 18 have an even more advanced understanding of death. By that age they can appreciate the meaning of the loss of someone whom they have known, as well as the effect that the person had on their life. If the person who passed away was very close to them, they may even try to take on some of the roles performed by the person they have lost.

Parents should always allow and encourage children to express their feelings, and especially let them know that it is okay to feel upset. Every child needs to know that the person they trust and upon whom they rely, loves them and will take care of all their needs and provide them with food and a safe home. Children also need reassurance that others whom they love will not leave them, and that there will be continued stability in their lives.

Death of a Parent, Spouse or Partner

When a parent dies, the situation is particularly difficult for a child, as they have to deal with not only their own grief, but at the same time, probably wants to help ease the grief of the surviving parent. In many such cases, a child is quite likely to start to take on many of the responsibilities of the deceased parent in order to provide help to the surviving parent. At the same time the son or daughter needs to allow their surviving parent to become more self-sufficient as soon as possible.

A surviving parent or spouse needs to be encouraged to build their own self-confidence and self-sufficiency in doing things for themselves. They also need time to overcome any feelings of being unwelcome in a coupled world. For example, a newly widowed person is likely to have fears of being alone, or of having to make unfamiliar decisions such as dealing with financial, legal or even domestic matters. In time they must develop a new level of self-esteem, self-worth and a forward-looking role as a single person so they are able to plan ahead in life.

IDEA Quite frequently there are a lot of things to be done at the same time you are dealing with the recent loss of someone close. At such a time it is very difficult to remember all the details of arrangements and conversations. So, just get a notebook to keep an accurate written record of all the practical matters that need attention, as well as conversations with attorneys, insurance companies, etc.

Losing a spouse is difficult for either partner, but often proves more difficult for men, as they are generally expected by others to be strong. In most cases the husband has probably relied heavily on their wife for a great many things throughout the marriage. Therefore, particularly for a man, it is very important that they go through the entire grieving process (discussed later in this chapter) or they can risk developing major stress. That, in turn, can lead to a variety of serious illnesses, and affect both their future personal and business life.

Funerals and Burial

The funeral provides a time for mourning and the expression of grief, and confirms the finality of death. It is a time when love can be expressed through stories or eulogies and nothing is expected in return. It is a meaningful ceremony that commemorates the life of the deceased, and it is a time that family, relatives and friends can participate in a thoughtful and significant way. It gives each one present an opportunity to express their thoughts, feelings and sympathy. The funeral offers the opportunity for the living to say "farewell" in a respectful and dignified way.

BEWARE Regardless of age, *never* force a child to go to a funeral. Conversely, if a child really wants to go to a funeral and you refuse to let them attend, they will almost certainly feel shut out. They can be confused by all the strange changes around them, and feel they are missing out on an important event in the life of the family.

If children have never attended a funeral but want to go, then prepare them for what they will see by explaining what will happen at the ceremony and the burial. By attending the funeral of someone they have known, they are likely to feel more a part of the family. Attending the funeral also gives them an opportunity to be comforted by others.

When the children are of elementary school age or younger and if they do not want to attend the funeral, have someone whom they trust stay with them during the service, to explain what is happening, comfort them and answer any questions.

It is quite normal for children to ask the same questions over and over as they grow and reach different stages of development. So at a time when there has been a death of someone very close, they may need to hear repeatedly about what is happening in the family, how you will manage and any changes that are taking place. Just be patient and keep answering their questions.

REACTING TO DISASTERS

Whenever any type of natural disaster or traumatic event occurs, both children and adults need reassurance. In particular, a child may need it explained that they are not to blame for the situation. They most likely want to have your confirmation that they are safe, loved and will continue to be protected.

Nowadays, unfortunately, it is almost impossible to avoid the barrage of potentially disturbing news that comes from the radio, TV, Internet and friends. Recent developments in technology and the media have made it possible for events to be broadcast around the world within minutes of the actual occurrence. The result is that we are frequently exposed to many types of disasters, including terrorism episodes, suicide bombings, natural disasters, epidemics, famine, and international crises. The list goes on and on.

Still, despite that, and depending upon the ages and levels of maturity of those in your household, with some effort it should be possible to monitor, at least at home, the amount of exposure to television and radio coverage of a particular disaster. Beyond the original shock, just viewing or listening to graphic news repeatedly can cause further trauma, or desensitize a person to violent aspects and their consequences.

Parents, teachers or other responsible adults can lessen the negative effects on children by watching the news with them whenever possible. This is particularly important whenever there has been a major tragic event that is broadcast over and over again. Your children should feel confident that they can discuss what they are hearing with you. After all, you are the person they rely upon and trust and the one they expect will explain things clearly to them in a calm way.

As an adult, you too will feel better and experience a sense of security upon watching traumatic news events if you do so with a close friend or family member who can share in your concern and sorrow. If you live alone, try to call friends or family, to talk about the events that have had an impact on you so that you can express your feelings and get support.

In the days immediately after any loss or disaster, a youngster's parents and loved ones should spend extra time with them. That time should be spent not only for talks focused on and related to the disaster, but also some of the time should be devoted to casual conversation and support.

For children, any natural disaster, whether an earthquake, hurricane, tornado, fire or flood can be very frightening. For adults too, these types of events can be frightening, and you should be willing and able to talk about natural weather phenomenon using words that are age-appropriate so that you are fully understood.

Never falsely minimize any danger, as that will not end a child's concerns. Children are very aware of their parents' worries most of the time and they are particularly sensitive during a crisis. Just admit your own concerns, and be sure to stress your abilities to cope with the situation.

No matter what we say or do, all types of disasters can be frightening at any age. However, the younger the person is, the more difficulty they may have in the future. So, if a child or an adolescent is directly exposed to a catastrophe, they are more likely than an adult to have difficulty dealing with related problems in the future. It is not unusual, and in fact it is quite common, for young people to believe that "nothing like that" would ever happen to them. If they are having such ideas, the ideas should be explored and discussed in a supportive manner and in a way that gently reminds a young person that certain kinds of disasters can happen to anyone.

A child's reaction to any traumatic event will depend on their age and how much destruction or even death they have seen during and after the disaster. The extent of any problems the child may encounter could also depend on their family history and if there has been any experience of prior psychiatric illness. When a close friend or a family member has been killed or seriously injured, or if the child's school or home has been severely damaged, there is a strong possibility that the child will experience some on-going difficulties, such as depression or post-traumatic stress disorder. Adults too, in similar circumstances, are likely to become depressed and suffer from subsequent stress disorders.

Both children's' and adults' reactions to a disaster can last a long time after the event itself, and professional counseling shortly after a disaster can be helpful in reducing long-term negative effects. Anyone who continues to find past events extremely upsetting would also benefit from professional counseling.

The "Correct" Way to Grieve

There is *no* "correct" or "right" way to grieve, and therefore each person needs to grieve in their own way. Particularly whenever there is a death of someone close to you, it is normal to grieve over a period of time. Also, the way each one grieves is usually going to be influenced by both their individual personality and cultural background. Grief is neither an instant process nor a single event. It's a natural reaction to any kind of loss, and it always requires a period of time to run its course.

Grief will occur whenever you experience a significant loss, such as the death of a parent, loved one or pet. But regardless of the cause, anytime you experience a period of grief, *one of the most important things is being able to respond to and accept the support and comfort offered by family and friends.* Naturally, there will be times during any grieving period when you feel better, but at other times you will feel down. You may even feel angry or express guilt over some aspects of the loss. In times such as these, you really need to talk about all your feelings with those you trust, and who will listen carefully when you want to talk.

At the same time that you are grieving you may also be experiencing some symptoms of depression; these feelings can be attributed to the bereavement, rather than a depressive disorder, unless they persist for more than two months.

Steps of Mourning

In order to get through a mourning and grieving period completely, here are a number of steps a person needs to go through in order to complete the grieving process.

The first of these steps requires a person to accept the reality and finality of the loved one's death.

This is then usually followed by a period when crying, and the pain of sorrow, are experienced. During this second phase (and later on) the grieving person requires a period of time in which they can begin to adjust to a new way of life, and a realization that life goes on without the deceased individual. It is at this point that the grieving person is likely to begin to take on some new responsibilities and start to make plans for the future and perhaps develop some new interests.

The last stage of the grieving process is when an individual realizes the need to find an acceptable way to memorialize the lost loved one. This is done so that the departed can live on in the heart and mind and not be forgotten.

When all the right steps have been taken and fulfilled, a person will quite likely discover that their own life can go on and that they can be happy in many new ways with family and friends.

Of course there will still be times, such as holidays, birthdays or anniversaries that can be difficult for the one who has been left behind to observe. When these times come around, it is important to find ways to talk about these occasions so that they are not ignored or forgotten, but are commemorated or celebrated in some new or meaningful way.

Recovering from Grief

The length of time it can take to recover and get past grief will depend on a number of factors, such as the age of the person grieving, the circumstances of the loved one's death, and the relationship the bereaved had to the person who died. The only "cure" for grief is time, and that can take a year or two, or even more. There is no specific time frame for grieving, and just because someone else thinks you should be "over it" does not mean that it is so for you.

Anyone grieving the loss of a loved one needs to realize that the relationship they had with the deceased has not ended. It has only changed. They need to find ways during the grieving process to accept the changes caused by the death, and move on.

Following any serious loss both adults and children need to understand that it is okay to feel sad or scared. They should do their best to share their feelings with family and loved ones. When adults are open about their own feelings, children realize that it's acceptable for them to express their feelings too. If people want to talk to you about your loss, do not change the subject and talk about other things.

In good times, when people are happy, we don't try to change their happiness. In the same way, when someone needs to grieve, we should not try to change how they are doing that either.

If you are the one grieving, try to do things that are routine, to help you get back into a somewhat familiar lifestyle. Just going out and walking or meeting a friend for coffee is a start. If that does not work or does not seem like a solution, then you should find a support group. There are many support groups all over the country and each one usually deals with a specific type of loss. There you will find people going through some of the same difficulties that you are facing who are also looking for comfort.

Just as there are beneficial ways to grieve there are certain things that are unhealthy as well. It is not good to keep feelings pent up inside. You need to talk about your feelings. In addition, it is not a great idea to replace the one you lost with another person very quickly or move to another place just to try to avoid your feelings.

It is unrealistic to think you should be over the loss in a very short time, and you should not grieve on your own: let family, friends or support groups that can help during this difficult time be a part of your life.

Depression

Both adults and children can experience depression when faced with the reality of a catastrophic loss.

Symptoms of adult depression include a depressed mood and/or a decreased interest in life and deriving less pleasure from previously enjoyed activities. Other typical symptoms of depression include persistent boredom or low energy, changes in weight and appetite, difficulty thinking and making decisions, feelings of worthlessness or guilt and in some cases recurrent thoughts of death or suicidal plans or attempts. These feelings can interfere with the ability to function, and a person is considered clinically depressed when he or she experiences these depressive symptoms for a period of two weeks or more.

In children extreme sensitivity to rejection or failure, and/or increased irritability, anger or hostility are also signs of depression. Other symptoms that can be experienced by children include difficulty having relationships and/or frequent complaints of physical illnesses such as headaches and stomachaches. Frequent absences from classes, poor concentration and lower performance in school are also symptomatic of depression. Major changes in eating or sleeping patterns, or attempts to run away from home, are common as well. Children and adolescents who cause trouble at home or at school may actually be depressed, but not realize it. When asked directly, children with any of these symptoms can sometimes simply state that they are unhappy or sad.

Adults as well as children are at a higher risk to become depressed if they experience a catastrophic loss and at the same time they are under stress or have attention, learning, conduct, or anxiety disorders.

Pay special attention to any child who usually plays with friends and suddenly begins to spend most of their time alone, showing little or no interest in anything. They could well be depressed. Because of their depression, they may say things such as they want to be dead, talk about suicide or use alcohol or drugs as a way to feel better. Any of these issues should be taken seriously and discussed. In the event that the behavior continues, professional help needs to be sought. Early diagnosis and medical treatment are essential for depressed children.

Depression is a real illness that requires professional help, and sometimes requires family therapy as well. It should not be ignored, as it will not get better by itself.

Post-traumatic Stress Disorder (PTSD)

Post-traumatic stress disorder is a condition that can result from experiencing, witnessing, or being involved in an overwhelmingly traumatic event. Symptoms of post-traumatic stress disorder (PTSD) will usually occur within three months after the trauma. Commonly the person has recurrent and intrusive recollections of the catastrophic event, or recurrent distressing dreams in which the event is replayed over and over again. Such a person will probably experience intense distress if exposed to cues that remind them of some aspect of the traumatic event.

People with PTSD persistently avoid thoughts, feelings or any conversations associated with the trauma. They may also experience a numbing of their general responsiveness, such as feeling estranged from others, or they are unable to have loving feelings towards others. It is common for people with PTSD to experience increased sleep disturbances, irritability, poor concentration, startle reaction and regressive behavior.

Children with PTSD disorder have repeated episodes in which they re-experience the traumatic event. Symptoms can occur at any time, even years later. The symptoms can manifest themselves in ways, such as "clinging" behavior, which includes following the mother or father around the house, or having nightmares. They could experience a loss of concentration, or they may become irritable, easily startled and jumpy. They can start to misbehave in school or at home as never before. Sometimes they will develop physical complaints for which a physical cause cannot be found. They may withdraw from family and friends, and show signs of sadness, listlessness, decreased activity and preoccupation with the events of the disaster.

Professional advice or treatment for children who have witnessed destruction, injury or death can help prevent or minimize the PTSD condition, and parents who are concerned should ask their doctor to refer them to a child psychologist or a psychiatrist. The same advice holds true for adults suffering from PTSD.

Stress Management

Whenever we perceive a situation as dangerous, difficult or painful, and believe that we do not have the ability to cope with it, we are likely to experience stress.

Such things as workplace demands, negative thoughts about oneself, financial worries, or a problem with friends, being in an unsafe neighborhood, or developing a chronic illness can all cause and increase levels of stress. Severe problems in the family, divorce, the death of a loved one, moving homes, changing schools or jobs, taking on too many activities or having unrealistically high expectations for our-selves will also result in stress. Stress can therefore be caused by a wide variety of situations, such as problems at home, work or in school.

So, whenever we are overloaded and are unable to adequately manage our stress it can lead to depression, anxiety, withdrawal, aggressive behavior, physical illness or poor coping skills. In addition, these typical reactions to stress can lead to drug or alcohol use. It is important to do everything possible to deal with stress in an adaptive way. Positive coping strategies need to be implemented to help prevent negative or destructive outcomes.

Anyone, at any age or at any time in their lives, can experience stress, so everyone can benefit from learning the best ways to cope with stress and stress management skills.

Ways to Cope with Stress

The good news about stress is that the same mechanism that turns on the stress response will also turn it off. Once we decide that a situation is no longer dangerous, changes start to occur in our minds and bodies that will help us relax and calm down. While it takes some determination on our part to ensure that we do not allow stress to get the better of us, there are many things we can do that will help reduce or eliminate stress. Most are easy to do such as:

- Eat regularly, minimize caffeine intake and learn relaxation exercises which will help reduce stress.
- Get involved in sports and other social activities.
- Avoid stressful situations.
- Choose to engage in activities like listening to music, talking to a friend, drawing, writing or spending time with a pet. Any of these things can help to reduce stress.
- Avoid illegal drugs, alcohol and tobacco.
- Decrease, or better still, eliminate negative thoughts about yourself.
- Learn to break a large task into smaller, more manageable tasks.
- Feel good about doing an "okay" job.
- Don't always strive or look for perfection all of the time.

These techniques will help you to develop stress management skills so that you will feel less helpless, more in control of your emotions and able to positively respond to stress.

As you become better and better able to deal with your personal stressful situations you will find an improvement in your reactions to trauma and the type of stress usually experienced in the event of a disaster. Once you reach that stage, in times of need you will find yourself better prepared and able to deal with emergencies or tragedies in your community. You also will be much more likely to get involved with volunteer groups knowing you are equipped to deal with stress in a realistic manner, and help those unable to help themselves.

The Strength in Community Plans and Relief Groups

Individual communities, and sometimes the entire country, will react to a specific disaster. The nation as a whole often will respond when there is such an event as a school shooting, a major natural disaster like the California wildfires or a manmade disaster such as the terrorist events of September 11th or the more recent Boston Marathon bombing.

As a result of all these and other types of disasters, families, schools, neighborhoods and larger groups throughout the country have started to create contingency plans for a variety of potential disasters *before* they occur.

There is no doubt that all groups, large and small, that use learning courses, discussion groups or activities to "rehearse" what they would do if there were a fire, earthquake, or some other type of emergency will be better prepared for any eventuality. With proper planning everyone can become familiar with such things as local community emergency sleeping arrangements, locations of tents, food resources, evacuation routes and so forth.

Planning and rehearsals will undoubtedly reduce personal anxiety and develop a sense of control. A good constructive way for adults to help children gain a sense of mastery and minimize their anxiety about a traumatic event is to make a game about the actual or potential disaster using available toys and things around the home with which they are familiar.

Psychologically it is very helpful for you and your family to participate in organized neighborhood programs, and national relief or aid responses, such as devoting time and effort to helping with food distribution or fund-raising. You could get involved with rescue training programs or help with activities that are needed to alleviate the problems caused by a disaster. Anything that you are trained to do that can help in an emergency will allow the police and fire and medical personnel deal with others in greater need.

There is also a certain satisfaction that comes with being better prepared and knowing that in times of emergency you can be of use and perhaps could save a life.

And of course, the life you save could be yours!

APPENDIX **B**

Charities and Volunteering

As the saying goes, "It is far better to give than to receive" So no matter what your financial or time constraints are, it is always possible to help someone else in one way or another. If you have little or no money available for charitable purposes, then use your skills and time. If you do not have time then you probably have sufficient income to be able to make some small donation to a cause that you deem fit. If you still believe you cannot do either of these charitable things, then just be kind to your neighbors. Look out for their interests, and they will look out for yours. The overall aim is that we need to become a community helping one another and not be selfish.

We need one another especially in these difficult times. If we do not look out for each other, we are making the work of criminals and terrorists that much easier. We each have a common interest in living a safer and more secure life, and we need each other in order to be able to do that.

CHARITIES AND VOLUNTEERING

Listed here are a number of charities' search engines, and a very brief description of each organization. As of this writing, each of these organizations is reputable. The list provides a starting point for you to begin to look for a group that would be of interest to you, and would win your support.

Search engines

Give.org- www.give.org

This site provides comprehensive descriptions and evaluations of a large number of national organizations provided by a non-profit watchdog. To donate to regional or local chapters, refer to the charities own web site or contact the local Better Business Bureau www.bbb.org. us or Wise Giving Alliance.

Special features include:
- Detailed tips on giving
- Information about tax deductions
- How to donate property
- How to donate without being taken advantage of by middlemen or by being pressured
- File complaints about organizations

GuideStar- www.guidestar.org

Provides data about more than 1 million non-profit organizations

Specific features of this site:
- Easy to navigate
- Information on organization's executives, programs and goals
- Charities listed are all legitimate non-profit organizations and meet IRS criteria
- Search listings for non-profit organizations for towns of all sizes
- Links to more than 300 disaster relief and assistance organizations

Network for Good.org - www.networkforgood.org

Focuses on allowing individuals to donate, volunteer or get involved in charities they care about.

Specific features include:
- Donate directly on-line to thousands of non-disaster groups
- Founded in 2001, administrative costs are covered by the AOL Time Warner Foundation, the Cisco Foundation and Cisco Systems, Inc. and Yahoo, Inc.
- 100% of donations go to the charities

JustGive.org- www.justgive.org

Provides access to more than 1.8 million organizations to which you can donate on-line. Many of the charities have been prescreened.

Special features include:
- Ability to search numerous charities by category
- Wedding/gift registry
- Charity wish list

SchoolPop - *www.schoolpop.com*
Now integrated with www.*OneCause.com*
A Percentage of your on-line and off-line purchases at Schoolpop partner merchants will be donated to your selected local school.

Special features:
- 74,000 participating schools
- 1000+ stores at which to shop.
- Shopping made easy by: category, brand name and percentage of profits donated
- Help on line so you can sign up your school to participate.

VolunteerMatch - *www.volunteermatch.org*
VolunteerMatch refers volunteers to more than 30,000 organizations.

Special features:
- 27 categories
- Search by zip code for organizations near you.
- To help you find a great place to volunteer.

Charities & Volunteering Websites
AmVets - *www.amvets.org*
This is an organization with a mission to provide support to America's veterans and their communities. Not funded by the federal government, the organization depends on contributions that are tax deductible. See how to help at www.amvets.org.
National Operator- # 1-877-7AMVETS (1-877-726-8387)

Charity America - *www.charityamerica.com*
CharityAmerica.com is an online "village" that unites donors, volunteers, businesses and qualified charities from across the nation. The web site provides access to the charities' profile page, mission statement, event information, volunteer opportunities, and contact

information. Donations can be made in the form of monetary and property donations, volunteering time and services and a percentage of purchases made online from affiliated stores. Contact: info@charityamerica.com Tel: 508-903-4100

Feed the Children - *www.feedthechildren.org*
Feed The Children is a nonprofit, Christian, charitable organization providing physical, spiritual, educational, vocational/technical, psychological, economic and medical assistance and other necessary aid to children, families, and persons in need in the United States and internationally. They provide food, clothing, medical assistance and educational opportunities to underprivileged children in 85 nations
around the world. A key goal is to help needy families move beyond relief assistance and become productive and self-sufficient members of their community.
National Operator- # 1-800- 627-4556

Make a Wish - *www.wish.org*
The *Make-A-Wish Foundation* grants the wishes of children with life-threatening illnesses to enrich the human experience with hope, strength, and joy. The Make-A-Wish Foundation has granted a wish to more than 250,000 children between the ages of 21/2 to 18 years around the world. Donations can be made directly to any of the local chapters or to the national chapter. To obtain information visit the website www.wish.org or contact: 1-855-889-WISH (1-855-889-9474)

Points of Light Foundation- *www.pointsoflight.org*
The *Point of Light Foundation*'s mission is to engage more people, more effectively in volunteer community service to help solve serious social problems. This Foundation works and networks, through their volunteer centers in every state to help encourage volunteerism. Contact your local Points of Light Center to match your interests and skills with volunteer opportunities.
National Operator- # 1-800-VOLUNTEER or 404-979-2900

Red Cross - *www.redcross.org*
The American Red Cross is a humanitarian organization led by volunteers that provides relief to victims of disasters and helps people, prevent, respond to and prepare for emergencies. The Red Cross is not a government agency and greatly appreciates community, business and personal donations of time, money and blood. Donations can either be given at a national or local level.

- National Operator: #1-800-733-2767
- To volunteer your personal services visit the Red Cross website or your local phone directory.

Salvation Army - *www.salvationarmy.org*

The Salvation Army in America is part of the overall organization that operates in more than 100 countries. In the USA, the Salvation Army delivers a wide range of social, medical, educational and other community services. Within the US there are over 7,000 centers for worship.

For donated goods pick-up- #1-800-728-7825 (1-800-SA-TRUCK)

United Way - *www.unitedway.org*

United Way of America is the national organization dedicated to leading the United Way movement in making a measurable impact in every community in America and 45 Countries and Territories. Each of the approximately 1,800 community-based United Way organizations is independent and governed by local volunteers. The United Way addresses local critical health and human care needs and raises funds through work place campaigns and fundraising. United Way provides education about the different services available in your community and helps to raise funds for organizations that may not be able to do so themselves. Workplace donation programs are attractive because small amounts are easy to give, but they add up over the year and create philanthropists out of everyone. If your workplace doesn't have a campaign and you would like to start one, or if you would like to make donations in USA call 703-836-7112 or contact your local chapter.

APPENDIX **C**

Using the 911 Emergency Number

The following sections provide guidelines for when to call 911, and when not to call the number. Everyone, including small children should know how and when to use this most useful number, correctly.

CRIME IN PROGRESS – SUSPICIOUS ACTIVITY
- Violent physical activity you believe is related to a CRIMINAL ACTIVITY
- Suspicious physical activity you believe is related to a CRIMINAL ACTIVITY
- Person pointing a weapon at someone, or children with weapons

LIFE OR SAFETY PROBLEMS
- Smell of GAS or ELECTRICAL SHORT, or something burning
- Smell of FIRE, or something burning or flooding
- In need of MEDICAL HELP, Ambulance, Paramedic, EMT, due to MEDICAL EMERGENCY
- Vicious, uncontained animals displaying a behavior that could be dangerous to children, elderly or the general public

DO NOT USE THE (911) EMERGENCY NUMBER FOR THE FOLLOWING
- To request a report – or information related to an already completed report
- To report loose, uncontained animals unless they display a behavior that could be dangerous to children, elderly or the general public
- For road conditions or weather information
- For the above types of questions call the local Police Business Phone Line

About the Author

Richard Watson grew up in Ireland. He began his career in sales and marketing in the UK and Ireland. In time, he became an investor, primarily in real estate. He moved to California with his family, and there he became interested in health related companies.

From an early age he has been involved in charitable work and has always had an interest in helping others and using his abilities to make a difference for the better.

For Richard, the tragic events of 9/11 created a sense of urgency in his life. He realized that for his family, and so many others, it was imperative to better organize one's life's details so that, in times of crisis, critical information could be accessed easily. As Richard realized how useful it would be to turn what had started as a personal project into a safety reference source with wide appeal the task became more extensive and much longer than originally contemplated to complete.

As a result, the safety and security information in this book reflects not only the author's personal life experience and wisdom, but is the outcome of extensive research and consultations he had, with a number of professionals in a variety of fields, from medicine to law to firefighting. A companion website, GettingSafer.com serves as a source of on-going and up-to-the-minute safety and security advisories.

Richard and his wife moved to New Jersey some years ago so as to be nearer to their children and grandchildren.

ACKNOWLEDGEMENTS

Lifeline: The Guide to Life Protection book is an updated version of an earlier book that was originally started with a simple idea: just produce a list of important things that most people neglect to do *(me included!)*. There are so many things that should not be put off, but they just keep getting put on the back burner. So, I started to make a list of some of these on paper and began to discuss my progress with family and friends. Ultimately the topics and ideas for this book began to take shape, and with lots of encouragement my original list of the important things to do, was expanded considerably.

This book is not just the result of my own effort; it is due in no small measure to the help I received from others as the book was being written. The support I received, through so many long weeks and months, from family and friends was invaluable and made the far-ranging Lifeline subject matter easier to complete.

In addition, I am indebted to many professionals I consulted for the time they spent, discussing and suggesting ideas and helping to provide guidance throughout the project.

Among the friends I especially want to thank are Malcolm Lewis and Alan Lewis. These brothers were among the very first people I spoke to about the concept. As we discussed the project they gave me immediate encouragement to go forward and many ideas that I researched and worked into the book.

As for the professionals, I must single out Dr. Arthur Cummins MD. My appreciation here is barely adequate for the tireless and endless help he gave me. Apart from his enthusiasm for the original book, his input, advice and numerous reviews of the medical information was invaluable. I treasure our close friendship, and I thank him for his whole-hearted support. In like manner, for his help with dental health matters, thank you to Dr. Jacob Fleischman, DMD.

We are so lucky to live in a time when so much information is readily available, if one just knows how and where to look. In this regard I acknowledge the numerous web sites that proved invaluable in terms of information gathering. I was able to obtain so much vital details from the web sites of organizations such as those of the Centers for Disease Control (CDC), Homeland Security, and Federal Emergency Management Agency (FEMA) and the Red Cross among many.

A sincere 'thank you' to the police and fire departments that I visited in both California and New Jersey for their help in providing information and assistance so willingly.

Danielle Towne provided invaluable research and help in the book's initial layout. The book benefited from her intelligence and skill in many areas, including the areas of health and especially one of her pet topics *(pun intended!)*, pets.

My gratitude to Richard Barndt, JD., LLM (Tax), who provided considerable help to simplify the topics in the legal chapter so you can gain a basic understanding of the matters covered, and generate ideas to discuss with your attorney.

On financial matters, I thank Tom Goddard, C.P.A, and especially Ian Kutner, CFP, for his willingness to share his many years of professional expertise with me. It was a joy to work with Ian on the financial chapter. He made some relatively complicated matters understandable, and helped generate the questionnaire for that section that, when completed by you, will become part of your Lifeline Personal Data System.

A most important element to achieving true peace of mind is related to psychological and emotional issues. In writing the material about coping with accidents, tragedies and more, I was helped by Dr. Michael Mantell, PhD, in California and by Dr. Nicola Weiss, PhD, in New Jersey. I greatly appreciate their professional opinions and all their help in making me keep this sensitive subject matter focused and as useful as possible for readers.

There were so many other sources of help, many of which were anonymous. For example, I learned a lot about safety and home protection material from people at Home Depot and Lowe's. The personnel from both companies were very generous with their time and information. Also, the credit reporting agencies, Equifax, Experian and TransUnion, were all very helpful in providing information and answering any questions posed to them.

My editor, Elizabeth Zack of BookCrafters LLC, was a real pleasure to work with. Her input overall was a great help, I believe, in making the original book easier to read and the content to flow. I appreciate her wide knowledge of the subject matters throughout the book, and her useful suggestions and prompts for worthwhile additions or changes.

All the time I have spent putting this work together was yet again made easier since I had the full support of my children Mark, Nicola and Lisa. Their belief in this project and their understanding when the endeavor seemed never-ending was invaluable.

To my wife Sandy, thank you for putting up with my long absences when I locked myself away as I struggled to write some of the more difficult subject matters. I know it has taken considerably longer than originally planned but I want you to know that without your support and love I could not have started, and your continued support and love has allowed me to complete this entire project.

NOTES